Creating the Functionally Competent Organization

An Open Systems Approach

JOSEPH A. OLMSTEAD

QUORUM BOOKS
Westport, Connecticut • London

Library of Congress Cataloging-in-Publication Data

Olmstead, Joseph A., 1921–
Creating the functionally competent organization : an open systems approach / Joseph A. Olmstead.
p. cm.
Includes bibliographical references and index.
ISBN 1–56720–532–1 (alk. paper)
1. Organizational effectiveness. 2. Performance—Management. 3. Performance—Evaluation. I. Title.
HD58.9.O46 2002
394.26973—dc21 2001049181

British Library Cataloguing in Publication Data is available.

Library of Congress Catalog Card Number: 2001049181
ISBN: 1–56720–532–1

First published in 2002

Quorum Books, 88 Post Road West, Westport, CT 06881
An imprint of Greenwood Publishing Group, Inc.
www.quorumbooks.com

Printed in the United States of America

The paper used in this book complies with the Permanent Paper Standard issued by the National Information Standards Organization (Z39.48–1984).

10 9 8 7 6 5 4 3 2 1

To Burnelle

Contents

Tables and Figures

TABLES

FIGURES

Preface

The purpose of this book is to present an integrated, coherent conceptual framework for thinking about organizational performance and to suggest a workable model for analyzing, assessing, and improving the performance of organizations of all types.

In a number of presentations, discussions, and applications of the models, numerous inquiries have been made about its theoretical foundations. Accordingly, in this book, I have described both a theoretical foundation and a conceptual model for assessing and developing functionally competent organizations. In over two decades of research and application, the model has proven to be highly effective as a basis for analyzing and improving organizational performance.

Throughout, there is an effort to avoid a simple listing of every relevant reference. Especially important and landmark references have been cited and an annotated bibliography of basic sources is included. Many of these significant publications appeared two, three, or four decades ago because organizational theory was in greater ferment then, and more significant writings appeared in those years.

The author is firmly committed to the use of references that are significant for the history of the several involved disciplines—organizational theory, organizational psychology, group dynamics, and leadership. In addition, there appears to be no reason for "reinventing the wheel" just to demonstrate familiarity with current literature that, for the most part, has become redundant.

The material presented in the book is the product of many years of research and development conducted under the sponsorship of the former Social and Rehabilitation Service of the Department of Health, Education, and Welfare; the U.S. Bureau of Mines; the U.S. Army Research Office; the U.S. Army Research Institute for the Behavioral and Social Sciences; the Defense Advanced Research Projects Agency; the Office of Naval Research, the Human Resources Research Organization (HumRRO); the Institute for Defense Analyses; and several proprietary business corporations.

Chapter 1

Introduction

In addition to presenting an integrated, coherent conceptual framework for addressing organizational performance and suggesting some practical models for use in analyzing, assessing, and improving the performance of organizations of all types, the book has a number of more specific objectives. They are:

1. To identify certain human factors found to be critical for the effective functioning of organizations.
2. To present a sound and systematic theoretical background for understanding the functioning of organizations and for identifying some critical organizational functions required for effectiveness.
3. To describe a sound and systematic conceptual framework for understanding the integration of organizations.
4. To present conceptual models for describing, analyzing, and assessing organizational functioning and to report the results of laboratory and field tests of the models.
5. To discuss implications of the test findings for the analysis and improvement of organizational functioning.
6. To propose procedures for assessing organizational functioning and for developing improved organizations.

RATIONALE

It is easy to establish an organization, and it is not hard to get some performance from it. However, it is exceedingly difficult to ensure that organizations so established always operate at high levels of effectiveness and, above all, consistently accomplish the purposes for which they are constituted (Drucker, 1999, 2001; Bouwen and Hosking, 2000).

Whatever the purpose, the effectiveness of an organization depends upon its ability to function as a unified system under current operating conditions (Hite, 1999). The necessity for coping with the highly turbulent, complex, and unpredictable environments of the modern world places a premium upon the capabilities of organizations to address and respond flexibly to a more or less constant flow of situations characterized by high levels of uncertainty. This emphasis upon flexible organizational responses to problem situations points up the role of organizations as problem-solving, decision-making, action-taking systems in which the basic purpose is to take direct unified action in highly turbulent and complex environments.

To be effective under such conditions, an organization must possess capabilities that produce a highly responsive and adaptive system of decision and action. In such a system, the means whereby information, decisions, and actions are brought into conjunction involves a complex interplay between individuals, positions, and levels. This constant interplay is a critical element in organizational responsiveness and makes flexibility highly important. Control and guidance of these processes in a flexible manner are a critical function of an organization.

The purpose of this book is to present an understandable and meaningful analysis of organizations at work, their dynamics, and influences that impact upon their capabilities to perform effectively. Organizations can have various types, configurations, purposes, and people who constitute them. Nevertheless, it is possible to identify the essential elements in organizational performance and to set forth some principles for leading and developing effective organizations (Galbraith, 1995).

This book is solidly based in Open Systems Theory and the social psychology of organizations. As discussed in Chapter 3, organizational performance and performance within organizations have been addressed from many different viewpoints. For this book, the concept of the *functionally competent organization* is proposed. It is conceived that organizations can be considered as unified systems based upon organizational competence.

Organizational competence is the central element in this discussion. The fundamental premise is that an organization should be viewed as a problem-solving, decision-making, action-taking system that functions within environments that change constantly. Competence is a way of classifying and systematizing essential organizational functions that must be performed and of making them more meaningful for everyday analysis and application.

The ability of an organization to perform these critical functions is what is meant by organizational competence. It is further conceived that organizational competence is a major operational determinant of organizational effectiveness. Competence is the capability of an organization to perform the critical functions (processes) that lead to achievement of effectiveness.

It is concluded that an open systems approach to organizations is the most meaningful and practicable means for understanding and improving performance. According to Open Systems Theory, an organization is an adaptive, equilibrium-seeking, open system; and the internal processes or functions through which adaptation occurs are significant subjects for attention.

In this view, the main challenge confronting modern organizations is coping with external stresses and continually changing conditions. When organizations are considered to be open systems—adaptive structures coping with various environments—the most significant attribute for understanding effectiveness is competence, or mastery over the environment. Following this view, the critical factors in understanding and improving effectiveness are the processes or functions by which the organization approaches its task and interacts with its environments. Identification and validation of essential organizational processes or functions provide an avenue to meaningful assessment of organizational functioning and to proven procedures for improving organizational performance.

In many organizations, the quality of process performance is not very good because, in order to control variability and thus ensure reliability, many leaders tend toward regulated and formal responses. They tend to prefer the certainty of standardized procedures with clearly demarcated and logically related stages, and, accordingly, they give little systematic attention to process performance. However, overreliance upon standardized responses tends to result in organizational rigidity, whereas, in the fast-changing environments of today, to be effective, an organization must maintain a high level of flexibility. This quality is essential in uncertainty situations, and it has its source in what has been called here *organizational competence.*

Leaders cannot be criticized too severely for overemphasis on standardized responses. Although most people who have given much thought to organizations are aware of certain more or less intangible aspects (which, here, have been called processes), these factors are often viewed as impossible to see and difficult to understand. Accordingly, little is ever done about them in any systematic way.

The conceptual framework presented here under the rubric of organizational competence offers a means for overcoming the problem. The competence components and their processes, together with the methodology for their measurement, provide concrete ways for analyzing internal functioning and for relating such functioning to both antecedent causal factors and ultimate achievement.

In application, competence and its components offer potential for both organizational diagnosis and development. It is possible to identify individuals, positions, or departments that are functional or dysfunctional in terms of performance of some or all processes. It is possible to determine who or what departments should perform each process, how well the processes are performed, and how they could be performed better.

The processes that have been identified provide both a framework for evaluation and bases for training and organizational development. Knowledge of requirements for effective process performance, when coupled with controlled experiences in execution, can be expected to result in decided improvements in the leadership and managerial performance of individuals. However, the greatest benefit is to be found in performance of the organization considered as a whole. Fundamental to the framework is the view that competence represents capability of the organization and is different from the sum of individual capabilities. Process performance involves organizational responses, and the quality of any single response event is determined by the entire network of antecedent relationships and responses. This suggests that organizational competence can best be improved by efforts that focus upon developing the organization as a system.

It has become axiomatic that human factors must receive full recognition in any reasonable consideration of organizational effectiveness. However, in attempts to do something about the human element, the most common approach in organizations is to focus upon the characteristics, skills, and deficiencies of individuals. This approach most often leads to emphasis upon selection procedures, performance evaluations and interviews, remedial training, and so forth. These and other activities that focus upon individual personnel are important and, indeed, essential for upgrading or maintaining the proficiency of an organization.

On the other hand, it is unreasonable to consider people without recognizing the impact of their environment upon them. People function within situational contexts, and these contexts define and limit behavior. An organization is a very powerful context and, accordingly, produces potent forces that circumscribe and channel the activities, attitudes, and motivations of personnel. For this reason, both individual behavior and group behavior within an organization are simply not the same as those outside it. This fact can never be safely ignored. The organizational context is indeed a most potent factor in individual and group effectiveness. This is fortunate because the organization is one thing that can be greatly influenced and controlled by leaders.

Essential Human Factors

An essential element in effectiveness involves competent performance by members of those organizational functions that are necessary for the development and integration of information, decisions, and actions and for the coordination of these elements at many levels of the organization. In later chapters, research is reported demonstrating the criticality of these functions for organizational effectiveness and the necessity for competent performance of them by all members.

It is apparent that performance of the functions is dependent upon human factors. Some technological assists can be provided, for example, highly sophisticated communication systems and equipment for rapid compilation and processing of data. However, the payoff in effectiveness ultimately reduces to the judgments and actions of organizational members both individually and collectively.

Because they play such essential roles in the performance of organizations, it is important to understand clearly and as concretely as possible how members function and how to train and lead them. The general purpose of this book is to improve such understanding through presentation of both (1) a conceptual rationale and model and (2) practical guidance for analyzing, assessing, and developing integrated organizations.

THE ORGANIZATION CONCEPT

The study of organizations has been approached from a variety of viewpoints, all of which seem to have some validity but differ widely in the attributes that they emphasize and in the aspects that they select for study. After evaluating these approaches, it was concluded that the most practicable for understanding organizations in all their variety would be an open systems approach. Systems concepts permit inclusion within one framework of the many different factors that may influence ultimate performance. In general, the conceptual framework for the book follows a systems viewpoint. It should be noted, however, that there has arisen recently some disagreement with systems approaches (Stacey, 2001; Stacey, Griffin, and Shaw, 2000).

For this book, an organization is conceived as a social system existing in physical and social environments over time. An organization is defined as a complex network of relationships of a number of people who are engaged in some activity for some purpose where the activity requires a division of work and responsibility in such a manner as to make the members interdependent. The people in this definition are physical organisms and psychological processes. The relationships among people are conditions in which the activity and psychological state of one person mutually influence those of another. A network of relationships is an abstraction of the relationships among a number of persons. The influence of a person is a function of both his or her psychological properties and the properties of the coordinating and decision-making roles assigned to him or her.

The stability of the organization through time in relation to its purpose is obtained through a sufficient coincidence of the psychological fields of its members. Shared understandings among members are essential for organizational achievement. A common means of communication, a common acceptance of purpose or objectives, and a common acceptance of duties and responsibilities are required for full effectiveness. The boundary of the organization as a unit of analysis can be established only in a relative manner. Relative autonomy is one means of doing this; another is purpose and perceived membership. In organizations, the particular services to be provided may be considered to constitute a purpose or mission.

The mode of organization is in part determined by the elements of purpose (i.e., the purpose dictates the method of distribution and execution of problem-solving, decision-making, and action functions). In turn, the distribution of these functions and the assignment of authority and responsibility to go with them define the formal structure of the organization. The purpose of an organization may be an important determinant of the way in which the organization is structured.

While an organization is a formal structure of positions operated according to the logics just described, it is also an adaptive social system. It is a set of formal relationships that can be manipulated in the interest of efficiency and effectiveness but is necessarily affected by conditions within its structure. The possibility of manipulating the formal system depends upon the extent to which the organization provides effective motivation to participants and conditions under which stability of relationships can be assured. Formal systems cannot be divorced from motivation and social relationships even within the most highly structured organizations.

Since an organization consists of individuals interacting within a formal system of coordination, it is the result of both formal and informal reciprocal influences. A proper understanding of an organization requires that it be possible to relate changes in official activities to both formal and informal patterns within the organization.

In summary, an organization is conceived as a number of persons performing some activity in relation to its external environments. The way the persons are arranged in relation to each other and to the task is the structure of the organization. The persons in the system are conceived as having various motivations and attitudes and as performing certain activities in certain ways. The ways in which they perform the activities are determined by their motivations and by how they perceive the organization, other members, themselves, and their roles.

The principal problem or task in writing this book was to describe a conceptual system that would include the various aspects just discussed, provide valid explanations of the relationships between them, and indicate directions for assessment and development of these relationships.

CHANGE MANAGEMENT

The Competence Model, described in detail later, provides a systematic framework for change management efforts. The book is dedicated to the proposition that organizations can be best developed by improvement of organizational competence, group competencies, and the competencies of individuals. Since an effective organization is a unified system, individual competencies feed into groups, and individual and group competencies feed into the competence of the organization.

If the above proposition is accepted, it follows that organizational change and improvement methods should be soundly based upon informed decisions—not guesswork, hunch, or the latest fads. "Informed decisions" refers to change management efforts to improve performance, as well as routine operational decisions, that are based upon systematically acquired data specifically designed to identify performance and competence problems at all levels (Anderson and Anderson, 2001). One purpose of this book is to set out some models for analyzing and developing functionally competent organizations.

THE PLAN OF THIS BOOK

Because they play such essential roles in the performance of organizations, it is important to understand clearly and as concretely as possible how organizations function and how to train, develop, and lead them. Here the general purpose is to improve such understanding through presentation of (1) a conceptual rationale and models and (2) practical guidance for analyzing, assessing, and developing integrated organizations. Accomplishment of this purpose requires that consideration be given to a variety of information related to individuals, groups, and organizations. The effectiveness of an organization is dependent upon the conditions that exist within it. Its performance and the performance of people within the organization are the resultants of a reciprocal relationship between the actions of people and existing conditions within the organization. Through examination of these essential aspects, it can be expected that better insight into successful organizational performance will be achieved.

Part I—Functionally Competent Organizations: Theory

For years the study of organizations remained one of the most confounding and conflicting areas of the social sciences; however, recently the parts have begun to fall into place. Now a number of propositions can be stated with confidence.

Part I is devoted to a theoretical and conceptual analysis of the approaches taken in later chapters. Chapters 1 and 2 introduce the book and discuss some of the central issues and problems involved in the performance and effectiveness of most organizations. Chapter 2 opens with a discussion of what is considered to be a problem in the effectiveness of organizations, namely, the ability to flexibly cope with current conditions within their environments.

Effectiveness requires that an organization have the capability to efficiently identify, assess, solve, and cope with events that are marked by rapid change and much uncertainty. In these chapters, the typical organization is analyzed, and some common problems or pitfalls in organizational functioning are identified.

Chapter 3 is devoted to a limited historical review and a critique of the major theoretical issues related to organizational performance. An Open Systems Theory and an emphasis upon processes and organizational functions are proposed as the model for organizational competence.

Chapter 4 is devoted to descriptions of research concerned with empirical tests of the Competence Model. Three large-scale studies of actual organizations are described. Implications of the results are discussed, and it is concluded that the main value of the Competence Model is that it offers (1) a systematic way of thinking about some otherwise exceedingly slippery organizational functions, (2) a workable framework for the assessment and diagnosis of organizational functioning and for the correction or improvement of dysfunctional elements, and (3) a meaningful and workable foundation for both individual and group training in organizational process performance.

In Chapter 5, the several elements of the Competence Model are set forth, described, and elaborated. Organizational attributes required for maximum effectiveness are stipulated. Components of organizational competence (functions) are identified and discussed. Quality requirements of each functional process are described. A three-part Competence Model is presented and discussed.

Part II—Requirements for Performance

In Chapter 6, the performance of individuals is addressed. The concept of competencies of individuals is introduced, and definitions and a rationale are presented. Some research on competencies is discussed. An Impact Model of performance is presented, and several classes of variables and component factors are identified and discussed. Utility of this model of individual performance is also discussed.

Chapter 7 is concerned with the performance of groups in organizations. The origins of groups within organizations are discussed and specified, and cohesion, or cohesiveness, is set forth as a significant and critical influence upon both the satisfaction and performance of group members. Likert's characteristics of an ideal group are listed and discussed. Several general factors that are determinants of group effectiveness are identified.

Part III—Functionally Competent Organizations: Application

The purpose of Chapter 8 is to present a concise, general framework for addressing the development of fully integrated organizations. Some concepts are introduced and defined, such as a human organization, organizational effectiveness, purpose, functional proficiency, and integration.

An overview of some essential organizational properties is presented, and the utility of a systems approach is discussed. Some social psychological requirements for organizational effectiveness are set forth.

The 12 necessary organizational characteristics are categorized, and necessary manager functions are listed and discussed with respect to integration.

Specifications for an effective training and development model are set forth, and assessment issues are discussed. A formal model for development of organizational integration is formulated and described, some assessment issues are discussed, and the model is evaluated. Implications are discussed, and the concepts are advocated as a solution to application for enhancing organization performance.

Chapter 9 is concerned with operationally defining competence. In this chapter, the principal focus is upon the conditions and activities for developing or enhancing organizational effectiveness through the improvement of organizational competence. The importance of Adaptability is stressed, and its reliance upon reality assessment is emphasized. The three attributes and competence are operationally defined in terms of relevant organizational functions. Each of the eight identified functions (processes) is defined and discussed, and quality requirements for each are set out. Performance of the processes is discussed, and specific criteria for assessing performance of each function are stipulated. Implications for the use of the Competence Model to assess performance are discussed.

In Chapter 10, a full Organizational Effectiveness Model is presented and discussed. The model sets forth several essential elements of an effectiveness model, and a figure illustrates the reciprocal relationships of the elements and the conditions and activities necessary for the development and maintenance of organizational competence and integration. The various relationships and the utility of the model are discussed. Six potential uses of the model are proposed.

An approach for improving competence is described, and procedures for analyzing and assessing the competence of existing organizations are discussed. Three methods for assessing competence performance within an organization are described. A discussion is devoted to ways of developing an integrated organization through enhancement of required organizational conditions and favorable developmental activities. Three different types of training activities are recommended. Each is described briefly, some specifications are presented, and implications for leadership in the developmental process are discussed.

In Chapter 11, the importance of work contexts is stressed. The two components of work contexts, structure and climate, are discussed, and considerations in developing favorable contexts are presented. A number of factors that control the performance of organizations are discussed, and the implications of this chapter for human factors considerations are analyzed.

In Chapter 12, a summary and some conclusions are presented. Three general objectives were developed for the book. Each is discussed in this chapter. In addition, this final chapter presents a concise, general framework for addressing problems of organizational performance and a summary of the elements involved in effectiveness. Several basic concepts are repeated, reviewed, and integrated. Finally, relevance of the material in this book is discussed in relation to several types of rapid-response organizations, as well as both conventional and unconventional organizations.

Part I

Functionally Competent Organizations: Theory

Chapter 2

Organizations and Their Functions

INTRODUCTION

The effectiveness of an organization depends upon many things. Some of the more critical elements are:

1. The formal body of plans, objectives, doctrine, policies, and procedures that have been developed to guide decisions and actions.
2. The adequacy of all of the variety of methods and techniques used in the performance of the work of the organization.
3. The quality of the equipment provided for use in the performance of required activities.
4. The training, skills, and proficiencies of the personnel.

Each of the above elements is critical for the effectiveness of most organizations, and, if any are deficient, effectiveness is impaired.

However, the logic of sound plans and doctrine to guide decisions; the adequacy of policies, procedures, and techniques; the quality of equipment; and the skills of individuals in executing technical operations are not sufficient to meet the increasingly demanding requirements of modern operations. *A remaining critical element includes the capability of the organization to function as a unified system in order to cope with the complex conditions of the modern world.*

Conditions in the Modern World

Today organizations of all kinds face unprecedented challenges. To be effective, every organization must efficiently cope with its operational environments and with problems that arise within them. This has always been important for success; however, recent developments in the world have made control of operational environments, external and internal, both more essential and more difficult.

We are presently moving at breakneck speed into an information age and an information economy. The ability to rapidly accumulate, assimilate, and disseminate large quantities of information makes the present-day operating conditions of many organizations exceedingly uncertain and unpredictable. This is true for business corporations and government agencies; crisis management organizations such as police departments and civil emergency organizations; as well as military units.

Whatever the purpose and mission of an organization, present-day operating conditions are characterized most often by:

1. High levels of turbulence within both the operating environment and the organization;
2. Increasingly unpredictable events arising from highly turbulent conditions;
3. Increasing rapidity of critical events;
4. Increasingly complex operations required to cope with threatening and uncertain events and their results.

When these conditions arc compounded by strong pressures generated by bottom-line management and bureaucratic gridlock, organizational stress becomes intense. The pressing need for world-class organizations capable of coping with highly turbulent, complex conditions and unpredictable events places a premium upon the capabilities of organizations to address and respond flexibly to a more or less constant flow of new situations characterized by high levels of uncertainty.

ORGANIZATIONAL EFFECTIVENESS

Organizational effectiveness is the accomplishment of missions or the achievement of objectives. Whatever its mission, the effectiveness of an organization requires that it efficiently identify, assess, solve, and cope with events or problems that arise within the operational environments. These are the classical functions of all organizations, and performance of them has always been critical for organizational success. It is clear now that functional proficiency and the integration of management and control systems play important roles in the performance of all organizations.

Required Capabilities

To be effective in turbulent and complex conditions, every organization must possess capabilities to:

1. Search out, identify, and interpret the properties of operational situations *as they develop*.
2. Solve problems *as they occur* within the context of rapidly changing situational demands.
3. Generate *flexible decisions* relevant to changing situations.
4. Cope with *shifting situational demands* with precise appropriateness.

It is apparent that the above capabilities require a highly responsive and adaptive system of decision and action. In such a system, the complex interplay between individuals, positions, and organization levels is a critical element in flexibility and responsiveness and, therefore, in organizational effectiveness. Control and guidance of these processes is an essential function in the management of any organization.

ESSENTIAL HUMAN FACTORS

Accordingly, an additional element in effectiveness involves competent performance of organizational functions that are essential for the development and integration of information, decisions, and actions and for the coordination of these elements at all levels within the organization. In later chapters, research is reported demonstrating the criticality of these functions for organizational effectiveness and the necessity for competent performance of them.

Performance of the functions is dependent mainly upon human factors. Some technological assists can be provided, for example, highly sophisticated communication systems and equipment for rapid compilation and processing of data. However, the payoff in effectiveness ultimately reduces to the judgments and actions of personnel in the organization, both individually and collectively. This is especially applicable to individuals who occupy key supervisory and control positions. These are usually individuals who are in the chain of authority and who influence execution of critical organizational functions.

THE TYPICAL ORGANIZATION

Most organizations are structures intended to function effectively in variable situations. This is especially true for quick-response organizations such as police and fire departments, crisis management teams, and military combat units, whose typical operational conditions are characterized by intense pressures from turbulent and rapidly changing environments. The functions of these units are to cope with such pressures and to overcome forces in the environments that generate the pressures. Although not as self-evident, the same is increasingly true for business and other types of organizations.

This emphasis upon organizational responses to problem situations points up the role of the organization as problem solver, decision maker, and action taker (Reitzel, 1958). Although individual members actually perform the problem-solving and decision-making activities, either singly or jointly, the necessity for global organizational responses makes it useful to conceive of an organization as a problem-solving, decision-making, and action-taking unit. Individuals are severely limited in their capacity to deal with complex situations. On the other hand, an organization makes it possible to analyze situations more understandably and, consequently, to develop more effective means of adapting to changing environments in order to accomplish missions.

The basic organizational technique is to (1) break down large problems into component parts, (2) assign responsibilities for dealing with the segments to specialized units (e.g., staff sections) and to various levels, and (3) coordinate these separate efforts in a system of organizational decision and action. The characteristic form of coping with complex problems is a controlled and directed problem-solving and decision-making system. Even though most organizations still adhere to the principle of manager responsibility for decision making, the complexity of problems and the organizational web in which a manager must operate reduce and qualify his or her function as a single, individual information processor and problem solver. It simply is no longer possible for a single individual to perform this function. Many organizations now have groups (staffs, committees) that may serve in either advisory or authoritative capacities.

The major and fundamental function of an organization is to act to achieve its objectives or to accomplish its missions. In general, its method is to coordinate the activities of organizational members so that all shall be properly related. More specifically, the method is as follows (Reitzel, 1958):

1. The members of the organization are assigned specific decision-making responsibilities and action roles.
2. The members are trained in some respects and indoctrinated in others to perform reliably in these assigned roles.
3. Both decision-making and action responsibilities are distributed in terms of types of problem situations and in terms of superior and subordinate levels of authority.
4. Standard operating procedures, including standard formats for the communication of information, decisions, and action plans, are developed; and these procedures are most rigorously enforced at the lower levels of responsibility.
5. The resulting structure and its standard procedures are then operated on the basis of a continuous flow of situation-decision-action.

Organizational Structure

The formal distribution of problem-solving, decision-making, and action functions and the assignment of authority and responsibility to go with them define the structure of the organization. The functions are arranged and systematized on the basis of ideas as to how they should be effectively performed and logically coordinated—on the basis of what have been called "the logics of organization."

In accordance with the logics, most organizations are characterized by (1) the rational determination of objectives, (2) hierarchical arrangements of personnel in terms of authority, responsibility, coordination, and control; (3) missions that require the collaboration of subunits to accomplish them; and (4) a certain degree of autonomy in matters strictly internal to the organization. Large units (e.g., divisions) are broken down into smaller components (e.g., departments), each having a fairly independent identity. The components are, in turn, usually divided into even smaller identifiable elements (e.g., sections and teams). Thus, most organizations are laid out so as to create a precise format in which each unit is clearly charted and its missions assigned.

Usually, the product is the well-known structure that resembles a pyramid, with a single position at the top and increasing numbers of positions at each succeeding lower level. The attachment of specialized units may flatten the pyramid somewhat, and some task force organizations may include two parallel pyramids. However, the most common structures resemble pyramids in some form. One variation may follow matrix-management procedures; with such organizations, however, many of the conventional logics still apply.

Leaders

The general functions of managers or leaders are to determine the courses of action to be taken within the purview of the mission and to oversee and coordinate the activities of all people and subordinate units so that such activities fit together and contribute efficiently to accomplishment of the mission. More specifically, it is the responsibility of managers or leaders to perform the "command and control" functions within and for the organization. In general, performance of command and control functions involves:

1. Solving problems in terms of both planning operations and supervising activities during ongoing operations.
2. Making multitudes of decisions ranging from major strategic determinations to those required to supervise some actions on a minute-to-minute basis.

3. Supervising ongoing activities of the organization as a whole and of subordinate units individually. This supervision involves both monitoring activities and providing guidance and direction.
4. Coordinating both own and subordinates' activities so that all contribute efficiently to objectives, as well as those encompassed by the larger mission, and
5. Coordinating activities with those of adjacent and supporting units and with higher organizational levels so that the unit's actions are congruent with both the larger mission and missions of similar units.

Command and Control

Most organizations are designed to operate according to a number of principles intended to maximize effectiveness through controls. They include the following:

1. There must be one central source of authority and decision making (unity of leadership).
2. There must be a clear-cut hierarchy of subordination (chain of authority).
3. There must be a routinized procedure for most activities (standardization of operations and functions).
4. Tasks and subtasks should be standardized, and personnel should be trained for specific tasks (specialization of functions).
5. Staff positions function in advisory capacities but carry no authority for making decisions (line and staff functions).

The basic purpose is to take directed, unified action in an environment that presents a continuous flow of uncertainty situations. *The principal device for maintaining control of this effort is the chain of authority, which runs through the heart of the organization, from the topmost level to the lowest point of supervision.* Individuals in the chain of authority, together with designated staff, perform the supervisory and control functions within most organizations.

Organizational Process

Ideally, the process of coping with uncertainty situations involves handling an operational cycle that flows up and down the chain of authority and consists of situation—information—decision—action—altered situation—new information—supplementary decision, and so on (Reitzel, 1958). Through its command and control function, the organization seeks to regulate this cycle without becoming inflexible in its responses.

In practice, however, the operational cycle is not usually so straightforward as described above. For one thing, although the logical starting point for the cycle should always be a specific situation, there are in reality no concrete boundaries for many situations. Thus, situations may overlap, or one may flow into another. Furthermore, there is no specific mechanism for recognizing a situation. Sometimes, information reveals a situation. Sometimes, action taken in one situation creates another situation elsewhere. Frequently, one organizational level, by decision or action, creates a situation for another higher or lower level. Thus, the cycle tends to operate erratically.

In addition, the process whereby information, decisions, and actions are brought into conjunction involves a complex interplay between and among levels. For example, as information flows upward in the chain of authority, parts are siphoned off, and bits are added. The flow of directives downward is similarly affected. At the same time, decisions and actions from intervening levels enter into the flow of information and directives.

This constant interplay is the essence of dynamic organizational process, and the extent to which leaders deal with it competently is a major determinant of effectiveness. The ability of leaders to control and direct the processes that drive an organization determines, in large part, its capability for coping with the pressures imposed by its environments.

PROBLEMS IN ORGANIZATIONAL FUNCTIONING

As discussed earlier, the functions of leaders or managers are to plan the actions required for accomplishment of the mission and to oversee and coordinate the activities of all personnel and subordinate elements so that such activities fit together and contribute efficiently to accomplishment of the mission. It is the responsibility of leaders to set objectives and develop effective plans based upon the best information available about (1) the mission, (2) external forces, (3) available resources, and (4) the internal environment. It is a further responsibility to oversee implementation of the plans and to adapt their ongoing implementation to changing operational conditions.

Unfortunately, everything does not always happen as planned. In the course of implementing planned activities, countless things can go wrong. Some problems that arise have their sources outside the organization. Other problems develop through error or default within it. All must be met and overcome as they occur. This necessity for flexible response to changing events seems to create major difficulties for many organizations.

Some General Pitfalls

A number of years ago, Schein (1970) set out some general problems or areas of difficulty encountered by most organizations in maintaining or improving effectiveness in response to changing environments. These have been adapted and are presented here as pitfalls in organizational functioning.

1. *Failure to sense changes in the environment and/or incorrectly interpreting what is happening.* This pitfall is clearly concerned with failure to obtain all relevant and current information and to apply correct meaning to the information obtained.
2. *Failure to communicate all relevant information to those parts of the organization that can act upon it or use it.* This pitfall refers to both the upward and downward communication of information. No organization can adapt to changes effectively and rapidly without continuous updating of information about the ongoing situation and of operational requirements.
3. *Failure of managers to ensure that all personnel and subordinate units make the changes indicated by new information or changed plans.* As Schein emphasized, effecting internal change in an organization requires more than merely the recognition or the announcement that such changes are necessary. A major pitfall is failure of managers to oversee and verify the implementation of required changes during ongoing operations.
4. *Failure to consider the impact of changes upon all parts of the organization.* This refers to failure to consider the effects of operational changes upon all subunits, especially support units. In short, focus upon operating elements without consideration of support or adjacent units may, on occasion, lead to disaster.
5. *Failure to obtain information about the effects of the change.* The problem here is essentially the same as failure to sense changes in the environment. The pitfall is failure to follow up on the effects of actions taken and, more seriously, failure of personnel at all levels to learn from the results so that mistakes will not be repeated, and profit can be obtained from success.

The above are common pitfalls that may occur in all types of organizations. They were presented to demonstrate that many of the problems encountered are not the result of tactical errors or bad judgment or poor execution, but, rather, their sources lie in deficient organizational functioning—in failure to adequately perform the problem-solving, decision-making, action-taking functions that are common to all organizations but that take specific form in different organizations. These functions are essential for developing the unified systems necessary for coping with the severe pressures imposed by current operating conditions.

Effects of Operating Pressures

A major concern in every organization should be to develop it to function at peak efficiency even under extreme conditions and to guard against disruption of its critical processes by pressures generated within its environments (i.e., by competition, severe financial conditions, difficult physical environments, or other adverse conditions). Disruptions of processes that are imposed by environmental pressures may initiate far-reaching consequences. Sometimes, they may actually determine survival of the organization.

The effects of environmental pressures are diverse and, occasionally, even contradictory (Herman, 1963). On the one hand, moderate pressure can result in closer integration, the development of appropriate problem solutions, and the enhancement of organizational processes. On the other hand, heavy pressure may lead to disruption of critical processes, which seriously limits viability of the organization.

Research evidence detailing the effects of extreme pressures upon organizational functions is sparse. However, there is a small body of literature concerned with the effects of crises upon the functioning of nonmilitary organizations (Williams, 1957; Herman, 1963; Drabek, 1965). A crisis is an event or situation that (1) threatens high-priority objectives of the organization, (2) presents a restricted amount of time in which a response can be made, and (3) is unexpected or unanticipated by the organization (Herman, 1963). Thus, a crisis is an emergency or extreme situation and, as such, is analogous to many of the high-pressure situations experienced by some organizations.

Emergency situations and the pressures generated by them mainly affect the problem-solving, decision-making, and adaptive processes discussed earlier. For example, it has been found that initial information about a potential threat tends to be given low value (Williams, 1957; Olmstead, Christensen, and Lackey, 1973; Bolger, 1986). Organizations are frequently caught unprepared because available information from the environment is overlooked or disregarded. Furthermore, recognition of the existence of an actual emergency or problem often lags behind the occurrence of threat or even behind the impact of the emergency itself. Frequently, fragmentary and local reports are available leading up to and following actual impact; however, it is only after these reports accumulate that a recognition emerges within the organization that a crisis has occurred or that a major problem exists.

Much behavior during the immediate threat and the onset of the crisis or problem is essentially a search for information. Accordingly, the time required to define the situation and to put responses into effect is critical. The length of time required depends, in large part, upon the communication that occurs within the organization. Yet, in many emergency situations, the total number of communication channels used for the collection and distribution of information is reduced (Janowitz, 1960; Herman, 1963; Olmstead et al., 1973; Bolger, 1986). For example, some communication channels are used extensively for all types of information, yet other channels may be used only a little for information that would be appropriate for them. This is in contrast to the fact that there is frequently information overload (Williams, 1957; Olmstead et al., 1973; Bolger, 1986). The number of channels employed is reduced but, in those channels that remain, the quantity of information may reach overload proportions. Sometimes, emergency channels are not planned.

Frequently, the compelling pressure to act and a compressed time perspective lead to increased errors in judgment. Furthermore, the required coordination of decisions and actions frequently is not supplied in the early stages. Then, as recognition of the gravity of the crisis increases, there is usually a tendency toward centralization of decision-making responsibilities (Herman, 1963; Olmstead et al., 1973).

When an organization is struck with a crisis (sudden, increased environmental pressures), the organizational processes often deteriorate or even break down completely (Olmstead et al., 1973). Under such circumstances, some organizations do not rapidly regain their abilities to function. For example, inadequate communication often means that a serious or large mistake or problem is required before it can be recognized by the headquarters staff and corrected. Because of lack of information, small mistakes or problems go unnoticed.

Finally, there frequently is a strong tendency to use stereotyped responses. The most familiar actions are those most likely to be taken, regardless of their suitability for meeting specific situational requirements.

The above examples are only a few of the ways that organizational processes may break down under the stress of environmental pressures. However, the important point is that those aspects of an organization that are most likely to be affected by operational stresses are the problem-solving, decision-making, and adapting processes—those processes that most determine the ability of the organization to cope with significant events in its environments.

Coping with Pressures

Such factors as knowledge, experience, and training restrict the tendencies toward breakdown of organizational functioning discussed above. This is what military and crisis management organizations attempt to accomplish through training, indoctrination, standard operating procedures (SOPs), contingency plans, and so on. There can be no doubt that the reliability so obtained is essential to integrated effort. On the other hand, overreliance upon stereotyped responses and standardized procedures tends to limit flexibility, a quality that is also essential in turbulent and uncertain situations.

A similar paradox is found in connection with adherence to well-accepted organizational principles and practices. A series of seeming dilemmas runs through many organizations.

1. Clear organizational lines are essential to operational effectiveness, but, if they become too fixed, they tend toward inflexibility.
2. Well-defined objectives increase the efficiency of the organization, but they often make it difficult to change direction easily.
3. Levels of authority assure an effective chain of command, but an extended hierarchy is another factor that encourages the development of inflexibility.
4. Clearly understood rules, methods, and standard procedures make it possible to operate consistently and with coordination, but they circumscribe subordinates' initiative as they increase in number.
5. The division of labor requires specialization of unit function, but specialization leads units into narrow perspectives of their responsibilities to the larger organization.

There is often a precarious balance between rigidity and flexibility in many organizations. The point at which this balance is struck can be a matter of considerable importance for effectiveness. Therefore, a major requirement is to establish and maintain a workable balance between these two aspects of the organized decision-making, problem-solving, action-taking process.

There can be no question that an organization operating within exacting requirements for coordination and control must rely upon formal structures, standard procedures, and indoctrinated practices to obtain many of its results. However, reliance solely upon such built-in controls is not sufficient to produce maximum effectiveness.

There is mounting evidence that maximum effectiveness can be achieved only when members of an organization address directly the quality of its functioning and develop capabilities that enable it to maintain functional integrity under the stress of extreme pressures. This capability for performing critical organizational functions and for maintaining structure and function under pressure is the main topic of this book.

The way in which an organization functions as an integrated unit is a matter for serious and careful consideration. Yet, all too frequently, such considerations are ignored. Reasons for this lack of attention to organizational functioning are difficult to surmise. One possible reason may be the ubiquity of organizational processes. They are always present in organizations, and their obviousness may lead to neglect. A more probable cause is the fact that organizational processes are the products of human behavior and, accordingly, are less tangible, more ambiguous, and more difficult to control than such concrete aspects of endeavor as procedures, plans, and efficient use of equipment. There seems to be a tendency in many organizations to give short shrift to the less concrete aspects of day-to-day operations. Yet, these intangible aspects may determine the difference between success and failure.

CONCEPT OF ORGANIZATIONAL COMPETENCE

The concept of organizational competence is a key element in this approach to the development and leadership of organizations. It derives from recognition that one of the most critical factors in the effectiveness of any organization is its ability to sense impacting events in its external and internal environments, to process the information sensed, and to adapt its operations to cope with the sensed changes.

The ability of the organization to perform these critical functions is what is meant by organizational competence. It is further conceived that organizational competence is a major operational determinant of organizational effectiveness. Where effectiveness is the ultimate outcome (mission accomplishment, achievement of objectives, productivity, etc.), competence is the capability of the organization to perform the critical functions (processes) that lead to achievement of effectiveness.

Organizational competence is a concept. It is a way of classifying and systematizing organizational functions that must be performed and of making them more meaningful for everyday application.

The fundamental premise of the concept is that an organization is a problem-solving, action-taking system that functions within environments that change constantly. In order for the organization to actively master its environments or to cope with events within them, adaptability is essential. Here, adaptability coincides with problem-solving ability, which, in turn, depends upon the flexibility of the organization. *Flexibility is the ability to learn through experience and to change with changing internal and external circumstances.*

In order for an organization to cope with its environments, it must be sufficiently flexible in its internal processes or functions to enable it to modify operations to meet the demands of new problems arising in its environments, both internal and external. This is especially important for organizations operating in high-stress situations, where rigidity can be fatal.

In turn, adaptability relies upon the organization's capability for reality testing. If the conditions requisite for an effective organization are to be met, the organization must develop adequate techniques for determining the real properties of the field in which it exists. The effective organization requires adequate reality assessment techniques if it is to cope with events in its critical environments. "Adequate reality assessment" refers to search and sensing processes sufficiently effective to provide the organization with information that permits it to develop accurate perceptions of the environments within which it must function. In short, *a correct understanding of the problem is necessary before it can be solved or overcome. The search, sensing, and communication processes involved in reality assessment help to provide that understanding.* What is contemplated for the improvement of performance is a carefully planned and systematic approach to the enhancement of organizational functioning.

Such a functional approach is required because the way in which an organization functions is one of the more important aspects of its capability for success or even survival. Organizational functioning (competence) is the foundation upon which all planning, strategies, and use of resources are built. If an organization does not function well, plans, strategies, and expenditure of resources are futile. Accordingly, organizational functioning is equal to planning, strategies, and use of resources as a critical determinant of effectiveness and survivability. Because of this importance, it is essential that organizational competence be given the same emphasis as other performance elements.

Most people who are concerned with the performance of organizations consider effectiveness to be control over environment. An effective organization is a unified system equipped with the knowledge, skills, and resources to control its environment, while an ineffective organization, for the lack of such capabilities, remains subject to forces over which it can exert little control.

Carried to the extreme, this insistence on the specificity of problems would render hopeless any attempt to obtain a prior understanding of things that affect organizational functioning. The saving factor is that problems occur in all organizations. Whatever their specific nature, all organizations possess certain universal properties that can be exploited, and, whenever a problem arises, its assessment in relation to basic organizational properties makes possible more insightful and lasting solutions.

Every organization has the following properties:

1. A structure of some sort, together with a set of either explicit or implied assumptions, premises, principles, or logics concerned with ways that the activities of the organization and its constituent groups should be arranged and executed.
2. Personal relationships, some of which are based upon work contacts, some on friendship, and some on group affiliation.
3. Communication processes through which, to one degree or another, there is a flow of information about the internal state of the organization, its constituent groups, the environments within which it functions, and the relationship of the organization to its environments.
4. Decision-making processes that guide the organization and its groups and determine its actions.
5. Influence processes, usually centered in formally designated leaders but sometimes based in individuals or groups not anticipated by the organization chart.
6. Resources to carry on activities, such as personnel, money, equipment, and materials.

7. Motivational and attitudinal characteristics, such as the forces drawn upon in mobilizing the efforts of people and the degree of favorableness and loyalty toward the work, the organization, its component groups, and its members.

Differences between organizations occur because of variations in the form and degree of the above properties and the specific configurations that evolve because of particular goals, tasks, and circumstances. However, every organization possesses the properties in some form and to some degree. Taken together, they constitute a foundation upon which assessment and developmental efforts can be based.

Dangers of Overcontrol

In many organizations, leaders' attempts to improve effectiveness most often take the form of modifications of the structural framework—that is, reorganization—and of increased emphasis upon the more formalized organizational constraints, such as policies and procedures. It would seem that many of these actions derive from an urgent desire to produce more reliable and predictable organizational performance by reducing the variability in human behavior insofar as possible.

Of course, attention to these aspects is important; however, excessive reliance upon them leads to organizational rigidity. Effectiveness under the complex conditions of today requires flexibility, a quality that has its principal source in the integrated functional processes discussed earlier.

INDIVIDUAL COMPETENCIES

Organizational competence depends upon the performance of individuals in acquiring and interpreting information, making choices concerning to whom acquired information is to be communicated, accurately and completely; making decisions concerning ways to cope with unusual or unanticipated situations; and executing actions that derive from such decisions—all performed at high levels of proficiency and cooperation. As discussed earlier, some technological assists may be available; however, the payoff in competence ultimately reduces to the judgments and actions of operating personnel.

In numerous studies of a wide range of jobs, a competency approach has been found to identify superior performers. This applies to skilled workers, as well as supervisors, managers, and executives.

A competency is an individual's *demonstrated* knowledge, skills, and abilities. Competencies go beyond traditional knowledge, skills, and abilities (KSAs); they are KSAs that are *demonstrated in a job context*. A cluster of demonstrated KSAs defines a competency and makes a real difference for organizational success. For example, planning is a competency. Rather than emphasizing a broad range of specific tasks and skills required for effective performance or attempting to establish the basic actions to be performed in a job, generic skills or competencies can be behaviorally defined and identified as basic to performance.

The fact is that many of the activities connected with work involve common elements or competencies. This is especially true for supervisors and managers, where the same competency may overlap many different tasks. An example is communicating, which may be necessary in many tasks performed by supervisors and managers.

A number of individual competencies have been identified for both nonsupervisory employees and supervisors and executives. Individual competencies are discussed in later chapters.

GROUP COMPETENCIES

Of equal importance, the performance of organizational processes is a team product, and much of the quality of process performance depends upon teamwork and the coordination of separate responsibilities and activities. Accordingly, equal to the skills of individuals is what is termed here as *the integration of structure and function*. This means that the positions, roles, and functions that make up an organizational system must fit together and support each other in their respective activities. Where the integration of structure and function does not occur, there may result missed signals, aborted decisions, overlooked information, and activities at cross-purposes. In the extreme, loss of integration may produce a collapse of essential functions, which can threaten survival of the organization. Group performance is a critical element.

Similar to individual competencies, group competencies are the properties and characteristics of effective groups. These competencies go beyond conventional performance elements. They are generic attributes that distinguish more effective from less effective groups.

A detailed discussion of group competencies and teamwork is presented in later chapters.

THE COMPETENCE MODEL

The Competence Model described above provides a systematic framework for change management efforts. Use of the model makes it possible to assess individual and group competencies, as well as organizational competence as a whole. Information and data obtained from such assessments provide bases for better-informed decisions concerning change management and performance improvement.

This book is dedicated to the proposition that organizations can be best developed by improvement of organizational competence, group competencies, and individual competencies. It follows that change management decisions and efforts to improve performance should rest upon the knowledge that an effective organization is a unified system consisting of interlocking parts—individuals, groups (sections, departments, work groups, teams, decision-making groups), and various levels of authority. Effectiveness depends upon the competencies of individuals, group competencies, and the competence of the organization as a whole in performing the functions required to accomplish its goals. Thus, individual competencies feed into groups, and individual and group competencies feed into the competence of the organization.

MANAGING CHANGE

If the above proposition is accepted, it should be apparent that change in organizational performance is achieved best by a total improvement effort directed squarely at organizational, group, and individual competence (Vroom, 1969). Furthermore, organizational change and improvement efforts should be soundly based upon informed decisions, not guesswork, hunch, or the latest fad.

"Informed decisions" means that change management and efforts to improve performance should be based upon systematically acquired data, specifically designed to identify performance and competence problems at all levels. The data should also indicate training or development requirements.

Although it is not proposed as a panacea, organizational competence plays a major role in the performance of organizations. Accordingly, it warrants significant attention in efforts to improve effectiveness. Competence and its integral concepts provide bases for a working framework or model that can be used for (1) analyzing the functional competence of an organization and its critical parts; (2) identifying dysfunctional elements; and (3) improving an organization's functioning through assessment, development, and training.

The remainder of this book sets out the proposed conceptual model, the relevant theoretical background, and recommended bases for developing competence and effectiveness in organizations.

RELEVANCE FOR ORGANIZATIONS

The Competence Model applies to all types of organizations. It can be a starting point for understanding and improving any organization.

Rapid-Response Organizations

Army and Marine tactical units are examples par excellence of rapid-response organizations. Rapid-response units are organizations that must identify and adapt effectively to events that occur in fast-changing and uncertain environmental conditions. Other examples of military rapid-response organizations are Navy fire-direction and fire-control centers and Air Force tactical control centers.

In civilian contexts, examples of rapid-response organizations are civil disaster organizations and police, fire, and forest-fire command centers. All such units are organizations that must collectively and continually adapt to uncertain, hostile, and fast-changing conditions.

In both military and civilian rapid-response organizations, each unit is governed by a command and control group closely resembling a battle staff. Furthermore, effectiveness is, in large part, determined by the execution of processes quite similar to those performed by military battle staffs.

The conceptual model described in this book (Chapter 5) is applicable to all types of rapid-response organizations. Similarly, the development and training procedures discussed are appropriate for most such organizations.

Other Organizations

Upon careful examination of the model, it becomes apparent that it can be applied to any organization, regardless of type. The concepts (reality testing, adaptability, identity), together with the seven processes derived from them, can be the starting point for understanding and improving the functioning of any organization. The seven competence processes include all of the essential general functions performed by all organizations. Aside from the types of environments encountered, the kinds of activities in which they engage, and the particular stresses that may arise, the greatest difference between military tactical units and other organizations, both military and civilian, is in the time frames within which problems occur and must be solved.

In contrast to rapid-response units, the time spans for operations and problems in more conventional organizations may extend over weeks, months, or even years, and problems may overlap so that it is difficult to know where one begins and another ends. The operations of tactical units are usually more clearly demarcated and shorter in duration. These differences make processes in nonemergency organizations somewhat more ambiguous, often complex, and sometimes difficult to trace.

Nevertheless, the seven processes that constitute competence include all of the essential functions performed by any organization, and, with care, they can be identified and traced. Attention to competence warrants major effort in any program intended to improve organizational effectiveness.

Attention to competence appears to be especially important in civilian organizations because of increasing needs to adapt to changing conditions in civilian life. The increasing rapidity with which change is occurring in modern society makes it essential for most types of organizations to learn to adapt flexibly to continuously fluid conditions. Such adaptation should occur with minimal internal turbulence. Notable examples are requirements for the military establishment to adapt to changed or reduced threat to national security, to changed sources of its personnel, and to new values in society.

Almost every industrial firm is faced with the necessity for accommodating to rapidly shifting markets, increased competition, fast-changing technology, and heightened public concern about pollution, ecology, and damage to the environment. Governments must stay abreast of their citizens' needs and desires. Even educational institutions must frequently modify goals and operations to meet the demands of constantly shifting constituencies.

Under such conditions, the survival of an organization requires a fine sensitivity to the often-subtle cues provided by critical environments, the ability to read such cues promptly and interpret them accurately, and the capacity for rapid but efficient modification of internal operations so that new developments can be met and mastered as they arise. Inadequacy in these capabilities can result in failure or destruction of the organization.

Chapter 3

Theoretical Background

The literature about organizations is characterized by many viewpoints, each of which seems to possess a certain degree of legitimacy. The problem is that the one thing, an organization, may be approached validly from a number of different standpoints. Thus, the systems developed by social scientists, business theorists, behavioral scientists, decision theorists, and operations researchers usually consist of widely different concepts and variables. Many years ago, Stogdill (1966) listed 18 separate ways of conceptualizing organizations and groups, and he said that this was not an exhaustive list. Yet, each approach has a certain relevance and each contributes to better understanding of organizations (Williamson, 1995).

One major contributor to the proliferation of approaches has been a certain duality that has existed throughout much recent history of the field. This division ultimately reduces to the old question of organizational requirements versus the needs of the individual. Although Barnard (1938) emphasized early the necessity for balance between the two elements, the work of most thinkers about organizations has reflected one emphasis or the other, but rarely both. Some major writers such as Argyris (1957) and McGregor (1967) even made this conflict the keystones of their systems. Only in recent years have a few theorists such as Bennis (1966) attempted to reconcile the differing viewpoints into an integrated position.

Recognition of these various approaches and of certain critical issues raised by them is essential to understanding the functioning of organizations. Accordingly, a brief historical analysis of the major relevant landmarks and issues in organizational theory is presented in this chapter. No attempt is made to present a comprehensive review of literature. Many such reviews have been published, and there is no reason for repeating them here.

Similarly, publications cited are those judged to have exerted greatest impacts upon the evolution of a valid conceptual approach to organizational functioning. Many of these significant publications appeared one, two, or three decades ago because organizational theory was in greater ferment, and, accordingly, many significant writings appeared in those years. Here, the major relevant theoretical positions are summarized, a few landmarks are reviewed, and significant considerations for understanding organizational functioning are discussed.

STRUCTURAL THEORIES

The problem of structure is a recurring theme in organizational theory. All organizations have to provide for the meshing of members' activities. Tasks must be allocated, authority (the right to make decisions) must be assigned, and functions must be coordinated. These requirements lead to development of a hierarchical framework that is called the "structure" of the organization.

The putative father of structural theory is German sociologist Max Weber (1947), who developed his concept of bureaucracy around the formal structure of organizations. Weber noted that, in an organization, authority is vested in positions rather than individuals and is exercised through a formal system of rules and procedures. The positions are arranged in a hierarchy, with each position exercising authority over all of those below it. According to Weber, the formalism characteristic of bureaucracies minimizes variability in problem solutions and maintains high standards of internal efficiency. From this viewpoint, "an organization is a social device for efficiently accomplishing through group means some stated purpose; it is the equivalent of the blueprint for the design of the machine which is created for some practical purpose" (Katz and Kahn, 1966, p. 16).

Weber wrote on bureaucracy around the turn of the twentieth century. Until recently, most structural theorists followed Weber in stressing the rational aspects of organizations. Most concerned themselves with deriving more and more ideal structures and with analyzing how such factors as objectives, size, geographical dispersion, and techniques of operation influence the shapes of hierarchical frameworks. Because scientists do not often get opportunities to manipulate the structures of existing organizations, much of this work was descriptive.

Most of the earlier theorists were concerned with increasing effectiveness through improved structural designs. However, in recent years, more attention has been given to the ways that attitudes, values, and informal goals develop within subordinate units despite structural controls and to the ways in which these unintended consequences can actually modify an organization's structure. This new emphasis began with Merton (1940) and continued with Dubin (1949) and Selznick (1957). As an example, Selznick demonstrated in a study of the Tennessee Valley Authority that Weber's description of a formal bureaucracy left out the problems that occur when organizational leaders delegate some of their authority, as inevitably they must. Delegation increases unit specialization and, thus, emphasizes conflicts of interest between units and the organization as a whole. Such conflicts hamper the effectiveness anticipated when ideal structures are designed.

These more recent developments have expanded the perspectives of structural theorists. Although there has remained a vigorous concern with organizational design (Thompson, 1966)—with linkages, levels, and bonds of organization (Haire, 1958; Marschak, 1959)—most modern-day theorists (Selznick, 1957; Dubin, 1959; Rapaport, 1959) have attempted to bring internal processes of some sort into their systems. Primary emphasis remains upon structure, but there is now recognition that disregard of human variability may have serious disrupting effects upon an ideally designed organization.

Structural theory has numerous critics. In particular, the older theories of bureaucracy have been attacked from many sides. According to Bennis (1966),

> Almost everybody, including many students of organizational behavior, approaches bureaucracy with a chip on his shoulder. It has been criticized for its confusion and contradictions, for moral and ethical reasons, on practical grounds such as its inefficiency, for its methodological weaknesses, and for containing too many implicit values or for containing too few. (pp. 5–6)

Some criticisms appear to be more valid than others. However, several limitations of structural theory are readily apparent and have particular relevance for this discussion.

The first major limitation is that structural theories usually focus upon the anatomy of organizations rather than upon their behavior. There can be no doubt that a knowledge of anatomy is important for understanding any organism; however, it is only a small part of the story. When viewed solely from the standpoint of structure, the greater portion of the organization is never seen.

This limitation would not be so critical if theoretical understanding were the only consideration. The trouble is that structural approaches have held predominance for so long and offer such easy answers that many practitioners—managers, executives, administrators—look to organizational design as the solution to problems whose sources often lie elsewhere. When difficulties arise within an organization, the most obvious solution is to redesign a job, change the authority structure, or modify the span of control, when, in fact, these aspects may be only tangentially relevant to the real problems.

A second limitation is that structural theories most frequently are concerned with derivation of ideal structures rather than with the design of real-life organizations. While ideal structures contribute to thinking about real organizations, many such analyses are simply irrelevant to practical situations.

A final limitation is that most structural approaches ignore the effects that the personalities and capabilities of members may exert upon the shape of an organization. A strong leader or team of leaders may exercise dramatic modifications upon the allocation of responsibility and authority. In a similar way, single positions or entire structures are sometimes modified to fit the competencies or limitations of incumbents. Structural approaches rarely take such things into account.

Despite these limitations, structural theories make valuable contributions to knowledge of organizational behavior. For example, an understanding of the ways in which such elements such as missions, objectives, size, and techniques of operation determine optimum structure is critical for efficient functioning, strength allocations, task organizations, and so on. Furthermore, the question of structure, of the linkage between positions, is closely associated with problems of information processing and decision making. The number of links in a system and the concomitant allocations of authority may have serious consequences for communication load and vulnerability to information loss. It is clear that structural concepts, when viewed in the proper perspective, have a place in a systematic theory of organizational functioning.

GROUP THEORIES

Weber himself eventually got around to expressing fear that the bureaucratic way of life tends to smother individual potentialities. He was the forerunner of a large number of writers who sounded the alarm against the practicing bureaucracy. Indeed, Bennis (1966) in a discussion of "the decline of bureaucracy," stated:

> [I]t would be fair to say that a great deal of the work on organizational behavior over the past two decades has been a footnote to the bureaucratic "backlash" which aroused Weber's passion: saving mankind's soul "from the supreme mastery of the bureaucratic way of life." (p. 7)

Bennis went on to conclude that very few writers of that period have been indifferent to the fact that bureaucracy is "a social instrument in the service of repression," treating a person's ego and social needs as a constant or as nonexistent or inert. Bennis contended that "these confined and constricted needs" insinuate themselves into the social processes of organizations in unintended ways (1966).

Bennis probably overstated the case when he envisioned a concerted movement to save humankind's soul from the supreme mastery of a bureaucratic way of life. Certainly, however, there has been a continuing flurry of writings concerned with the inhibiting effects of organizational life. These are discussed in the section on individual theories. However, the earliest and still continuing attack came not so much from a concern for the repressive effects of organizations as from discovery of a basic fallacy in classical structural theory. This fallacy was that structural theory fails to recognize the effects of informal groups upon motivation, behavior, and performance in organizations.

Group theories of organization stem from two unrelated sources. The first was work begun by Elton Mayo (1933) at the Hawthorne plant of Western Electric and continued by Roethlisberger and Dickson (1939). These researchers identified the influence of the face-to-face informal group upon motivation and behavior in a work situation. However, for them, there was no essential conflict between a worker and the organization. Rather, they contended that satisfying workers' social and psychological needs is congruent with the organization's goals of effectiveness and productivity.

Directly descending from Mayo were Whyte (1959, 1961), Homans (1950), and Zaleznick and Moment (1964). Working with data drawn from business organizations (usually obtained by intensive case study of a single firm), these theorists developed such findings as the following. The output of workers is determined as much by their social relations as by their abilities and skills; noneconomic rewards are extremely important in the motivation and satisfaction of personnel; group-held norms and attitudes play a major role in individuals' evaluation of their work situation; and informal leaders can develop who may possess more actual power than appointed supervisors.

The second source of group theories was the work of Kurt Lewin (1947), who stressed the importance of group forces in influencing and motivating people. Following Lewin, there appeared a long series of studies, of which the most notable for this book are the leadership studies of Lewin, Lippitt, and White (1939), the participation studies of Coch and French (1948), and the work on morale and productivity by Katz and Kahn (1952).

The work of Lewin's successors reached a landmark with the publication of Likert's *New Patterns of Management* (1961). In this book Likert proposed a "modified" theory of management in which he stressed the importance of group forces in worker motivation, the necessity for managers and supervisors to serve as "linking pins" between the various groups and levels within an organization, and the essentiality but relative independence of both productivity and morale.

Although the lineal descendants of Mayo and Lewin have remained apart in their general approaches, many common elements can be identified. In both approaches, the principal emphasis was changed from Weber's rational bureaucracy to an organizational model that took account of "unanticipated consequences" (i.e., feelings, attitudes, norms, sentiments, and perceptions). Thus, the behavior of an organization was viewed as less mechanistic but more unpredictable.

The acceptance of social relationships as a major variable in organizational behavior was a significant development in the theory of organizations. The strong reaction of group theorists to the older, rational models was highly valuable in calling attention to a hitherto ignored facet in organizational functioning—the influence of informal groups. On the other hand, the aversion of group theorists, especially the Lewinians, to anything resembling hierarchical control within organizations has been something of a limitation. So far, attempts to relate group behavior to organizational functioning in systematic ways have been limited. Likert came closest, but his concepts became rather pallid when he discussed groups in relation to hierarchical levels. Likert (1967) eventually moved into a fourfold typology of organizations based upon eight dimensions. He concluded from extensive research that more successful organizations tend toward "System Four" management. System Four organizations are characterized by a supportive climate, group decision making, considerable self-control, and high performance goals. The major variables appear to be the nature of the management climate (directive versus supportive) and the individual versus group orientation of the organizational structure. Likert, of course, advocated an overlapping group structure, which is his well-known "linking pin" concept.

Many group theorists have been reluctant to give full weight to formal authority relationships. In fact, this reluctance has been so pronounced that Cartwright (1959), one of the more eminent group theorists, accused group psychology of being "soft on power." Especially for groups within hierarchical organizations, power is a critical variable. Because organizations are structured on the basis of authority relationships, groups within organizations are different from those outside, and the two can never be treated the same. This fact should never be ignored in any consideration of organizational functioning.

INDIVIDUAL THEORIES

The rubric *individual theories* embraces for convenience two approaches that are only remotely related. On the one hand, a rather large group of empirical researchers and a smaller number of theorists are concerned with psychological factors that affect the performance of individuals within organizations. On the other hand, a small but increasing number of writers, in violent reaction against rational, structural theories and the practices based upon them, have emphasized the conflict between organizational requirements and needs of the individual. Both approaches are concerned with the performance of individuals. However, the first approach addresses itself to improving performance through better selection, classification, training, leadership, and so on. The second approach starts with the notion of a basic incompatibility between organization and individual and then attempts to modify organizations and their practices in ways intended to permit greater opportunities for need satisfaction by personnel.

Fitting the Person to the Organization

The first approach centers around those activities commonly considered to be within the purview of traditional industrial psychology. Stemming from a long and respectable history of applied work, there has developed a considerable body of studies concerned with such concrete problems as selection, training, conditions of work, methods of payment, incentives, and human engineering. In these areas, a genuine contribution has been made in fitting the person to the job. Until fairly recently, the contribution has been mainly in terms of methods. Most work has relied upon analyses of single problems in unique situations rather than systematic studies of generalized phenomena.

This limitation has subjected individual theorists to criticism by a number of writers who desire a more systematic understanding of the problems studied. For example, in a significant publication, Pugh (1966) contended that all of the studies on industrial selection have "contributed little more to the understanding of human behavior than a series of (usually modest) validity coefficients" (p. 289). Pugh credited the individual theorists for being the only ones who have tackled the problem of the validity of data, but he also contended that their emphasis upon a "factorial-statistical" approach has usually resulted in a theoretically arid formulation.

Perhaps a more serious limitation of the traditional individual approach is that many attempts to improve performance of individuals do not take the organizational context into full account. Personnel selection again provides an illustration. Selection procedures are desired so that an organization can be composed of the most adequate individuals. Yet, even though the adequacy of each individual can be important, the operational processes characteristic of the particular organization and the ways that members' activities are integrated and coordinated can be equally critical.

Recently, this traditional approach to individual effectiveness appears to have been embarking on a new stage of development. Over the past three decades, there has developed a growing body of data concerned with motivation and its more complex relationships with performance.

Of course, motivation has been recognized in industrial psychology for a long time. However, only recently have psychologists begun to produce genuinely sophisticated studies and theories concerned specifically with the composition of those motives most relevant to performance within an organization (Gellerman, 1963). Outstanding among these theorists has been Maslow (1954, 1970), whose approach to human motivation has been widely accepted because his Needs Hierarchy Theory has considerable explanatory power with respect to human motivational behavior and personal satisfaction in organizational settings.

The relationship between job satisfaction and productivity has been a big issue for a long time. Originally, it was assumed that satisfaction and performance must be highly related. Then, it was shown that job satisfaction and productivity are not necessarily complementary (Brayfield and Crockett, 1955; Kahn, 1960). This was puzzling for a while until Herzberg, Mausner, and Snyderman (1959) demonstrated that job satisfaction itself is not a unitary concept and that certain conditions at work only prevent losses in morale but do not push toward greater motivation, while others exert strong uplifting effects upon attitudes or performance. Although Herzberg later endured some strong criticism on methodological grounds, his theory was well received among organizational practitioners because, like Maslow's approach, it makes sense.

Finally, Porter and Lawler (1968) derived a remarkably elegant model of human occupational motivation based on expectancy theory. These writers and an extensive list of researchers who have followed them have developed and refined a model that is noteworthy for its parsimonious, yet comprehensive, consideration of moderator variables mediating motivation, performance, and satisfaction and the relationships between them.

These developments in the study of motivation also offer promise for improved understanding of organizational behavior. Although still concerned with the effects of motivation upon the performance of individuals, most present-day theorists give full recognition to the influence of organizational conditions upon motivation and, more important, to the effects of social motivation upon group and organizational performance.

At this point, it is important to note that recognition of the essentiality to performance of motivation came relatively late (Mayo, 1933, and the individual theorists after World War II). In the early stages, the fact that motivation is an attribute of individuals was taken to indicate a more or less permanent state within a person. A person was believed to be highly motivated to work—to perform—or not. The idea was to select individuals who are highly motivated.

The value of the motivation theories of Maslow, Herzberg, and Porter and Lawler lies in the full recognition that, although motivation is an attribute of the individual, the motivational state of any one person is not a constant. Within limits, motivational states vary according to what happens to individuals, how they perceive their situation, and their expectations about what is happening to them.

For individuals within organizations, much that happens is determined by the organization. Thus, elements in the organizational environments are major determinants of the motivational states of members.

The importance of this fact lies in the shift from the notion that the individual is solely responsible for his or her motivational level to recognition that conditions within the organization are major determinants. Therefore, a principal part of the responsibility for the motivation of personnel lies with those persons who are charged with control over organizational conditions, that is, with the management or leadership of the organization.

Fitting the Organization to the Person

Whereas the just described approach has focused mainly upon fitting the person to the organization, another approach is more concerned with fitting the organization to the person. In one way or another, theorists of the second approach see the basic problem as a conflict between the psychological needs of individuals and the formal requirements of organizations as put forth by the structural theorists.

By far the most clear in his conceptualizations was Argyris (1957, 1962), who built a complete system around the notion of the basic incompatibility of the individual and the organization. According to Argyris, this incompatibility results in frustration, which can be inferred from "pathological behaviors" and "defense mechanisms" exhibited by many individuals employed in organizations. In his earlier work (1957), Argyris was mainly concerned with effects upon lower-level personnel, and his solutions involved restructuring organizations toward greater decentralization and enlarging jobs so that "self-actualization" would have more chance to bloom. In later work (1962), Argyris addressed himself to the problems of executive, and he advocated modification of impersonal value systems in organizations and the development of "authentic" relationships.

Although he started from a somewhat different initial position, McGregor (1960, 1967) based his analysis upon the same essential conflict as Argyris. McGregor began with recognition that "if there is a single assumption which permeates conventional organizational theory, it is that authority is the central, indispensable means for managerial control" (1960, p. 18). McGregor then proceeded to his now-famous comparison between "Theory X" and "Theory Y." He attempted to show the limitations of authority based on role and status (Theory X) as compared with authority based on objectives (i.e., task or goal requirements) (Theory Y). McGregor stressed the integration of task requirements with needs of the individual. However, where Argyris advocated restructuring job and organization,

McGregor recognized that leadership is the means whereby the needs of the individual and the requirements of the organization can be reconciled. For him, leadership was "the creation of conditions such that members of the organization can achieve their goals best by directing their efforts toward the success of the enterprise" (1960, p. 187)

About the same time, several other writers (Blake and Mouton, 1964; Shepard, 1965) were stressing the importance of organizational leadership as the main integrating factor. In their views, if leaders see their organizations as organic rather than mechanistic—as adaptable rather than controlled by rigid structure—emphasis within the organizations will shift from arbitration to problem solving, from delegated to shared responsibility, and from centralized to decentralized authority. Thus, the needs of individuals and requirements of organizations are reconciled.

The second approach of the individual theorists is important because it forces attention to internal processes in organizations and the way that human components affect them. Effectiveness within an organization requires trading and negotiation by all participants. The extent to which problems are solved and objectives are accomplished is strongly determined by the degree of accommodation that can be achieved.

As a final point, it should be noted that all of the approaches mentioned in connection with both group and individual theories tend to emphasize interpersonal and group factors as causal elements in organizational effectiveness. They tend to ignore or, at least, de-emphasize the cognitive processes of problem solving as equally important determinants.

DECISION THEORIES

Whereas group and individual theorists have tended to play down cognitive processes, other writers have focused squarely upon problem solving and decision making as controlling factors in organizational effectiveness. Although the study of decision making, particularly that performed by individuals, is a relatively independent area, it has made a significant contribution to the understanding of organizations.

Theories of organizational decision making have their origin in economic theories of consumers' choice (Edwards, 1954). Classical economic theory started from an assumption that a person is entirely rational in his or her choices. The economic person was presumed to be completely informed, infinitely sensitive, and totally rational. In his or her decisions, not only were the alternatives in the choice known, but also each alternative was known to lead to a specific outcome. Thus, classical economic theory was essentially one of decision under conditions of absolute certainty (Taylor, 1965).

Classical theory has undergone numerous modifications, the most notable of which occurred with the advent of game theory (von Neumann and

Morgenstern, 1944). Game theory recognized the concept of decision making under uncertainty or risk; however, it still rested upon the assumption of rationality. Furthermore, game theory remained a theory of decision making by individuals.

A decision made by an individual in isolation is one thing, but a decision made by him or her in an organization is another. In the latter case, the considerations to be taken into account become much more complex. A landmark in the development of theories of decision making in organizations was Simon's book *Administrative Behavior: A Study of Decision-Making Processes in Administrative Organization* (1947). Simon retained the idea that decision behavior within organizations is "intendedly rational" and that decisions are made by individuals within organizations and not by organizations as entities. However, he also recognized the inadequacy of classical economic theory for understanding behavior within organizations. Accordingly, he distinguished between the role of facts and the role of values in decision making. Questions of value are questions of what *ought* to be. Simon contended that decision makers employ values as well as facts in making choices. Limits upon rationality in decision making are imposed by lack of all the possible facts. Therefore, in Simon's view (1957a), decision makers must "satisfice"—find a course of action that is "good enough"—rather than maximizing returns, as would be possible if they had full knowledge of the consequences attached to every alternative. Simple as it may sound, Simon's concept of "satisficing" opened totally new vistas in theories of organizational decision making.

The contrast between the economic person and Simon's administrative person emphasizes an important point. Rationality is central to behavior within an organization. However, if the members of an organization were individuals capable of the kind of objective rationality attributed to the classical economic person, theories of organization would have no purpose. In Simon's words:

> [I]f there were no limits to human rationality, administrative theory would be barren. It would consist of the single concept; always select that alternative, among those available, which will lead to the most complete achievement of your goals. (1957b, p. 15)

Then Simon went on to contend that the need for an administrative theory resides in the fact that there are practical limits to human rationality and that these limits are not static but depend upon the organizational environment in which the individual's decision takes place. The task of administration (organizational leaders) is to so "design" the environment that the individual approaches as closely as practicable to rationality (judged in terms of the organization's goals) in his or her decisions.

The most significant point in the above statement is that decisions are influenced by the organizational environment. Internal relationships and operational processes can and do exert critical effects upon the nature and quality of decisions. Thus, decisions can never be completely rational. This theme was expanded into a full theory of organization by March and Simon (1958).

In the classical economic theories and Simon's administrative theories, the decision maker is the individual. On the other hand, Cyert and March (1964) formulated a theory of the organization as decision maker. They built upon the classical model of rational behavior; however, they recognized an important fact. Organizations are constantly attempting to adapt to their external and internal environments, and fully rational adaptation is constrained by some fairly strong limits on the cognitive capacity, the computational speed, and the internal goal consistency of organizations.

To describe how organizations cope with these constraints, Cyert and March posited four critical modifications to the classical axioms of rationality:

1. *Quasi-resolution of Conflict*—organizations do not have a simple preference ordering of goals. Instead, they exist with considerable conflicts of interest, which are resolved either through compromise or sequential attention to goals.
2. *Uncertainty Avoidance*—organizations tend to avoid uncertainty rather than deal with it by calculations of expected returns as in economic theory.
3. *Problemistic Search*—decisions to search for solutions are dictated by the existence of problems rather than calculations of expected returns.
4. *Organizational Learning*—organizations learn from their experiences and modify procedures over time.

The notion that numbers of people make decisions as a unit was not a new idea in group dynamics. However, in decision theory, it is a relatively recent concept. When the temptation to anthropomorphize can be resisted, when it can be recognized that what is involved are a number of individuals arriving at decisions jointly, the concept of organizational decision making provides possibilities for promising insights into some of the more complex aspects of organizational behavior. For example, the four modifications described in the discussion of Cyert and March open the door to the analysis of organizations in terms of ongoing processes. Where previous theories viewed decision making in terms of essentially static models, Cyert and March saw it as a dynamic process occurring in response to continuous changes in the environment and constantly modified on the basis of new information. Thus, decision making is viewed as an adaptive response of the organization.

The importance of viewing decision making in terms of organizational processes cannot be overemphasized. Even today, much current research and theory ignore the circumstances under which the decision is made and under which the decision maker is acting (Hayes-Roth and Hayes-Roth, 1979; Hunt, 1980). Much of the work in the field makes it appear that the specific act of choosing among alternatives is the core of the decision-making process and that prior or subsequent events need not be considered. Yet, in real organizations, the events leading to the act of choice and those following are often the more critical ones. Frequently, the outcome is fore-ordained by the time that the act of choice is reached and, often, decisions are not implemented as intended. It begins to become clear that decision making cannot be separated from other organizational processes.

One final point remains with regard to decision theories. Just as group and individual theories overstress interpersonal and motivational factors, decision theories place primary emphasis upon rational aspects of cognition and perception. Accordingly, like the group and individual approaches, decision theories offer only partial explanations of the complex phenomena encountered in organizations.

THE ISSUES AND A RESOLUTION

The effort to formulate a general theory of organization has not as yet been totally successful in producing firm and significant explanations regarding how and why some organizations are effective and others are not. Probably the most significant reason for the lack of progress is that, until recently, theorists and researchers have concerned themselves with relatively small and often unrelated segments of the overall problems. This was suggested by March and Simon (1958) many years ago when they pointed out that most propositions about organizational behavior can be grouped in three broad categories:

1. Propositions assuming that organization members, particularly employees, are primarily *passive instruments*, capable of performing work and accepting directions but not initiating action or work or exerting influence in any significant way.
2. Propositions assuming that members bring to their organizations *attitudes, values*, and *goals*, that they have to be motivated or induced to participate in the system of organization behavior, that there is incomplete parallelism between their personal goals and organization goals, and that actual or potential goal conflicts make power phenomena, attitudes, and morale centrally important in the explanation of organizational behavior.
3. Propositions assuming that organization members are *decision makers* and *problem solvers*, and that perception and thought processes are central to the explanation of behavior in organizations.

After 40 years, the above analysis still holds. It should be noted that Category 1 encompasses the bureaucratic theories, as well as the many other theories and propositions concerned with structures, procedures, policies, and other formal aspects of organizations. Category 2 summarizes a large number of studies in psychology and sociology that have stressed the nonrational forces at work in organizations committed to operating on the basis of rationality and discipline, to include the group and individual theories discussed earlier. Category 3 includes decision theories and covers those studies devoted to the analysis of strategies and choice.

As March and Simon made clear, there is nothing contradictory about these three sets of propositions. Organizations involve all of these things. However, this is precisely the problem with most organizational theories. Whereas an adequate understanding of organizational behavior has to take account of the instrumental (bureaucratic) aspects, the motivational and attitudinal aspects, and the rational aspects, most researchers and theorists have focused on only those partial elements that seemed particularly significant for their interests. The result has been, to say the least, an imperfect picture of organizational behavior.

Most recently, several researchers (Burns and Stalker, 1961; Lawrence and Lorsch, 1967; Dalton, Lawrence, and Lorsch, 1970) began to examine design aspects of organizations in relation to the kinds of technology used and the functions served by various organizational divisions. Schein (1970) termed these researchers "Neostructuralists." In brief, the approaches of the Neostructuralists are important because they recognize that, for an organization to function effectively, both structure and functional behavior requirements must be considered.

These conclusions suggest that some ways of thinking about organizations may not be fully adequate. Bennis (1966) made the same point when he contended that it is no longer realistic to view an organization as an analog to the machine, as Max Weber argued. Furthermore, Bennis contended that it is not reasonable to view the organization solely in terms of the sociopsychological attributes of the people who are involved. Instead, the better approach is that organizations are to be perceived as open systems defined by their primary task or mission and encountering environmental conditions that change constantly.

Bennis went on to contend that "The main challenge confronting today's organization . . . is that of responding to changing conditions and adapting to external stress" (1966, p. 44).

Bennis has been the most articulate critic of the more customary ways of thinking about organizations. He contended that the traditional approaches are "out of joint" with the emerging view of organizations as adaptive, problem-solving systems and that conventional criteria of effectiveness are not sensitive to the critical needs of the organization to cope with external stress and change (1966). According to Bennis, conventional methods of evaluating effectiveness provide static indicators of certain output characteristics (performance, productivity, and satisfaction) without revealing the processes by which the organization searches for, adapts to, and solves its changing problems. Yet, without understanding of these dynamic processes of problem solving, knowledge about organizational behavior is woefully inadequate. He concluded that "the methodological rules by which the organization approaches its task and exchanges with its environments are critical determinants of organizational effectiveness" (1966, p. 47).

Bennis proposed that the major concern should be with "organizational health," defined in terms of "competence," "mastery," and "problem-solving ability," rather than "effectiveness," if "effectiveness" is considered in terms solely of final outputs. He then postulated some criteria for organizational health (1966):

1. *Adaptability.* Adaptability coincides with problem-solving ability, which, in turn, depends upon flexibility of the organization. Flexibility is the freedom to learn through experience, to change with changing internal and external circumstances.
2. *Identity.* Adaptability requires that an organization know what it is and what it is to do. It needs some clearly defined identity. Bennis says that identity can be examined in two ways: (1) by determining to what extent the organizational goals are understood and accepted by the personnel and (2) by ascertaining to what extent the organization is perceived veridically by the personnel.
3. *Reality testing.* The organization must develop adequate techniques for determining the real properties of the environment in which it exists. The psychological field of the organization contains two main boundaries, the internal organization and the boundaries with the external environment. Accurate sensing of the field is essential before adaptation can occur.

Thus, Bennis viewed an organization as an adaptive system, and he contended that the processes through which adaptation occurs are the proper focus of analysis. When the processes are understood, greater potential exists for improvement of organizational performance.

A few other writers have recognized the potentiality of studying the problem-solving processes used by an organization. For one, Altman (1966) stated:

> Performance effectiveness should be viewed from a much larger perspective, to include so-called "process variables" as intrinsic antecedents of performance outputs. Thus, we reject the approach of small group performance [or organizational performance] solely from a "black box" point of view, but propose instead a strategy that peers into the box and attempts to understand the sequential development of performance as it progresses from input to output. (1966)

GENERAL SYSTEMS THEORY

In their search for a conceptual framework that encompasses the many varied aspects of organizations, Bennis (1966), Schein (1965, 1970), Katz and Kahn (1966), and a number of other writers turned to General Systems Theory (von Bertalanffy, 1956). In Systems Theory, an organization is viewed as existing in an environment with which there are more or less continuous interchanges. As a system, the organization is regarded as having inputs (resources such as material, people, and information) on which it operates a conversion process (throughput) to produce outputs (products, services, actions, etc.). Both the inputs and outputs must take account of environmental changes and demands (Emery and Trist, 1965).

According to Systems Theory, the organization simultaneously engages in two general kinds of processes: (1) those concerned with adaptation to the environment and (2) those concerned with internal development and execution. Thus, it uses its internal processes and energies to continually react to changes in its environment in order to maintain equilibrium with it.

Of particular interest to organization theorists is the concept of equifinality. According to this principle, a system can reach the same final state from different initial conditions and by a variety of paths (Katz and Kahn, 1966). It has special significance for organizations because it points up the importance of ongoing processes adapted from specific situations as major determinants of outcomes. Whereas bureaucratic theories rely upon rules, policies, and precedents to dictate action, and theories of decision rely on rationality to indicate the obvious solution, Systems Theory recognizes that actions are governed by dynamic processes through which problems are approached as they arise and in accordance with their particular nature.

One of the most fully developed approaches is that of Parsons (1960). According to Parsons, all organizations must solve four basic problems:

1. *Adaptation*—the accommodation of the system to the reality demands of the environment and the actual modification of the external situation. Each organization must have structures and processes that enable it to adapt to its environment and mobilize the necessary resources to overcome changes in the environment.
2. *Goal achievement*—the defining of objectives and the attaining of them. Processes are required for implementing goals to include methods for specifying objectives, mobilizing resources, and so on.
3. *Integration*—establishing and developing a structure of relationships among the members that unifies them and integrates their actions. The organization must develop processes aimed at commanding the loyalties of the members, motivating them, and coordinating their efforts.
4. *Latency*—maintenance of the organization's motivational and normative patterns over time. Consensus must be promoted on values that define and legitimate the organization's goals and performance standards.

Parsons applied his theory to all types of social phenomena. Probably because of his interest in a theory of general social systems, he painted his analysis of formal organizations with a fairly broad brush (Parsons, 1956). However, Katz and Kahn (1966) built upon Parsons's work, together with that of Allport (1962) and Miller (1955), to develop a comprehensive, wide-ranging theory of organizations that is solidly within the Systems Theory framework. Katz and Kahn attempted nothing more than a complete explanation of organizational behavior with Systems Theory concepts. Although certain aspects of organizations require a little forcing to fit systems concepts, the attempt was reasonably successful in putting into proper perspective such ideas as interchange with environments, operation by process instead of procedure, and the interrelationships among functional units.

Systems Theory embraces a much more comprehensive set of concepts than is possible to describe here. An outline provided by Schein (1965) summarizes those ideas that have the most relevance for this discussion:

1. The organization should be conceived as an open system that is in constant interaction with its several environments. It takes in raw materials, people, energy, and information.
2. When an organization is conceived to be a multiple-purpose system, its functions are seen to involve multiple interactions with its environments. Many subsystem activities cannot be fully understood without considering these multiple interactions and functions.
3. An organization consists of many subsystems that are in interaction with one another. It is becoming increasingly important to understand the functioning of the subsystems—groups, roles, or other types of subsystems.
4. Since organizational subsystems are mutually dependent, a change in one subsystem likely affects the actions of other subsystems.
5. An organization exists in numerous environments that consist of other systems. These environments place demands upon and constrain the organization in numerous ways. Therefore, the functioning of the organization must be understood by explicit examination of the environmental demands and constraints.
6. A viable concept of organization is perhaps better defined in terms of flexible processes of import, conversion, and export, rather than stable characteristics such as size, shape, or structure.

The swing to a system emphasis by such respected theorists as Bennis, Katz and Kahn, Parsons, Schein, and Selznick signaled a significant new development in ways of thinking about organizations. Where, previously, attention was mainly focused upon the invariant aspects of organizations—the unchanging aspects of procedures, policies, structures, and role relationships—there was now recognition that the variant aspects may be the real key to understanding organizational behavior and controlling it.

ORGANIZATIONAL PROCESSES

Thus, it became apparent finally that it is plainly necessary to focus upon the dynamics of organizations. Since an organization is an adaptive, equilibrium-seeking, open system, the processes through which adaptation occurs are significant subjects for attention. Processes are those activities performed by an individual, group, or organization over time to solve a problem or perform a task (Steiner, 1972). Process is a series of actions, each of which is determined by those occurring previously and determines those that follow.

The main challenge confronting organizations is coping with external stress and continually changing conditions. When organizations are considered as open systems—adaptive structures coping with various environments—the most significant attribute for understanding effectiveness is competence, or mastery over the environment. If this view is valid, then the critical factor in understanding and improving effectiveness is the processes or functioning by which the organization approaches its task and interacts with its environments.

Schein (1965) has suggested an actual sequence of activities or processes used by organizations in adapting to changes in environments. Schein called this sequence an "Adaptive-Coping Cycle." The stages of Schein's adaptive-coping cycle are as follows:

1. Sensing a change in the internal or external environment.
2. Importing the relevant information about the change into those parts of the organization that can act upon it.
3. Changing production or conversion processes inside the organization according to the information obtained.
4. Stabilizing internal changes while reducing or managing undesired by-products (undesired changes in related systems that have resulted from the desired changes).
5. Exporting new products, services, and so on that are more in line with the originally perceived change in the environment.
6. Obtaining feedback on the success of the change through further sensing of the state of the external environment and the degree of integration of the internal environment.

As demonstrated in Chapter 4, Schein's Adaptive-Coping Cycle makes it possible to identify and isolate those processes where performance may be inadequate. In addition, the relative contribution of each process to overall effectiveness may be specified accurately.

It is important, therefore, to understand precisely how these processes affect and contribute to organizational effectiveness. It is equally important to understand what factors influence functioning of the organizational processes and, in a particular organization, what determines whether the processes can resist disruption. With such understanding it is possible to know how to assess organizational performance and how to improve performance in this critical area.

Chapter 4

Research Results

In this chapter, an operational model for organizational competence is described, and both laboratory and field tests of the model are reported. In Chapter 8, an operational Integration Model is presented and assessed for its feasibility in organizational training and development.

The research studies are reported here in some detail to demonstrate how both experimental and empirical research can be conducted with large, complex organizations.

ORGANIZATIONAL COMPETENCE

The concept of *organizational competence* is intended to encompass within one term the functions or processes required by organizational systems for effective accomplishment of missions or objectives. The concept derives from the analysis of Open Systems Theory and concepts described in Chapter 3, especially those of Bennis (1966) and Schein (1965, 1970). It also derives from the recognition that one of the most critical determinants of the effectiveness of any organization is the ability of that organization to accurately identify, solve, and cope with problems that arise in constantly changing environments. The capability of the organization to perform these functions is what is meant by organizational competence, and, in addition to proficiency, integration is a major determinant of competence.

It is conceived that organizational competence is a major operational determinant of organizational effectiveness. Where effectiveness is the final outcome (mission accomplished, productivity, achievement of objectives, etc.), competence is the ability of the organization to perform the critical operational functions (processes) that lead to the achievement of effectiveness.

When the organizational processes that constitute competence are performed well, they enable an organization to cope with problems arising within its operational environments. When handled poorly, their effects may negate many of the positive effects contributed by efficiency in other areas of activity.

The ability to maintain organizational competence under heavy pressure is closely related to the ability to sustain effectiveness. If the processes break down when the organization is subjected to external pressures, effectiveness is impeded. On the other hand, if the processes continue to function adequately, effectiveness should be maintained or enhanced.

The Research Context and Strategy

The series of studies reported here were conducted with (1) simulated U.S. Army battle staffs, (2) actual U.S. Army units engaged in field training exercises, (3) two nationwide surveys of county social welfare agencies, and (4) three proprietary business corporations.

The research staff was fortunate in being able to initiate the research program with Army tactical units. Military combat operations often have moderately clear beginnings and endings, and they are usually tightly controlled. It is frequently possible to make actual and detailed observations of the activities and relate them to outcomes. Accordingly, the research staff was able to conduct pilot tests and data collection under reasonably controlled conditions before moving into observations of actual organizations at work. In conventional civilian organizations, the time frames are usually not so clearly demarcated and can extend over weeks, months, and even years.

The ultimate research strategy, partly planned and partly fortuitous, was conducted in the following order:

1. Simulated Army battle staffs, under experimentally controlled conditions
2. Army units engaged in actual field exercises
3. Social service agencies nationwide
4. Proprietary business organizations

THE COMPETENCE MODEL

As elaborated in Chapter 5, organizations are conceived to be open systems engaged in interaction with a number of significant environments (the physical environment, opposing organizations, higher organizational levels, adjacent units, supporting elements, etc.) that are external to the organization. In order for an organization to be effective (i.e., to accomplish missions or to achieve assigned objectives), it must assess accurately all of its significant external environments, as well as its own internal environment; process information resulting from such assessments; determine all required actions; and execute the actions such that they lead to accomplishment of assignments or the achievement of objectives.

In short, an organization must be capable of assessing accurately the operational requirements of the situations in which it is engaged and of performing all functions needed to meet the requirements. In this book, execution of required organizational functions has been termed organizational competence.

Components of Competence

Organizational competence is conceived to be composed of three components (see Bennis, 1966, ch. 3):

1. *Reality Testing*—capability of the organization for assessing the operational situation facing it—the ability to search out, accurately perceive, and correctly interpret the properties and characteristics of its environments (both external and internal), especially those properties that have particular relevance for the functioning of the organization.
2. *Adaptability*—capability for solving problems that arise from changing environmental demands and operational requirements and for acting flexibly and with effectiveness in response to these changing requirements.
3. *Integration*—capability for maintaining structure and function under stress and a state of relations among subunits that ensures that coordination is maintained and that the various subunits do not work at cross-purposes. (Bennis called this attribute "Identity"; see Chapter 3.)

Taken together, these three components constitute organizational competence. The adequacy of the components, both collectively and individually, strongly influences the effectiveness of an organization. Furthermore, the ability of an organization to maintain adequate performance in each component while under pressure from external forces is critical for its effectiveness and its survival.

Organizational Processes

As developed from Chapter 3 (Schein, 1966, pp. 52–54), seven organizational processes or functions are the constituent elements of organizational competence, together with integration. The processes are:

1. *Sensing*—the process by which the organization acquires information concerning the states of, or events occurring in, the environments, both external and internal, that are significant for the effective accomplishment of objectives. The specific nature of sensing activities that are required may differ according to the type and mission of the organization and the character of the environments that are significant to it. Whatever their specific nature, all sensing activities involve seeking, acquiring, processing, and interpreting information.
2. *Communicating Information*—those activities whereby information concerning an organization's environment is made available to those individuals who should act upon it. This process involves the initial transmittal of information by those who have sensed it, the relaying of information by intervening levels, and the dissemination of the information throughout the organization. Most important, the process also includes discussion and interpretation—those communicative acts through which clarification is attempted or implications of the information are discussed.
3. *Decision Making*—those activities leading to the conclusion that some action should be taken by the organization or someone within the organization. This process is limited to the deliberative acts of one or more persons and is usually evidenced by the initial communication of the decision by the decision maker(s). Decisions may be made that lead to coping actions, stabilizing actions, formal sensing actions, and feedback actions. In addition, decisions not to act may be made.
4. *Stabilizing*—the process of taking action to adjust internal operations or otherwise taking action to maintain stability and functional integration within the unit in the face of potential disruption that might result from events in the environment or from actions taken within the organization.
5. *Communicating Implementation*—the process whereby decisions and resulting requirements are communicated to those individuals who must implement them. In addition to the straightforward transmission of orders or instructions, this process includes discussion and interpretation—those communicative acts through which clarification is achieved and implications for actions are discussed. Of particular importance in this process are those activities of individuals who relay instructions between the original decision maker and the individual(s) who ultimately implement the decision.
6. *Coping Actions*—those activities involving direct action against external and internal environments. This process is concerned with the actual execution of actions at points of contact with the target environments. Accordingly, it is the ultimate determinant of effectiveness. Whereas all other processes influence the performance of coping actions, these actions, in turn, determine the effect of the organization upon the target environment.
7. *Feedback*—the process of assessing the effects of a prior action through further sensing of the external and internal environments and evaluating the effects of the prior actions.

Each of the above processes is related to one of the components of organizational competence. The relationships are as follows:

Competence Component	*Organizational Process*
Reality testing	Sensing, communicating information, feedback
Adaptability	Decision making, communicating implementation, coping actions
Integration	Stabilizing

Competence is concerned with the quality of performance within an organization. Although each process must be performed at least to a minimal amount, frequency of process performance is not a major factor. The essence of competence is quality—how well the processes are performed. The following criteria illustrate the qualitative requirements of each process:

1. *Sensing*
   a. Accurate detection of all available information.
   b. Correct interpretation of all detected information.
   c. Accurate discrimination between relevant and irrelevant information.
   d. Relevance to mission, task, or problem of all attempts to obtain information about the environment.
2. *Communicating Information*
   a. Accurate transmission of relevant information.
   b. Sufficient completeness of transmission to achieve full and adequate understanding by recipient.
   c. Timely transmission of information.
   d. Transmission to appropriate recipients.
   e. Correct determination of whether information should be transmitted.
3. *Decision Making*
   a. Correctness of decision in view of circumstances and available information.
   b. Timeliness of decision in view of available information.
   c. Consideration in the decision process of all contingencies, alternatives, and possibilities.
4. *Communicating Implementation*
   a. Accurate transmission of instructions.
   b. Sufficient completeness to transmit adequate and full understanding of the actions required.
   c. Timely transmission to recipients, in view of both available information and the action requirements.
   d. Transmission to appropriate recipients.
5. *Actions: Stabilizing, Coping, and Feedback*
   a. Correctness of action in view of both the operational circumstances and the decision or order from which the action derives.

b. Timeliness of the action in view of both the operational circumstances and the decision or order from which the action derives.
c. Correctness of choice of target for the action.
d. Adequacy of execution of the action.

Thus, competence is the adequacy with which an organization performs its critical processes or functions. When the processes are performed adequately, they assist an organization to be effective. When handled poorly, they may negate many positive effects contributed by efficiency in other areas. Integration is an organizational attribute that, when fully developed, enhances performance of the organizational functions.

Organizational competence is the quality of performance of an organization's command and control system. Therefore, the importance of competence is self-evident. Competence, or the quality of process performance, displayed by command and control (management) personnel *as a team* plays a most potent role in the operations for any organization.

It should be noted that, in addition to effective performance of essential functions, integration and competence are dependent upon existing conditions within an organization.

TESTS OF THE MODEL

Two major tests of the organizational competence model in military organizations were conducted by research personnel of the Human Resources Research Organization (HumRRO) under the designations of Project FORGE and Project Cardinal Point. Results of the tests are described in the following sections.

Project FORGE

A detailed description of Project FORGE appears in the Technical Report by Olmstead, Christensen, and Lackey (1973) and an Institute for Defense Analyses Monograph by Olmstead (1992).

Project FORGE (Factors in Organizational Effectiveness) was conducted at Fort Benning, Georgia, from July 1968 to June 1971. The project was designed to accomplish several broad research objectives:

1. To determine the relationship between organizational competence and organizational effectiveness within U.S. Army combat units.
2. To evaluate the separate contributions of each of the components of competence and determine the relative contributions of the seven organizational processes used to operationalize the components.

3. To determine the effects of environmental pressures upon competence and determine the relationship between effectiveness and the ability of the organization to maintain competence under pressure from its environments.

To accomplish these objectives, researchers observed and assessed the activities of simulated battle staffs as they performed in realistic tactical situations, evaluated their military effectiveness, measured their performance on the hypothesized organizational processes, and analyzed the relationships between measures of effectiveness and indices of competence, its components, and its processes.

Method

Ten 12-man groups of Vietnam-experienced Infantry officers, ranging in grade from senior major to first lieutenant, participated in an eight-hour role simulation of a light infantry battalion engaged in combat operations in Vietnam. Player-subjects occupied battalion levels; experimenter/controllers occupied brigade and company levels. Thus, the full simulation was a complex, three-level organization. All inputs into the simulated battalion were made by military experimenter/controllers, who filled the roles of officers at brigade (higher), platoon (lower), and adjacent unit levels. Through the use of preplanned and tightly scheduled messages, controllers created a dynamic and realistic situation that provided continual and changing environmental inputs requiring rapid and flexible organizational responses from the simulated units. The simulate scenario consisted of 128 probes (problems) made up of 376 separate input messages. Although activities of the players were uninterrupted, the simulate was designed in four administrative phases, three of which differed in the intensity of environmental pressures, as determined by frequency, complexity, and criticality of inputs.

The bases of data were (1) players' ratings of realism, involvement, and pressure experienced during the simulation and (2) all communications (radio, written, and face-to-face) of members of the simulated organizations. Communications of the players were the source of data for evaluation of both organizational competence and organizational effectiveness.

The analysis of organizational competence included (1) content analysis of each unit of communication according to a system that classified it in terms of 12 descriptive categories and identified the organizational process performed by the unit; (2) assignment of a score to each unit in terms of how well the process represented by it was performed; and (3) the development of group scores for each organizational process, competence component, and competence as a whole. Scores for processes, competence components, and competence were rated according to the quality of process performance.

Organizational effectiveness was determined by the military outcomes of the 128 probes. Experienced officers examined transcripts of communications concerning each probe and assigned an effectiveness score according to predetermined criteria concerning contribution of the outcome to mission accomplishment. Group effectiveness scores were summations of scores for the 128 probes.

Results

Players rated the simulation as (1) more interesting than other command post exercises in which they had participated, (2) quite realistic in the problems and procedures used, (3) high in the extent of player involvement, and (4) high in probability that battalions that were effective in the simulation would also be effective in a real situation. Furthermore, players' ratings of the amount of pressure experienced during the various phases were in accord with the experimental design. It is concluded that the validity of the simulation was high, which permits confidence in the substantive findings of the study.

During the simulation, the 10 groups averaged 1,377 contacts. These contacts resulted in a mean of 1,800.7 scoring units per group. Group mean units per probe were 14.1. These data indicate that each group produced a large number of communications for scoring, thus ensuring that scores developed from them are genuinely representative of the groups' performance.

An analysis of frequency of process performance in relation to organizational effectiveness resulted in a correlation coefficient of .33, which was not significant ($N = 10$). This finding indicates that effectiveness was not related to the frequency with which processes were performed by the simulated organizations.

For this study of 10 groups, the most important finding concerns the relationship between organizational competence and organizational effectiveness (see Table 4.1). The obtained correlation coefficient of .93 is highly significant ($p < .01$) and indicates a strong relationship between the two variables. Under the conditions of this study, competence accounted for 86 percent of the variance in effectiveness. Therefore, it appears that competence was a principal determinant of organizational effectiveness.

Zero-order correlations of competence components with effectiveness resulted in coefficients of .96 for reality testing, .79 for adaptability, and .11 for integration. Thus, both reality testing and adaptability were related significantly to effectiveness. The relationship of integration to effectiveness was quite small and not significant. This lack of relationship is explained, in part, by the few occurrences of stabilizing, the one process of which integration was composed. The results concerning stabilizing and integration are deemed to be inconclusive because of insufficient data in this study.

A multiple correlational analysis between the competence components and effectiveness resulted in a corrected coefficient of .94. Beta weights were .79 for reality testing, .25 for adaptability, and −.08 for integration. Relative contributions to effectiveness were 76 percent for reality testing and

Table 4.1
Intercorrelations: Major Variables and Subvariables

Variable	1	2	3	4	5
1. Effectiveness	–	.93**	.96**	.79**	.11
2. Competence		–	.94**	.92**	.33
3. Reality Testing			–	.73*	.10
4. Adaptability				–	.43
5. Integration					–

**p < .01; *p < .05. Correlations are based upon eight degrees of freedom.

Table 4.2
Intercorrelations: Effectiveness, Competence, and Processes

Variable	1	2	3	4	5	6	7	8	9
1. Effectiveness	–	.93**	.92**	.83**	.70*	.11	.71*	.72*	.03
2. Competence		–	.95**	.72*	.86**	.33	.77**	.77**	.18
3. Sensing			–	.72*	.79**	.32	.58	.65*	.06
4. Communicating Information				–	.30	–.33	.58	.47	–.08
5. Decision Making					–	.63	.59	.67*	.37
6. Stabilizing						–	.14	.17	.49
7. Communicating Implementation							–	.68*	.29
8. Coping Actions								–	.18
9. Feedback									–

** p < .01; *p < .05. Correlations are based on eight degrees of freedom.

20 percent for adaptability, while the contribution of integration was negligible (–.008%). It is apparent that reality testing and adaptability were critical determinants of organizational effectiveness. Reality testing contributed more than adaptability, which demonstrates the importance of information acquisition and information processing to the effectiveness of military organizations.

For all processes except stabilizing and feedback, correlations with effectiveness were significant beyond the .05 level of confidence (see Table 4.2). Sensing produced the highest correlation (.92), communicating infor-

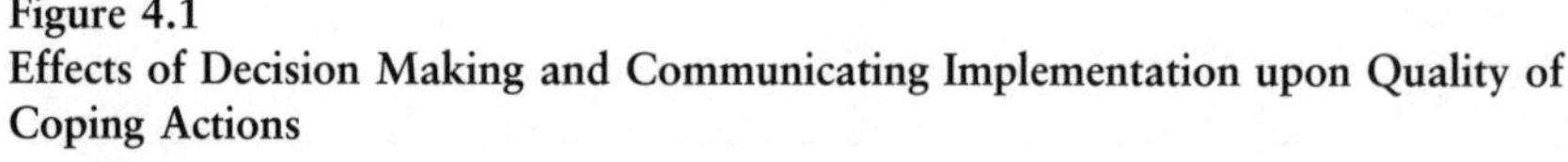

Figure 4.1
Effects of Decision Making and Communicating Implementation upon Quality of Coping Actions

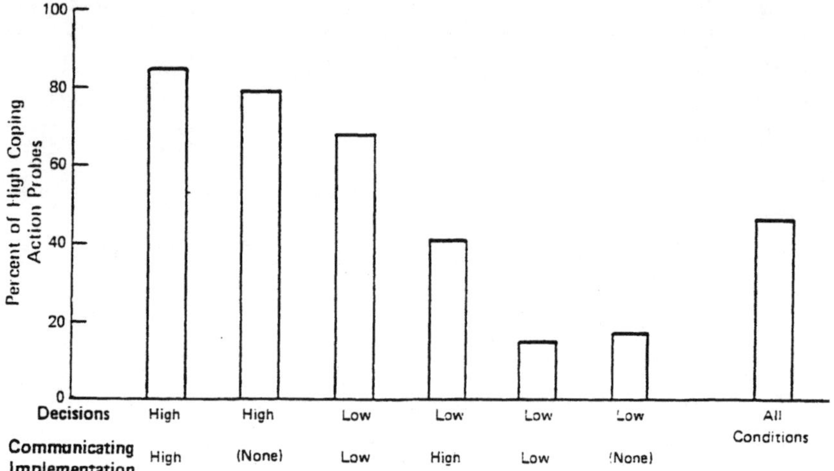

mation was second highest (.83), and decision making, communicating implementation, and coping actions were somewhat lower and approximately equal (.70, .71, .72).

An important finding is the linkage among the five processes found to be significantly related to effectiveness (see Figure 4.1).

Performance of processes that occur later in the Adaptive-Coping Cycle was found to be dependent upon the quality of early ones (see Figure 4.2).

This finding indicates that the capability of an organization for coping with the environments depends upon equally effective performance of each process, both separately and in combination (see Figure 4.3).

To analyze the effects of environmental pressure upon competence, performance of the five groups that were highest in effectiveness (high effectiveness groups) was compared with that of the five groups that were lowest in effectiveness (low effectiveness groups) (see Table 4.3).

Analysis of variance procedures were used to compare the competence of the classes of groups across the three pressure phases (low, moderate, and high).

Competence of the high effectiveness groups was significantly better than for low effectiveness groups in all phases. In addition, when faced with a change in mission and operations under moderate pressure, competence deteriorated for both groups, but much more drastically for low effectiveness groups (see Figure 4.4). After deterioration in competence occurred, low groups continued to function at a reduced level for the remainder of

Figure 4.2
Effects of Sensing, Communicating Information, and Decision Making upon Effectiveness

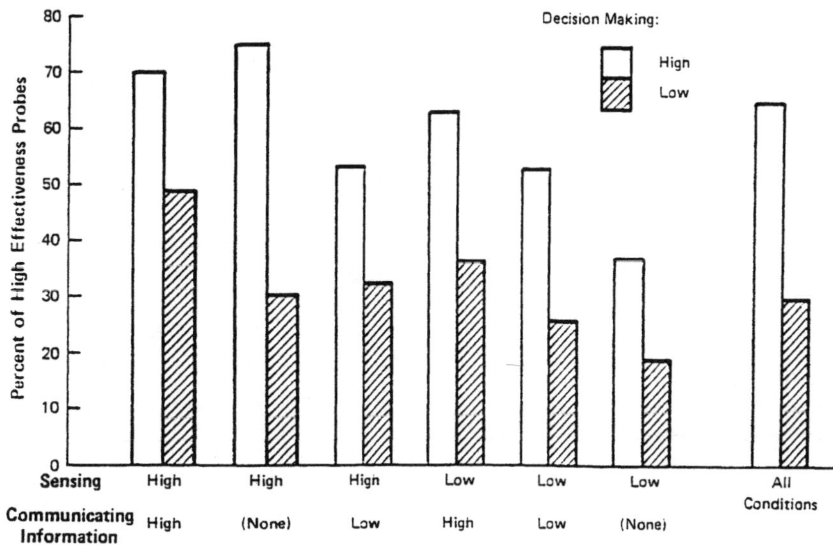

Figure 4.3
Effects of Decision Making, Communicating Implementation, and Coping Actions upon Effectiveness

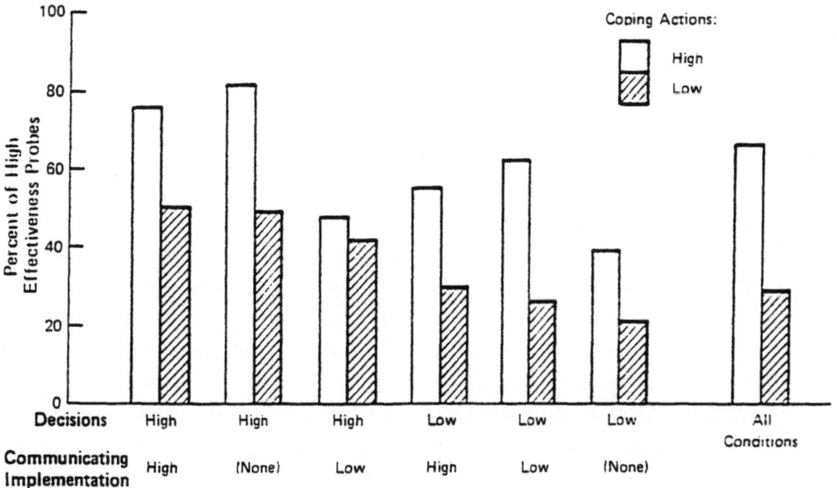

Table 4.3
Competence Performance of High Effectiveness and Low Effectiveness Groups under Differing Degrees of Environmental Pressure[a]

	High Effectiveness Groups		Low Effectiveness Groups	
Pressure Condition	Mean (N = 5)	SD	Mean (N = 5)	SD
Low (Phase II)	146.5	15.0	136.2	12.3
Moderate (Phase III)	135.2	12.8	114.1	16.0
High (Phase IV)	143.4	12.5	122.0	6.7

[a]Scores are mean Probe Competence Scores for each phase.

Figure 4.4
Mean Probe Competence Scores for High and Low Effectiveness Groups under Environmental Pressure

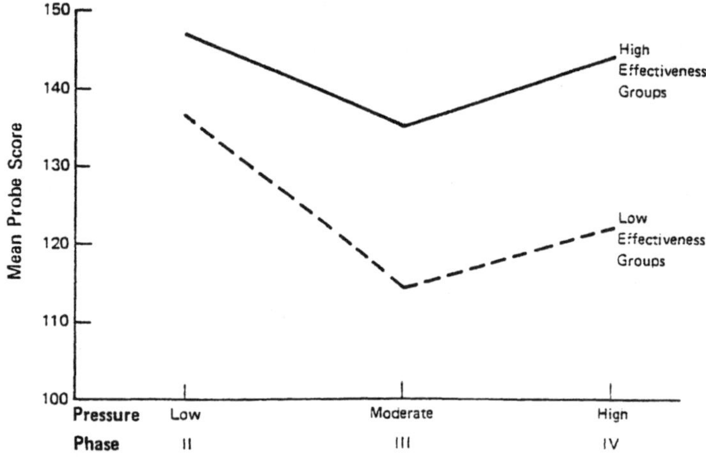

the simulation, whereas high effectiveness groups recovered their initial level of competence and maintained it even under high pressure conditions.

A similar analysis for competence components showed that reality testing deteriorated with change in mission and increased pressure but recovered for both classes of groups (see Table 4.4.).

Patterns of reality testing for the two types of groups were similar, although performance was consistently better for high effectiveness groups (see Figure 4.5). On the other hand, patterns for adaptability were different.

For high effectiveness groups, scores for adaptability remained essentially

Table 4.4
Competence Component Performance of High Effectiveness and Low Effectiveness Groups under Differing Degrees of Environmental Pressure[a]

		High Effectiveness Groups		Low Effectiveness Groups	
Competence Component	**Pressure Condition**	**Mean (N = 5)**	**SD**	**Mean (N = 5)**	**SD**
Reality Testing	Low	84.3	6.3	76.1	6.6
	Moderate	74.2	5.2	63.1	7.5
	High	88.0	9.3	73.7	4.8
Adaptability	Low	61.3	9.1	59.8	5.9
	Moderate	59.8	9.3	50.7	7.8
	High	57.3	3.5	48.0	3.9
Integration	Low	1.0	1.4	.4	.5
	Moderate	1.1	1.4	.3	.6
	High	.1	.2	.4	.5

[a]Scores are mean Probe Competence Component Scores for each phase.

the same throughout the three pressure phases. However, adaptability scores for low effectiveness groups showed a continual degradation as pressure increased. Therefore, it appears that effectiveness of low groups was lower because of (1) consistently lower performance of reality testing and (2) a breakdown in adaptability processes under increased environmental pressure.

Aborted decisions are those for which no implementing actions are performed. A comparison between high effectiveness and low effectiveness groups showed that, throughout the simulation, low groups aborted more decisions (see Figure 4.6). In addition, when they experienced the high pressure phase, the mean increase in aborted decisions for high effectiveness groups was only .4; for low effectiveness groups, it was 7.6. Under the stress of strong environmental pressure, processes for implementing decisions broke down much more often in the low effectiveness groups but continued to function reliably in the high effectiveness groups.

An analysis of process performance by organizational position showed a clear pattern. Sensing was performed predominantly by maneuver company personnel. Communicating information was performed most frequently by the battalion operations officer, and decision making was most heavily centered in the battalion commander, operations officer, and company com-

Figure 4.5
Mean Probe Scores for Two Competence Components for High and Low Effectiveness Groups

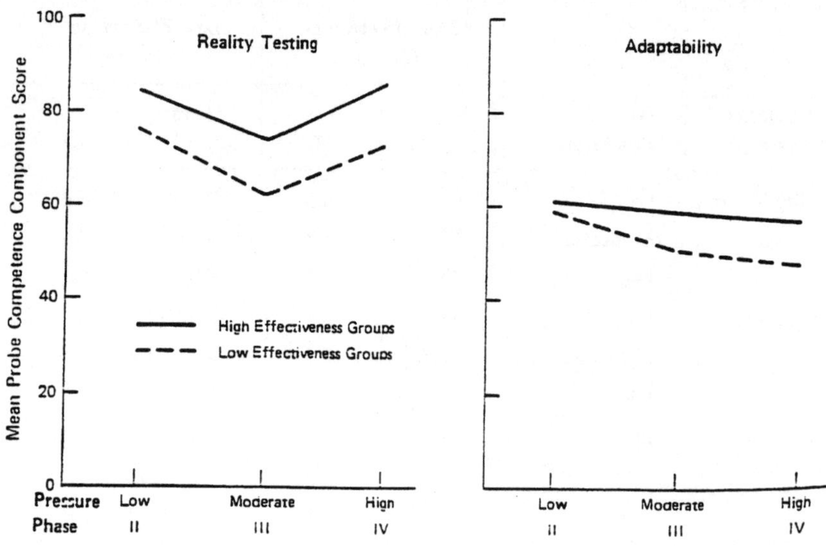

Figure 4.6
Aborted Decisions of High Effectiveness and Low Effectiveness Groups

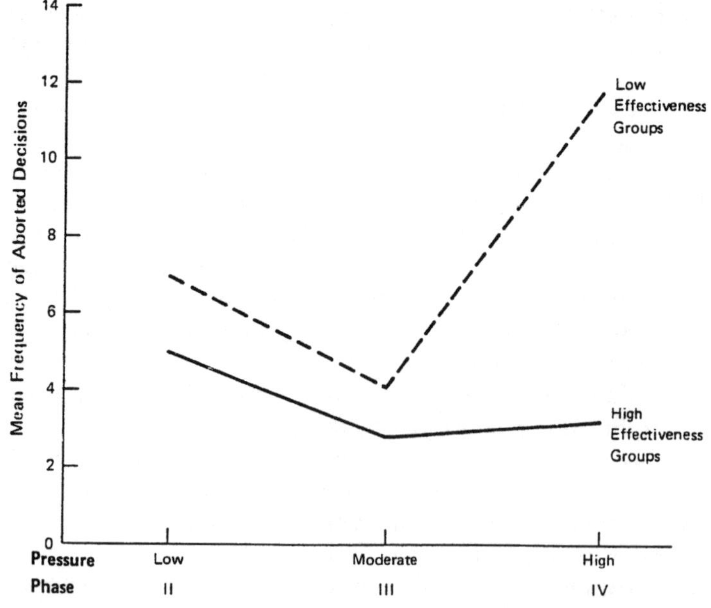

manders. Although not performed often by anyone, stabilizing was performed most frequently by company commanders; feedback actions were not performed often enough to yield a discernible pattern. Staff officers performed communicating implementation most often, while coping actions, as expected, were executed predominantly by company commanders.

Conclusions

The results of this study permit the following conclusions:

1. Organizational competence is a principal determinant of the effectiveness of organizations.
2. Competence is concerned with the quality of organizational processes. The frequency with which processes are performed is not an important determinant of effectiveness.
3. When the processes constituting competence are performed proficiently, an organization is more effective. When the processes are not performed proficiently, effectiveness is reduced.
4. The organizational processes that constitute competence contribute differentially to effectiveness; however, most contribute in significant degrees, and the causal linkage between the processes makes it essential that all be performed proficiently.
5. The ability of an organization to respond flexibly to changes in its operational environments is related to its competence.
6. The ability of an organization to maintain effectiveness under pressure from its environments is related to its competence.
7. The conceptual framework used in this study is a valid and practical means for understanding, analyzing, and evaluating the internal functioning of an organization.
8. The conceptual framework provides a meaningful, concrete basis for developmental efforts intended to improve the internal functioning of complex organizations.

The principal contribution of this study is a concrete demonstration of the importance of organizational competence as a determinant of effectiveness, of the relative contributions of the various processes, of the systematic relationships that exist among them, and of the ways in which change and pressure affect the performance of organizations and, accordingly, warrants major attention in efforts to improve effectiveness.

Project Cardinal Point

A detailed description of Project Cardinal Point appears in a report by Olmstead, Elder, and Forsyth (1978).

Project FORGE confirmed the validity of the Competence Model as a viable approach for understanding the performance of complex combat units through analysis of the functioning of their battle staffs. However, two weaknesses in the study were:

1. A tightly controlled, scenario-based laboratory simulation was used as the research vehicle. Although this method was perfectly legitimate for an initial study of such complex phenomena, there still existed questions as to whether battle staff performance would be similar under field conditions.
2. Ad hoc groups were used in FORGE. Accordingly, some nagging doubt always remained as to whether existing battle staffs, which have been formed within units and have worked together over time, would produce results similar to the groups in Project FORGE.

For these and some other reasons of credibility, it was deemed desirable to test the model with operating battle staffs under realistic free play, field conditions insofar as possible. Furthermore, as a step toward utilization of the FORGE results, it was considered desirable to determine whether the Competence Model could be used meaningfully to train and improve the performance of battle staffs.

Accordingly, Project Cardinal Point was devoted to two main objectives:

1. Verify the relationship between combat outcomes of battle simulations and the process performance (organizational competence) of battalion battle staffs in such simulations.
2. Determine the feasibility of training military personnel to observe, assess, and feed back assessments of the process performance of battle staffs while they participate in battle simulations or field exercises.

Method

All data were collected in association with Cardinal Point II, a large training exercise conducted by the 8th Infantry Division in Europe during July and August 1978. Research personnel from HumRRO and the U.S. Army Research Institute for the Behavioral and Social Sciences (ARI) were guests of the 8th Division, and full support and cooperation were provided by the division. However, the exercises were conducted for training purposes, and data collection activities were secondary and adapted to the training goals of the division.

For each battalion, Cardinal Point II was an 11-day exercise consisting of a combination of Field Training Exercise (FTX), battle simulation (PEGASUS), and live firing. The data presented here were collected during participation of battalion battle staffs in the battle simulation phase of Cardinal Point II.

PEGASUS was the vehicle used in the battle simulation phase, during which focus was upon the battle staffs while they engaged in controlling and coordinating operations. PEGASUS is a two-sided, free-play, manual, board simulation that makes possible a training situation in which a battalion command group interacts with controllers playing superior unit levels and board players serving as lower-unit company commanders. In Cardinal Point II, actual company commanders in each participating battalion served as board players.

The exercise was planned and directed by an Exercise Director. Activities of controllers were supervised by a Chief Controller. PEGASUS permits use of an enlarged map of any terrain upon which to depict disposition and movement of forces. Friendly-force board players (company commanders) maneuver their units according to instructions from the battalion command group so as to engage in combat with opposing force (OPFOR) units maneuvered by OPFOR controllers. In Cardinal Point II, OPFOR controllers were 8th Division intelligence officers who were specially trained and indoctrinated in PEGASUS procedures as well as in the tactics of potential opposing forces.

Engagement outcomes are computed by use of combat results tables developed specifically for use with PEGASUS. Play is activated by an operations order issued by Brigade Commander. In the order, a mission is assigned to a battalion, and typical intelligence and other information are provided. Initial friendly and OPFOR unit strengths may be varied, according to the training plan, and therefore differing force ratios may be played. PEGASUS is a flexible, two-sided, free-play battle simulation that provides dynamic and realistic opportunities for battle staffs to exercise and practice required command and control activities.

In the PEGASUS phase of Cardinal Point II, each participating battalion constituted a task force operating in coordination with another player battalion task force under the command and control of a brigade headquarters. The Brigade Commander served as Chief Controller and Chief Evaluator, as well as PEGASUS Brigade Commander.

During one iteration, two battalion task forces conducted simulated combat operations in adjacent lanes of the 8th Division training area. Battalion task force command posts (CP) were located on the actual terrain in the respective lanes, while subordinate unit operations conducted by company commanders of the battalion took place on game boards (depicting the actual terrain) in a central location at the training area headquarters. Communication was by conventional radio nets.

The task force CPs moved as dictated in the operational plans or by the tactical situation. Periodically, company commanders traveled forward to the task force CPs to receive orders, conduct reconnaissance, or take part in critiques conducted by evaluators.

During the two-month duration of Cardinal Point II, seven iterations of the PEGASUS exercise were conducted. In five iterations, two battalions participated simultaneously. In two iterations, only 1 battalion participated at a time. Thus, a total of 12 battalions participated.

Each iteration required four days to complete. Participation of the battle staffs was continuous, day and night, during each four-day period. Within that period, four modules were completed, with each module consisting of one or more types of combat operations.

With minor deviations, the types of combat operations covered by the respective modules were the same for all units. Similarly, the sequence in which the operations were executed were the same. On the other hand, specific events within a module varied considerably between units because PEGASUS is a free-play simulation, and OPFOR players were free to insert special problems (e.g., chemical and nuclear play or communications jamming), as deemed useful for training purposes.

Process Performance: Observation and Feedback

Two Organizational Effectiveness Staff Officers (OESOs) assigned to the 8th Division participated in the battle simulation phase of Cardinal Point II. Throughout each iteration of the battle simulation, one OESO was stationed in each battalion Tactical Operations Center (TOC). The OESOs systematically observed the activities of battle staff members as they proceeded to plan and supervise execution of each operation. OESO observations were addressed to identification and assessment of the quality of performance of the various organizational processes by the battle staff. Focus of the observations were the questions, "What process is occurring? How well is it being performed? How could it have been performed better? What were its effects upon outcomes?" The OESO met periodically with the Battalion Commander and reported the results of his observations.

Results of the ratings were not discussed because the ratings were conducted solely for research purposes. Rather, discussions between OESOs and commanders took the form of informal feedback sessions in which the OESO reported his observations, and the two individuals discussed implications for the functioning of the battle staff. This procedure of prompt feedback to the commander enabled him to obtain immediate assessment of the quality of process performance within the battle staff and, if deemed advisable by him, afforded the opportunity to make on-the-spot adjustments in procedures, policies, and behavior of members of the battle staff. In many instances, at the commander's discretion, OESOs also reported results of observations to all command group members and assisted in analyses of ways that process performance could be improved.

Thus, an OESO served as eyes and ears of a commander with respect to the quality of the performance of organizational functions within the battle staff and provided a mechanism through which on-the-spot feedback could be made available to the commander and members of the battle staff. In addition, OESO ratings of process performance were one major source of data for this study.

Prior to the beginning of the battle simulation phase of Cardinal Point II, HumRRO staff members devoted two days to intensive training of OESOs to observe and assess process performance of battle staffs. It is important to note that both OESOs were combat-arms officers, with experience in battalion staff activities. These qualifications and experience, coupled with their OESO training, made observation more meaningful and made translation and application of the conceptual model more credible and decidedly more effective.

Data

Data were collected on 12 battalion battle staffs. Included were seven Mechanized Infantry and five Armor battalions. Following completion of each module, OESOs rated process performance, and OPFOR controllers independently rated combat effectiveness of the battalions. For each battalion, there were available four ratings on organizational competence (one for each module) and four on combat effectiveness, with personnel who conducted ratings independent of each other.

OPFOR controllers varied their inputs depending upon the tactical situation. In addition, different types of operation (e.g., attack, hasty defense, etc.) were judged to vary in terms of difficulty. To obtain some indication of relative difficulty of the four modules, the Chief Controller and the Chief OPFOR controller rated difficulty of each module for each unit on a five-point scale. Mean ratings across units were computed to obtain an index of difficulty for each module.

Results

Quantitative data were available from OESO ratings of battle staff process performance and OPFOR Controller ratings of combat outcomes of PEGASUS battle simulations. For each battalion, total scores for the exercise and scores for each of the four modules constituting the exercise were obtained. Table 4.5 shows data for the seven organizational processes, organizational competence (sum of the process scores), and combat effectiveness.

Process Performance and Combat Outcomes

Spearman rank order correlation was computed between battalion organizational competence and combat effectiveness scores for the exercise. The statistic provides an index of the relationship between process performance and combat outcomes across the four modules of the exercise. For this relationship, Rho was .71 ($p. < .01$, one-tailed test). A significant and strong relationship was found between battle staff performance of organizational processes and combat outcomes of battle simulations. *When*

Table 4.5
Summary Data for Process Performance and Combat Effectiveness—Cardinal Point

	Module[a,b]								Exercise (Sum of Module Scores)	
	1 (2.45)		2 (3.54)		3 (4.25)		4 (3.17)			
Variable	**Mean**	**SD**	**Mean**	**SD**	**Mean**	**SD**	**Mean**	**SD**	**Mean**	**SD**
Sensing	2.25	.75	3.08	.52	3.25	.62	3.67	.49	12.25	1.48
Communicating Information	1.83	.96	2.75	.62	3.17	.58	3.58	.69	11.33	2.06
Decision Making	3.58	.51	3.75	.45	3.67	.49	4.00	.00	15.00	1.34
Stabilizing	3.08	1.31	3.25	.97	3.33	.89	3.42	.90	13.08	3.70
Communicating Implementation	3.42	.78	3.58	.52	3.41	.69	3.67	.49	14.08	1.92
Coping Actions	3.33	.79	3.50	.52	3.58	.52	3.58	.52	14.00	2.13
Feedback	2.00	.74	2.67	.65	3.17	.84	3.42	.52	11.25	2.13
Organizational Competence	18.91	2.96	22.25	3.54	23.50	3.52	25.25	2.83	89.91	11.60
Combat Effectiveness	4.72	1.00	5.62	1.28	4.79	1.65	6.13	1.04	21.25	3.10

[a]Numbers in parentheses following module designations are difficulty ratings; maximum difficulty = 5.00.

[b]Possible score ranges

	Module	Exercise
Processes	1–4	4–16
Competence	7–28	28–112
Combat Effectiveness	2–10	8–40

the process performance of battle staffs was better, combat outcomes of the battalions were better also. When the process performance of battle staffs was less effective, combat outcomes were lower.

The distribution of battalion combat effectiveness scores was split at the median, and the six highest and six lowest battalions were grouped. For the six highest battalions, mean combat effectiveness was 23.83 with standard deviation of 1.71. For the six lowest, mean combat effectiveness was 18.66 with standard deviation of 1.50. The difference in combat effectiveness between the two groups was significant ($t = 5.57$, $p < .01$).

Mean process scores were computed for each group. A comparison of

Table 4.6
Comparison of Process Performance of More and Less Combat-Effective Battalions—Cardinal Point[a]

Process	More Effective Battalions		Less Effective Battalions		t	p[b]
	Mean	SD	Mean	SD		
Sensing	12.80	1.55	11.40	1.14	1.96	< .05
Communicating Information	12.67	1.97	10.00	1.09	2.90	< .01
Decision Making	15.83	.41	14.17	1.47	2.67	< .05
Stabilizing	15.33	1.63	10.83	3.92	2.59	< .05
Communicating Implementation	15.33	1.21	12.83	1.72	2.91	< .01
Coping Actions	15.33	1.63	12.67	1.75	2.73	< .05
Feedback	12.83	1.47	9.67	1.37	3.86	< .01
Organizational Competence (Total Process Scores)	99.33	6.72	80.50	5.96	5.05	< .01

[a]Scores shown are exercise (4 modules) means.
[b]One-tailed test.

process performance of more and less combat effective battalions is shown in Table 4.6. Comparisons are solely within the group of units on which data were collected, and comparisons of more and less effective units carry no implications for the actual combat readiness or effectiveness of the units involved. From this table, it is evident that process performance of battle staffs of units with the more favorable combat outcomes was uniformly superior to that of battle staffs in units with less favorable combat outcomes. Differences between the two groups were significant for all processes and for organizational competence.

The correlation between organizational competence and combat effectiveness scores and the difference in process performance between more and less effective battalions indicate a strong relationship between combat outcomes, as reflected in battle simulations, and the quality of the organizational processes that occur within a battle staff.

Impact of Feedback

The OESOs reported to and discussed their process observations with Battalion Commanders following completion of each module. An impor-

Table 4.7
Paired t Statistics for Module Differences in Organizational Competence—Cardinal Point

	Module[a]			
Module	**1**	**2**	**3**	**4**
1	–	3.98	7.69	7.82
2		–	2.09	5.32
3			–	3.02
4				–

[a]Degrees of freedom = 11; p < .05 = 1.796, p < .01–2.718 for one-tailed tests.

tant question concerns the impact of that feedback upon the process performance of the battle staffs.

The impact of feedback was evaluated by comparing organizational competence scores for the four modules (see Table 4.7). A simple one-way analysis of variance was used to test the effects of modules. Module effects were significant.

Table 4.7 shows t statistics for differences between module means for organizational competence. All differences were significant.

From Table 4.5, it can be seen that mean process performance (organizational competence) increased throughout the exercise, and an analysis of variance showed that differences between all modules were significant, indicating that OESO feedback exerted positive effects upon the process performance of battle staffs. It is recognized that the possibility of simple practice effects was not controlled; however, the facts that the tactical operations conducted in each module were different and that the modules differed in level of difficulty suggest that the contribution of practice to increased process performance would be minimal. Since process performance improved significantly in each succeeding module, it is concluded that main sources of the improvement were the changes and learning that resulted from the feedback provided by the OESOs.

Of particular interest are the differences between Modules 1 and 2 and 1 and 4 (Table 4.5). Performance in Module 1 occurred prior to any feedback or discussion of organizational processes. Accordingly, scores for the first module constitute baseline data against which scores for the succeeding modules can be compared.

Differences between performance in Modules 1 and 2 provide the most clear-cut demonstration of the impact of feedback. The mean improvement of 3.34 points for Module 2 is the largest increase between any of the modules and suggests that the initial feedback exerted the greatest impact upon process performance. On the other hand, continuing increase in succeeding modules suggests that cumulative effects result from repeated occurrences of feedback.

From Module 1 to Module 4, process performance improved an average of 6.34 points per battle staff. Least improvement was 3 points for a unit that, because of a high initial score, had only a small margin for improvement. Greatest improvement for a unit was 13 points. Process performance of all battle staffs improved across the four modules.

Interviews with the two OESOs revealed that, although some Battalion Commanders had initial reservations about the potential value of process feedback, most commanders rapidly perceived its utility and used the provided information to make on-the-spot adjustments in staff procedures, role relationships, and even leadership styles during the course of the exercises. OESOs cited numerous instances of constructive changes initiated by the commanders and of improved coordination and teamwork, with resulting improvements in overall battle staff performance.

In view of the above findings, it was concluded that OESO feedback of process observations had a significant, positive impact upon performance of the organizational processes and that these observations and subsequent feedback to unit commanders contributed substantially to improved combat outcomes of the battle simulations.

Conclusions

The results of the research conducted in Project Cardinal Point warranted the following conclusions:

1. The results verify the findings of Project FORGE and, therefore, validate the Competence Model of organizational performance.
2. Organizational competence (the quality of organization process performance) is a principal determinant of combat effectiveness, and, hence, of organizational effectiveness.
3. Feedback of process observations by trained observers during training programs exerts positive impacts upon the effectiveness of organizations.
4. It is feasible to train management staffs to improve their performance of critical organizational processes that contribute to effectiveness.

One weakness of Project FORGE was that ad hoc groups were used to form the battle staffs that were studied. Another weakness was that, in FORGE, the battle staffs performed in a fully simulated situation (i.e., they were not in the field). In Project Cardinal Point, participants were actual battalion battle staffs engaged in the conduct of simulated combat operations under field conditions. Since the results for Project Cardinal Point were remarkably similar to those of Project FORGE, it can be concluded with confidence that the processes subsumed under the rubric of organizational competence are important contributors to organizational performance. To the extent that the command and control system of a unit influences the performance of that unit, organizational processes are determinants of organizational performance.

HEW Studies

The studies conducted for the Social and Rehabilitation Service of the former Department of Health, Education and Welfare included an intensive analysis of social service agencies and the effects of organizational context upon the performance of individuals and the performance and competence of agencies. The principal objective was to determine the impact of organizational structure and climate upon social welfare and rehabilitation workers, their attitudes, and their performance. A secondary objective was to identify the perceptions of the workers toward a number of specific aspects of their agencies and their work environments. Two separate and independent studies were conducted. Each study followed the same research design, and all procedures were identical between the two studies.

In the first study, data were collected in 12 public welfare, 9 private welfare, and 10 public rehabilitation agencies throughout the nation (Olmstead and Christensen, 1973). At each location, research teams collected information about the organization, its structure, and policies of the agency; interviewed a staggered sample of service delivery personnel; and administered a comprehensive questionnaire to all workers of the agency.

The surveyed agencies in the first study employed a total of 6,397 people, of whom 1,662, a sample of service delivery personnel (workers and supervisors), were interviewed. The sample contained 1,219 females and 443 males. Mean age was 36.05 years. Mean years of education was 15.60 for the total sample.

The data presented here are results of the first study. The second study of 17 additional public welfare agencies was conducted in 1975 (Olmstead, Christensen, Salter, and Lackey). In the main, the results were essentially the same as for the first study.

The results are presented here in some detail because they illustrate how large-scale, theory-based, multiple-variable research can produce meaningful data for both theory verification and use for planning and organizational development.

Method

The conceptual framework for the study followed an Open Systems approach as discussed in Chapter 3. The basic framework for the study was devised as a means for systematizing the many different variables with which the study was concerned and for hypothesizing the relationships that could be expected to exist. The impact model of performance illustrated in Figure 6.1 was used here in the study of social service agencies.

The impact model consists of three classes of variables (see Figure 6.1), which must be examined together for a full understanding of their relationships. They are Impact Variables, Mediating Variables, and Dependent Variables.

Impact Variables

Impact variables are factors within the organization that can be changed or manipulated through management decision, training, or other organizational actions and thus impact upon or influence the other classes of variables—the activities, attitudes, motivations, and performance of employees. Climate and structure are the two classes of impact variables, and they constitute the organizational context. Climate is the sum of those properties that reflect the organization's internal state and characteristic ways of working, and climate factors are those attributes responsible for its particular atmosphere. Structure is concerned with the relationships and practices that result from the allocation of authority and responsibility by an organization and includes not only the formal framework of roles but also the hierarchies of power, communication, status, and function.

In summary, a social service or rehabilitation organization was conceived as a number of persons performing some activity in relation to its external environment. The way that the persons are arranged in relation to each other and to the task is the structure of the organization. The persons in the system were conceived as having various motivations and attitudes and as performing certain activities in certain ways. The ways in which they performed the activities were determined by their proficiency, by their motivations, and by how they perceived the organization, other members, themselves, and their roles.

The problem for the study was to devise a conceptual system that would include the various aspects just discussed, provide explanations of the relationships between them, and indicate directions for evaluations of their relationships. The model set out in Figure 6.1 was the product of the deliberations.

Results

Full details of the results can be found in the publication by Olmstead and Christensen (1973). In summary, formal structure was found to be a significant determinant of agency climate when its dimensions were differentially weighted. Greatest weight is contributed to climate by a dimension called dispersion. It appears that climate improves when an agency consists of several geographical locations. This probably can be accounted for by the fact that the various offices are smaller. It appears that as size of office increases, climate becomes less favorable, and vice versa. Finally, configuration contributes some weight. As agencies became taller (increased number of levels) and as spans of control became larger, climate became less favorable.

It was also found that certain components of climate are determined not only by structure but also by other climate factors such as supervision and communication. The overall climate of an agency is determined by its agency type, its structure, and several major influencing factors that have been included as parts of the climate.

Agency climate was strongly related to the perceptions, attitudes, values, and need satisfactions of employees and was found to be a major determinant of these processes. However, structure had no significant, direct correlation with them, and it was concluded that its influence is only indirect through its impact upon climate.

Climate was a very strong determinant, accounting for 79 percent of the variance in employee satisfaction. Most dimensions of climate are related to satisfaction; however, the strongest contributors were agency goals, agency policies, supervision, and communication.

The variable of agency performance consisted of two dimensions: agency goal achievement, the ratings of the extent to which an agency is successful in achieving its goals, and adequacy of agency performance, the ratings of the adequacy with which an agency performs its mission in comparison with other agencies like it. Members of medium-sized and small agencies were approximately equal in ratings of agency goal achievement; however, large agencies were lower in goal achievement.

Determinants of Agency Performance

The result of a multiple correlation analysis of the two dimensions, formal structure and climate, with agency performance was an obtained coefficient (R) of .82, which is large and highly significant. Structure and climate combined account for 67 percent of the variance in rated agency performance. Structure contributed 5.37 percent, and climate contributed 61.70 percent, making climate the larger determinant by far.

Formal structure correlated with agency performance at −.31. This negative relationship was slightly significant and indicates that an increase in formal structure is accompanied by a decrease in agency performance. On the other hand, the correlation between climate and agency performance is high and positive (.80), indicating that an increase in favorableness of climate is accompanied by an increase in agency performance.

Table 4.8 shows correlations between agency performance and dimensions of formal structure and variables of climate. Within structure, size shows the highest relationship (−.61), which is negative. As size increases, ratings of local agency performance go down. In addition, dispersion (.31) and complexity (−.34) are somewhat related to agency performance. As an

Table 4.8
Correlations between Agency Performance and the Components of Formal Structure and Climate

Component	r	p
Formal Structure:		
Configuration	–.22	NS
Dispersion	.31	< .05
Size	–.61	< .01
Complexity	–.34	< .05
Concentration of Authority	–.25	NS
Support Components	–.24	NS
Climate:		
Agency Goals	.90	< .01
Agency Policies	.81	< .01
Supervision	.64	< .01
Group Relations	–.06	NS
Structuring of Activities	–.62	< .01
Agency Practices	.15	NS
Stability of Work Environment	.64	< .01
Communication	.80	< .01

Degrees of freedom = 29; NS = not significant.

agency becomes more geographically dispersed, performance tends to increase somewhat, but as the structure becomes more complex, performance decreases.

From Table 4.8, it can be seen that six of the eight climate variables are highly correlated with agency performance; only group relations and agency practice had no significant relationship to it. The magnitude of these correlations confirms the effects of climate. Agency performance is enhanced when goals and policies are clear; supervision is effective; formalization, standardization, and controls are low; the work environment is stable; and communication is frequent and effective. Decrements in these factors are usually accompanied by decreased agency performance.

Organizational Competence

The components of organizational competence proved to be highly correlated with organizational effectiveness in the studies of military organizations. Competence is the capacity of an organization for adapting its internal processes to the requirements of changing external environments and for coping with situational demands rapidly, accurately, and appropriately. It consists of two components and includes an additional element, each of which must be performed well if an organization is to be effective. The components are reality testing, the ability of the organization to obtain a correct understanding of the critical environments within which it must function, and adaptability, the ability of an organization to adjust its activities to cope with the requirements that are placed upon it by its environments; the additional element is stabilization or integration, the ability of the organization to maintain internal structure and function while coping with the demands placed upon it.

For the study of social service delivery organizations, each component was classed as a variable and seven organizational processes, the key elements in organizational competence, were used as dimensions. Through the seven processes, it was possible to obtain measures of some specific effectiveness-related activities and, thus, overcome some of the possible biases frequently attributed to more global ratings of performance. Each organizational process was represented by one dimension, and each dimension consisted of three scales.

The dimensions are not discussed separately here. Competence was highest in private welfare agencies, second highest in rehabilitation agencies, and lowest in public welfare agencies. For all agencies taken together, the mean was slightly above the midpoint of a 100-point scale and indicated that competence is rated as only moderate in most agencies. According to analysis of variance results, the differences were highly significant, suggesting that agency type was a factor in organizational competence.

Table 4.9 shows a comparison of competence according to agency size. Medium-sized agencies were highest in competence, with small agencies a close second and large agencies lowest. Analysis of variance results for size were significant, indicating the existence of actual differences. Accordingly, size is also a factor in organizational competence.

Determinants of Competence

A multiple correlation analysis for formal structure and climate with organizational competence produced an obtained coefficient (R) of .86, which is high and very significant. However, the simple correlations showed that structure was not related to competence in any significant degree and that climate was the sole contributor (73.5%) to the variance in competence in social service agencies.

It was concluded that climate is a principal determinant and that organizational structure is not a major determinant of competence. When climate is high in favorableness, the competence of agencies is also high. Since competence is related to the effectiveness of organizations, enhancement of climate is assumed also to enhance effectiveness through its strong impact

Table 4.9
Organizational Competence by Agency Size

Component	Large		Medium		Small		All Agencies	
	Mean	SD	Mean	SD	Mean	SD	Mean	SD
Reality Testing:								
Sensing (Possible Range 0–150)	95.15	9.06	103.76	8.41	102.31	5.02	100.52	8.38
Communication of Information (Possible Range 0–150)	89.96	7.80	98.88	9.52	100.43	6.86	96.50	9.17
Feedback (Possible Range 0–150)	77.26	10.62	92.93	11.37	87.40	7.60	86.09	11.75
Adaptability:								
Decision Making (Possible Range 0–150)	86.51	11.50	100.40	10.47	98.59	5.99	95.34	11.22
Communicating Information (Possible Range 0–150)	84.20	7.57	98.21	10.75	94.31	7.31	92.43	10.38
Coping Actions (Possible Range 0–150)	97.72	8.14	108.44	7.29	107.01	8.31	104.52	9.03
Stabilization:								
Stabilizing (Possible Range 0–150)	74.73	11.66	93.29	13.89	86.40	9.53	85.08	13.91
Organizational Competence (Possible Range 0–150)	524.10	56.52	601.08	59.08	585.48	35.47	571.22	60.29

Table 4.10
Correlations between Variables of Climate and Organizational Competence

Variable	r	p
Agency Goals	.86	< .01
Agency Policies	.80	< .01
Supervision	.75	< .01
Group Relations	.15	NS
Structuring of Activities	–.59	< .01
Agency Practices	–.27	NS
Stability of Work Environment	.55	< .01
Communication	.90	< .01

Degrees of freedom = 29.

upon competence. Table 4.10 shows the relationship between the variables of climate and organizational competence.

Agency goals, agency policies, supervision, and communication were strongly correlated with competence. When these factors are high, competence increases. Stability of work environment and structuring of activities were high–moderate, with the correlation for structuring activities being negative (i.e., when this factor is low, competence is high).

Group relations and agency practices were not related to competence in any significant way in this study. In other research, not reported here, both group relationships and organizational practices have been found to be related to performance and effectiveness.

Significance of Organizational Competence

The results in this study of organizational competence provide some significant new understandings about the performance of organizations. Competence measures are a way of evaluating specific activities and of obtaining estimates of performance that permit more precise understanding of the causes of effectiveness or the lack of it.

Competence focuses upon the internal processes that enable organizations to react effectively to requirements placed upon them by external forces that are critical for them. For social service agencies, such sources may be governmental agencies at all levels, boards, citizen groups, clients, unions, or any other element important to the functioning and survival of the agency. The processes comprising competence must function effectively and in coordination if an agency is to be responsive to the demands placed upon it by these critical elements.

When the processes of competence function well, an organization acquires the information that it needs to make accurate evaluations of conditions within its environments, processes the information so that informed decisions can be made, makes decisions rationally, and executes the resulting programs and actions effectively and efficiently. When the processes do not function well, organizational responses are frequently ineffective, inefficient, and inappropriate.

The data presented here demonstrate that the climate within an organization is one principal determinant of its organizational competence. When the climate factors are favorable, employees are able to perform the required organizational processes well because a favorable climate produces a workforce at all levels who know the requirements of their respective jobs in relation to goals and policies. They also possess the necessary information to make intelligent and appropriate decisions, they can perform their duties in accordance with such decisions, and they possess both the skills and the motivation to coordinate their activities for the best interest of the organization.

From these results, it is evident that organizational competence determines the flexibility and responsiveness of an organization. High-quality performance of the competence processes makes it possible for an organization to adapt rapidly and effectively to changing environmental requirements. Poor performance leads to organizational rigidity, which is characterized by slow adaptation to change, stereotyped responses to new and different situations, and ultimate inability to satisfy requirements placed upon it.

The concept of competence refers to the ability of an organization to manage certain processes so as to flexibly and effectively cope with requirements placed upon it by its critical environments. Essential for competence are the seven processes discussed throughout this book. The high-quality performance of these processes has been shown to be strongly related to organizational effectiveness.

Data on competence in this study included ratings by the employees of their agencies' effectiveness in performing each process and also ratings of the amount of emphasis placed upon effective performance of each process within the agency. It was anticipated that emphasis and effectiveness would be related. If an agency emphasized a particular process, it was likely to be performed more effectively, and, if effectiveness was low, it was likely that the process did not receive much emphasis from the agency.

Ratings were obtained on both effectiveness and emphasis for each of the seven processes. The relative sizes of the scores followed the same pattern for all agency types. The order of ratings from highest to lowest for both effectiveness and emphasis were:

- Coping actions
- Sensing

- Decision making
- Communicating implementation
- Communicating information
- Stabilizing
- Feedback

It should be noted that scores were not spectacularly high for any scale. Furthermore, emphasis scores were always higher than effectiveness scores, indicating that workers perceived that effectiveness did not match the emphasis placed upon the processes. However, differences between effectiveness and emphasis scores varied between agency types.

Comparisons across criteria enabled identification of impact factors that consistently had the highest relationships with all or most criteria. If the model for agency priorities was followed, these factors would receive the earliest attention and greatest effort. If agency resources were limited, attention could be given only to those factors with the highest priorities. Significant determinants for the several criterion variables are shown in Table 4.11.

Listed below in recommended order of priority are those impact variables that were deemed most important for attention by management of service delivery agencies. Standards for determining priorities were number of criterion variables affected, with the required minimum of at least two, and relative sizes of relationships to criterion variables.

- Agency goals
- Agency policies
- Communication
- Supervision
- Structuring of activities
- Stability of work environment
- Size of agency
- Dispersion of agency

In a second nationwide study of 17 public welfare agencies (Olmstead et al., 1975), the study reported above was repeated with essentially the same results.

IMPLICATIONS

Organizational competence is the adequacy with which an organization performs certain critical processes or functions. When the processes are performed adequately, they assist an organization to be effective. When

Table 4.11
Significant Determinants for Criterion Variables

Satisfaction	Individual Performance	Absenteeism	Turnover	Agency Performance	Competence
Communication (.93)	Communication (.33)	Agency Size (.41)	Agency Practices (–.36)	Agency Goals (.90)	Communication (.90)
Supervision (.84)	Supervision (.34)	Complexity of Structure (.38)	Dispersion (.35)	Agency Policies (.81)	Agency Goals (.86)
Agency Goals (.80)	Agency Goals (.31)	Agency Goals (–.34)		Communication (.80)	Agency Policies (.80)
Agency Policies (.75)		Supervision (–.34)		Supervision (.64)	Supervision (.75)
Structuring of Activities (–.57)		Agency Policies (–.31)		Stability of Work Environment (.64)	Structuring of Activities (–.59)
Stability of Work Environment (.49)				Structuring of Activities (–.61)	Stability of Work Environment (.55)
Agency Size (–.47)				Agency Size (–.61)	Dispersion (.45)

Figures in parentheses are Pearson product-moment correlation coefficients.

handled poorly, they may negate many positive effects contributed by proficiency in other areas of activity.

Survey techniques were used to evaluate competence in 31 social service and rehabilitation agencies nationwide and in 17 public welfare agencies in nine states. In both studies, very strong relationships were found between agency effectiveness and (1) organizational competence, (2) each of the components of competence, and (3) each organizational process. Agency effectiveness was measured in terms of agency productivity and judged quality of agency performance.

Taken together, the two military studies and the two studies of civilian agencies demonstrated that the Competence Model is generally applicable to all types of organizations. In addition, three studies in proprietary business organizations, not reported here, have confirmed the results.

The results of the research discussed in this chapter confirm the validity of the Competence Model as a viable approach for analyzing and understanding the performance of complex organizations. *The principal contribution of the studies is concrete demonstrations of the following*:

1. The importance of the processes subsumed under organizational competence as determinants of the effectiveness of organizations.
2. The relative contributions to effectiveness of the various organizational processes.
3. The systematic relationships that exist among the processes.
4. The ways in which change and pressure influence performance of the organizational processes.
5. The ways in which the organizational context influences both organizational competence and organizational effectiveness.

The studies described in this chapter also reinforce the concept that organizational competence is a system attribute. That is, organizational processes must be performed well by all members of an organization. Ideally, the processes take the form of coordinated activities that bring information, decisions, and actions from many sources into conjunction through a complex interplay between positions and between organizational levels. Through such interplay, the various activities of the organization are integrated and produce the unified action required by an effective system.

Accordingly, maximum effectiveness can be expected when (1) members at all levels are equally proficient in performance of the organizational processes and (2) their separate activities are integrated into a unified system of decision and action. In short, *organizational competence involves two elements: (1) proficiency of all individuals in process performance and (2) teamwork among all levels so that performance of organizational processes by individuals is fully coordinated. Teamwork results from integration of structure and function.*

It is now clear that organizational competence plays a principal and critical role in the performance of organizations, and, accordingly, it warrants major attention in efforts to improve effectiveness. It is also apparent that the findings and concepts discussed in this chapter have considerable potential utility for the improvement of organizational effectiveness.

The main values of the Competence Model are that it offers the following:

1. A systematic way of thinking about some otherwise exceedingly slippery organizational functions.
2. A workable framework for the assessment and diagnosis of organizational functioning and for the correction or improvement of dysfunctional elements in an organization.
3. A meaningful and workable foundation for both individual and group training in organizational process performance.

The processes associated with organizational competence can be operationally defined. Once made operational, the Competence Model provides concrete bases for (1) the assessment and (2) the improvement of organizational functioning. Recommended procedures for assessment, diagnosis, and training are described in later chapters of this book.

Chapter 5

Functionally Competent Organizations

This chapter is a summary of the conceptual framework that has resulted from the research discussed in Chapters 3 and 4. It describes a unitary system with relevance for both research and application.

When organizations are conceived as open systems, it becomes evident that many operational failures may not be the results of individual error, personal bad judgment, or poor execution. Instead, their sources may lie in deficient organizational functioning—in failure of the organization, as a system, to adequately perform the problem-solving, decision-making, action-taking functions that are common to all organizations but may take specific forms within particular types. These functions are essential for performance under the intense pressures and problems encountered in modern operational contexts.

Ideally, the process for organizations to cope with uncertainty situations involves handling an operational cycle that flows up and down the chain of authority and consists of situation—information—decision—action—altered situation—new information—supplementary decision—and so on. Through its command and control function, the organization seeks to regulate this cycle without becoming inflexible in its responses.

The constant interplay that occurs is the essence of dynamic organizational process, and the extent with which it is handled competently is a major determinant of organizational effectiveness. The ability to control and direct the processes that drive an organization determines, in large part, the capability of that organization for coping with the pressures imposed by its various operational environments.

To be effective under such conditions, organizations must possess capabilities to:

1. Search out, accurately identify, and correctly interpret the properties of operational situations *as they develop*.
2. Solve problems *as they occur* within the context of rapidly changing situational demands.
3. Generate *flexible* decisions relevant to changing situations.
4. Cope with *shifting situational demands* with precise appropriateness.

The necessity for flexible, unified responses to changing events creates some major difficulties for many organizations. Thinking of actions as the product of an organization rather than of individuals makes it possible to analyze situations more understandably and, consequently, to develop more effective means for coping with problem environments.

ORGANIZATIONAL ATTRIBUTES

Over the past 50 years, extensive research (Bennis, 1966; Schein, 1970; Olmstead et al., 1973; Olmstead, 1992) has identified certain attributes that constitute the underpinnings for organizational effectiveness (Olmstead, 1997a). In summary, to be successful, every organization needs three basic attributes:

1. *Reality Assessment*—the capability to accurately assess the reality of situations facing the organization, the ability of the organization to search out, accurately perceive, and correctly interpret the properties and characteristics of its environments (both external and internal), particularly those properties that have special relevance for the missions and operations of the organization. In short, every organization must have the capability for accurately determining the real conditions within its important environments. "Real" refers to the way conditions are, not how they are supposed to be or how they are desired to be.

   To survive and succeed, every organization must have structures and processes that enable it to assess the current reality demands of its particular environments.
2. *Adaptability*—the capability for solving problems that arise from changing environmental demands and for acting with flexibility in response to the changing demands.

   To survive and succeed, each organization must have structures and processes that enable it to mobilize the necessary and appropriate resources for adapting to changes in its environments and to act so as to overcome such changes.
3. *Integration*—the maintenance of structure and function under stress and maintenance of a state of relations among subunits that ensures that coordination is sustained and that the various subunits do not work at cross-purposes.

   Integration derives from a sense of identity, and, in order to develop and maintain integration, organizational members must possess knowledge, insight, and a reasonable consensus regarding organizational objectives, missions, and the activities required for the accomplishment of missions and objectives.

In addition, technical proficiency is a requirement.

COMPONENTS OF ORGANIZATIONAL COMPETENCE

In the research, there was also derived from the attributes a set of organizational processes that have been verified as major determinants of effectiveness. Taken together, the set of processes have been subsumed under the rubric *organizational competence.*

Organizational competence is analogous to another term, *functional competence*, which refers to the quality of performance (i.e., how well an organism performs the critical or essential functions required for it to be effective). Function is the general term for the natural activity of a person or thing that is required in order to accomplish its created or designated purpose. Organizational functions are the activities of an organization that *must be performed* if the organization is to accomplish its purposes.

In Open Systems approaches to organizations, functions are called processes because they occur over time, and their beginnings and ends may be sometimes difficult to identify. The specific nature of a process and the way it must be executed may differ with type, purpose, mission, and objective of an organization. However, it can be concluded with high confidence that the seven basic processes described in the following section apply, in some form, to every organization, regardless of its type.

Organizational competence refers to the capability of an organization to function as a unified system in order to cope with complex conditions in the present-day world. It is concerned with the quality of system functions (processes) that are critical to the effectiveness of organizations.

Organizational competence is a major operational determinant of organizational effectiveness. Where effectiveness is the ultimate outcome (mission accomplishment, achievement of objectives, productivity, etc.), competence is the capability of the organization to perform those critical functions (processes) that lead to effectiveness.

In a series of studies (Olmstead and Christensen, 1973; Olmstead, Elder, and Forsyth, 1978; Olmstead, 1992) conducted in both simulated and operational settings, seven organizational functions or processes were found to be critical to organizational competence and, therefore, to effectiveness. The organizational processes found to be critical include most of the functions performed by personnel in any organization. Stated in general terms, the processes are:

1. *Sensing*—the acquisition of information concerning the environments, both external and internal to the organization, that are significant for the effective accomplishment of objectives. Examples of significant external environments are the economy, the competition, higher organizational levels, adjacent departments, and weather. The specific character of sensing activities that may be

required can differ according to the type of organization, its mission, and the particular environments that are significant to it. However, whatever their specific nature, all sensing activities involve seeking, receiving, acquiring, processing, and interpreting information. They are those activities through which an organization obtains as accurate an understanding as possible of all of the environments in which it must function and of the requirements that must be met in order for it to accomplish its purposes.

2. *Communicating Information*—those activities whereby information that has been sensed is transmitted within the organization to those individuals who should know about it or act upon it. This process involves both the initial transmission of information by those who have sensed it originally and the dissemination of the information throughout the organization to those individuals who need it for effective performance of their duties. Most important, the process also includes discussion and interpretation—those communicative acts through which the members of an organization attempt to clarify information and its meaning and to determine the implications of the information.
3. *Decision Making*—the deliberative acts of one or more persons that lead to a conclusion that some action should be taken by the organization. The decision-making process is not limited to those important decisions made by a manager but, rather, includes all decisions, however large or small, made by any member of the organization, if they impact upon activities. Decisions also include conclusions that actions should not be taken.
4. *Stabilizing*—those actions intended to maintain organizational stability or unit integrity or to prevent internal disruptions and negative side effects that might result from ongoing actions or changes in such actions; also actions intended to adjust procedures or internal activities so as to accommodate to changes in mission-related activities. The purpose is to maintain internal structure and function.
5. *Communicating Implementation*—those activities through which decisions and the requirements resulting from decisions are communicated to those individuals or units that must implement the decisions. In addition to the straightforward transmission of directives, plans, orders, and instructions, the process includes discussion and interpretation—those two-way communicative acts through which clarification of requirements is achieved and implications for actions are discussed. Of particular importance in the process are the activities of linking individuals, who relay instructions between the original decision maker and personnel who ultimately implement the decision.
6. *Coping Actions*—those actions through which an organization copes with its environments and with changes therein, activities involving direct execution of actions against target environments. This process is primarily concerned with the actual execution of actions at points of contact with the target environments and with how such actions are carried out.
7. *Feedback*—those activities of the organization intended to provide it with information about the results and outcomes of actions taken so that the organization can learn from its successes and mistakes and adjust future activities accordingly.

For any particular problem, event, or situation, the seven processes are conceived to occur in the sequence shown above. The sequence is called the Adaptive-Coping Cycle (Schein, 1970). Thus, when a problem arises or a change occurs in the environment, the organization first must sense the problem or change, followed by communication of the sensed information, make decisions concerning how to cope with the problem or change, and so on through the cycle.

Of course, in actual practice, the cycle is not always so clear-cut or straightforward. It tends to operate erratically, with much redundancy and backtracking at many points. Nevertheless, there is considerable evidence that processes that occur later in the cycle are dependent upon the quality of those that occur earlier (e.g., the quality of decisions depends upon the amount and quality of information available to decision makers—upon the amount and quality of information that has been sensed by various elements of the organization and communicated to decision makers). Similarly the quality of actions taken to cope with the environment depends upon the character of earlier decisions and the communication used to obtain implementation. This leads to the obvious conclusion that maximum effectiveness requires that all processes be performed equally well. It also means that the correction of dysfunctional processes results in improvement in overall process performance and, therefore, contributes to improved effectiveness. For convenience, the processes have been labeled "Organizational Performance Elements" (OPE).

INDICATORS OF QUALITY

Competence is concerned with the quality of process performance within an organization. Although each process must be performed at least to a minimal degree, the frequency with which the processes are performed is not a determinant of effectiveness. The critical requirement is quality (i.e., *how well the processes are performed*). The following criteria illustrate the qualitative requirements of each process:

1. *Sensing*
   a. Accurate detection of all available information, including active seeking of information from higher and lower levels as well as all available sources elsewhere.
   b. Correct interpretation of all detected information.
   c. Accurate discrimination between relevant and irrelevant information.
   d. Relevance to mission, task, or problem of all attempts to obtain information.
   e. Accurate and relevant processing of acquired information.
2. *Communicating Information*
   a. Accurate transmission of relevant information.

b. Sufficient completeness in transmission to achieve full and adequate understanding by recipient.
c. Timely transmission of information.
d. Correct determination of whether information should be transmitted.
e. Transmission to appropriate recipients.

3. *Decision Making*
    a. Timeliness of decisions in view of available information.
    b. Correctness of decisions in view of circumstances and of available information.
    c. Consideration in the decision process of all contingencies, alternatives, and possibilities.
4. *Communicating Implementation*
    a. Accurate transmission of directives, orders, and instructions.
    b. Transmission to appropriate recipient.
    c. Sufficient completeness to communicate adequate and full understanding of actions required.
    d. Timely transmission of directives, orders, and instructions in view of both available information and the action requirements of recipients.
5. *Actions: Stabilizing, Coping, and Feedback*
    a. Correctness of action in view of both the operational circumstances and the decision or directive from which the action derives.
    b. Timeliness of the action in view of both the current circumstances and the decision or directive from which the action derives.
    c. Correctness of choice of target for the action.
    d. Adequacy of execution of the action.

The organizational processes that have been discussed constitute a basic framework for analyzing some of the more intangible but exceedingly important aspects of organizational performance. Use of the framework makes it possible to:

1. Assess the quality of performance of parts or entire organizations;
2. Identify processes that are dysfunctional or poorly performed;
3. Identify strengths and weaknesses in organization or unit process performance and determine sources of deficiencies;
4. Identify individuals, groups, or units in which process performance requires improvement; and
5. In general, assess organizational performance in a manner that produces sound and credible bases for feedback or training.

Similarly, the framework provides a credible basis for clarifying roles and developing teamwork.

DETERMINANTS OF COMPETENCE

Three principal elements determine the competence of an organization:

1. Proficiency of individuals.
2. Proficiency of groups.
3. Integration of structure and function.

Competence depends upon the skills of individual personnel in acquiring and interpreting information, making choices concerning to whom acquired information is to be communicated, accurately and completely; making decisions concerning ways to cope with unusual or unanticipated situations; and executing actions that derive from such decisions—all performed at high levels of proficiency and coordination. Although some technological assists may be available, such as data-processing equipment and sophisticated communication devices, the payoff in competence ultimately reduces to the judgments and actions of operating personnel.

Of equal importance, the performance of organizational processes is a team product, and much of the quality of process performance depends upon teamwork and the coordination of separate responsibilities and activities. Accordingly, equal to the skills of individuals are group proficiencies and the integration of structure and function. This means that the positions, roles, and functions that make up an organizational system must fit together and support each other in their respective activities. Where the integration of structure and function does not occur, the result may be missed signals, aborted decisions, overlooked information, and activities at cross-purposes. In the extreme, loss of integration may produce a collapse of essential functions, which can threaten survival of the organization.

The Role of Integration

Careful examination of the above descriptions of the seven processes makes clear that the several functions or processes contribute directly to the two fundamental organizational attributes of reality assessment and adaptability. The functions of sensing, communicating information, and feedback contribute to reality assessment. Decision making, communicating implementation, and coping actions result in adaptability. Stabilizing is important for maintaining integration.

Whereas capabilities for reality assessment and adaptability result directly from performance of relevant functions by personnel of the organization, integration is an attribute that enhances such performance. It is a condition that may vary according to circumstances or events that impact upon an organization, and, in large degree, it determines the extent to which critical organizational functions are coordinated and effective.

Integration is:

1. The maintenance of organizational structure and functions under stress, and
2. A state of relations among the various organizational parts that ensures that coordination is sustained and that the parts do not work at cross-purposes.

Integration is activated and controlled by a number of conditions within an organization, and the extent to which it is sustained depends upon these conditions. The degree of integration that develops depends upon the presence and extent of the required conditions.

Conditions Conducive to Integration

In one sense, it can be argued that the main function of an organization is to make favorable conditions for the achievement of its goals. Efforts are made to increase, as much as conditions permit, the probabilities of success in accomplishing the organization's objectives, mission, or purposes. The making of decisions, the specification of methods and the improvement of procedures, the designation of responsibilities and the assignment of duties, the direction of work, and the execution of tasks—all of these processes have one legitimate organizational purpose: to increase the chances of successfully accomplishing the organization's objectives. Upon this point rest all of the criteria by which the effectiveness of organizational activities is evaluated.

Probabilities of success are increased only by taking relevant and appropriate actions. For organizations, whose very survival may depend upon the successful achievement of objectives, the actions require high levels of competence by numbers of people working together. The effectiveness of such an action system requires the coordinated efforts of individuals performing parts of a total task so that the activities of each person contribute, in some fashion, to accomplishment of the overall objectives. In these terms, it is not surprising that the effectiveness of an organization with respect to the achievement of its objectives should be so closely related to the sociopsychological conditions within it.

When an organization is viewed as an open system, its stability in relation to its mission, its objectives, and the performance of critical processes is obtained through a sufficient coincidence of the psychological fields of all personnel. For an organization to be maximally effective, shared understandings among all members are essential. A common means of communication, a common acceptance of purposes and subpurposes, a common acceptance of the distribution of duties and responsibilities, and a common motivation to do whatever is needed are required for effective performance as an organization.

Numerous factors play a part in determining whether the system processes discussed earlier are performed effectively and whether they are resistant to disruption under pressure. Knowledge, experience, and skills of individuals influence functioning of the processes. Standard operating procedures and contingency plans reduce the potentiality for disruption. However, integration is a vital aspect of organizational experience that cannot be understood as codified procedures, routine functions, personal characteristics, or formal organizational relationships. This aspect involves more than simple activity. Rather, it involves the interaction of individuals and groups that results in shared understandings and common perspectives. In this interaction, such as occurs between members of a well-functioning team, there is no simple, one-to-one relation between an isolated cause and effect. Instead, there is a more or less continuous process of action and reaction. Over time, the product of this interaction is a condition that is critical for the maximally effective functioning of organizational processes. For this discussion, the condition has been termed *integration*.

Factors Affecting Integration

Following are brief discussions of the major factors that influence integration and performance in organizations.

Roles

The concept of role is a principal means of explaining individual behavior in organizations and for linking such behavior to the organizational processes. Roles are at once the building blocks of organizational systems and the frameworks of requirements with which such systems control their members as individuals. Each person in an organization is linked to other members by the functional requirements of his or her role, which are implemented through the expectations that those members have of him or her. It is important to stress that roles are ideational (i.e., they are ideas about how behavior ought to occur, rather than being the actual behavior).

The functioning of organizational processes is determined in large part by the role perceptions of individual members. The problem-solving, decision-making, and adapting processes are affected by the extent to which there are clear, accurate, and shared perceptions of role requirements by all members of the organization.

Goals

Organizations face the problem of adapting to environmental change without losing their basic character and distinctive capabilities. On the one hand, if the goals around which activities are mobilized are adhered to despite environmental change, there may be losses and inefficiencies or even threats to survival. On the other hand, if goals are changed too frequently, there is the risk of members' losing sight of the principal missions of the organization.

The importance of goals lies in the necessity for the efficient conduct of complex activities and for keeping activities on track. When goals are clear, operational, and shared, and when people are emotionally committed to their accomplishment, misperceptions, conflicts, false starts, cross-purposes, and wasted effort are kept to a minimum. The overall (superordinate) objectives of the organization, the objectives of subordinate units, and the goals of participants are in general harmony, and all aim toward accomplishing the mission of the organization. In turn, this should result in more efficient functioning of the organizational processes.

Norms

An often neglected set of requirements in organizations and in teams includes those actions that are not specified by role prescriptions (job descriptions) but that facilitate the accomplishment of organizational objectives. Any organization's need for some actions of a relatively spontaneous sort is inevitable. Planning, standard procedures, and role prescriptions cannot foresee all contingencies and cannot anticipate all environmental changes that may occur. The resources of personnel for innovating and for spontaneous cooperation are thus vital to effective functioning. However, this spontaneous behavior requires some control to funnel it into organizationally approved channels. This control cannot be provided by the more formal role prescriptions. Norms serve this function.

Norms are attitudes and codes of behavior held in common by all, or most, of the members. When well developed, this superstructure of customs, standards, and values regulates the behavior of members and provides them with the bases for assessing nonroutine situations and for governing their actions in such situations, where no official guidance is available.

It is evident that the patterned activities that make up the organizational processes are so intrinsically cooperative and interrelated that the kinds of norms that develop must inevitably influence their functioning. *This influence is most likely in terms of the extent to which participants execute the process functions above and beyond the minimal limits prescribed by formal role prescriptions.*

Group Relations

When group members work together toward common objectives over time, role structures, norms, and patterns of interaction develop. These group attributes exert a lasting influence upon the ways that members go about their tasks, the levels of motivation that are achieved, and the extent to which a sense of identity develops within the group and the organization. A sense of identity is Bennis's third ingredient of organizational health, and, when highly developed, it contributes to the evolution of integration within an organization.

Group relations influence the performance of organizational processes in at least two ways. First, group relations determine the extent to which members develop shared perspectives concerning organizational problems and practices. Second, group relationships influence the motivation of members to perform the activities related to organizational processes.

Cohesion is the major element in determining the impact of group relations upon the development of norms, values, and stable role structures and upon performance. The cohesiveness or cohesion of a group refers to feelings of solidarity and pride that exist among the members. Cohesiveness is central to any undertaking to develop teamwork; however, the relationship between cohesiveness and effectiveness is not simple. A group is not necessarily effective from the organization's viewpoint merely because it is highly cohesive. An additional essential requirement involves strong norms that value high-quality performance or, in other terms, integration with organizational requirements and organizational structure and function.

In general, integration is enhanced through the existence of conditions that cause members to develop common perceptions of events and problems, to evolve shared perspectives of themselves and their organization (identity), and to become consistently and harmoniously committed to the activities and objectives of the organization. Such conditions are specified below.

IMPLICATIONS

Organizational competence represents the capability of an organization and is different from individual capabilities. Although most often performed by single individuals, the processes discussed here involve organizational responses, and the quality of any single response event is determined by the entire network of antecedent relationships and responses. Thus, organizational competence and integration can best be improved by efforts that focus upon developing the organization to function as a system.

It is important to recognize that competence is an attribute of an organization, not of roles or individuals. This fact is important because it governs how one views an organization and whether performance is analyzed, assessed, and developed as an attribute of individuals, groups, or entire units. On the one hand, an executive who views process performance as an attribute of individuals or of particular roles (positions) will devote all of his or her efforts to training individuals. On the other hand, if he or she recognizes that performance of processes is an attribute of organizations, he or she will devote his or her efforts to development of the organization as a unified system.

It has sometimes been stated that the premier function of organizations is to orchestrate the application of the skills and energies of their members to solutions of problems larger than any of them could handle separately. "Orchestrate" suggests many critical and coordinative activities; however, above all others, the term implies the necessity to provide conditions that are conducive to the effective performance of organizational members. Most such conditions can be assessed, and required improvement actions can be identified.

Some principal organizational conditions necessary for effective performance include:

Factors that enhance proficiency

- Effective structure and job design.
- Efficient procedures and practices.
- Excellent training for everyone, including leaders.
- Communication practices that supply each individual with information and knowledge necessary for intelligent performance of duties.

Factors that enhance motivation

- A system that makes careful provision for incentives, reward, and approval of good performance.
- Procedures that make information about individual and group progress available to everyone.
- Opportunity for individuals and groups to experience success in performance of tasks.
- Opportunities for challenge and growth for each individual.
- Opportunities for optimum independence in the performance of jobs.

Factors that promote a common desire to belong to the organization and identify with it

- Good administrative, supervisory, and leadership practices at all levels.
- Good working conditions and good equipment.
- Opportunity for each individual to perform as a conscious member of a larger whole.
- Means of providing occasional, explicit acknowledgment of organizational progress to all members and of recognition of the shared responsibility of such progress.
- Opportunities for personnel to influence decisions about matters that affect them.

A full model for organizational competence is shown below.

The Competence Model

I. Organizational competence
   A. Organizational attributes
      1. Reality testing
      2. Adaptability
      3. Integration
   B. Organizational functions (Processes)
      1. Sensing
      2. Communicating information
      3. Decision making
      4. Stabilizing
      5. Communicating implementation
      6. Coping actions
      7. Feedback
   C. Required integration conditions
      1. Roles
      2. Goals
      3. Norms
      4. Group relations

II. Individual competencies

III. Group competencies

IV. Necessary organizational conditions (Elements for Intervention)
   A. Factors that enhance proficiency
   B. Factors that enhance motivation
   C. Factors that promote a common desire to belong to the organization and identify with it.

Together, the several elements constitute a model that can be used to assess organizations and to improve them. Both the necessary conditions and some proposed procedures for assessing organizational competence are addressed in later chapters of this book.

Part II

Requirements for Performance

Chapter 6

Performance of Individuals

All organizational activities rely upon the performance of individuals. Both group competencies and organizational competence derive ultimately from the actions and performance of individuals.

INDIVIDUAL COMPETENCIES

The concept of individual competencies was introduced in Chapter 2. The discussion is elaborated here.

Competency Defined

A competency is an individual's *demonstrated* knowledges, skills, and abilities (KSAs). Competencies go beyond traditional knowledges, skills, and abilities; they are KSAs that have been demonstrated in a job context. Some researchers have extended the concept to KSAO, as in knowledges, skills, abilities, and other, to indicate something more than a conventional KSA. A cluster of demonstrated KSAs defines a competency and makes a real difference for organizational success. For example, planning is a competency.

Utility

Rather than emphasizing a broad range of specific tasks and skills required for effective performance or attempting to establish the basic functions to be performed in a job, generic skills or competencies can be (1) behaviorally defined and (2) identified as basic to performance.

Rationale

This approach asserts that, in daily job performance, an individual is faced with problem situations requiring decisions or actions. When the problems are routine or familiar, they are handled with little thought about the process. When problems arise that require conscious solving, competencies are needed to structure the information, create ways of handling the problems, determine alternative solutions, and evaluate results of solutions selected.

The characteristics of competencies are:

1. They are abilities that have a unique hierarchy of component skills.
2. They are pervasive and recur across most job tasks.
3. The development of competencies is dependent on mastery of a knowledge and skill base.
4. Integration of lower-order knowledge and skills is required for demonstration of competencies.
5. When mastered, competencies can be applied in a variety of job contexts.

In numerous studies of a wide range of jobs, the job competency assessment approach has been found to identify superior performers. This applies to skilled workers, as well as supervisors, managers, and executives. The approach has an advantage over techniques based upon job dimensions derived by factor analysis or critical-incident analysis, both of which usually provide only descriptive accounts of average performance in routine situations.

The fact is that many of the activities connected with work involve common elements or competencies. This is especially true for supervisors and managers, where the same competency may overlap many different tasks. An example is communicating, which may be necessary in many tasks performed by supervisors and managers.

Competencies are valuable in serving as bases for:

1. Assessing performance of individuals.
2. Assessing training needs.
3. Designing training or development programs.
4. Designing assessment centers.

Research on Competencies

A variety of approaches or methodologies has been used to identify tasks and skills in job performance. The predominant methods have involved task analysis, critical-incident analysis, or factor analysis. All have made significant contributions to the identification of relevant tasks and skills. However, they share certain limitations that affect their utility for determining behaviorally defined skills that can also cut across jobs, positions, and technical areas.

The limitations include:

1. Some attributes identified in certain studies are expressed in terms of attitude and value judgments that cannot be systematically observed or measured.
2. Some tasks, especially in soft skill areas, are described in terms too vague for an assessor to use meaningfully.
3. Job functions that are identified frequently lack behavioral referents that would allow for observation and measurement.
4. Job task analyses can describe the technical aspects of a job very well but not the personal attributes or interpersonal skills required to do the job.
5. Job task analyses may describe everything that a person does in a given job, but not what is done that actually accomplishes the task, what represents effective performance, or what behaviors actually make the difference in performance.

Attempts have been made in several empirical studies to determine the limited set of skills or competencies required of people in various leadership roles. Rather than emphasizing a broad range of tasks and skills required for effective leadership or attempting to establish the basic functions of leaders in performing their duties, these studies identify competencies or generic skills that can be behaviorally defined and that are basic to performance of the leadership function.

The existence of such generic leadership skills was suggested by Peterson and Rumsey (1981). The purpose of their study was to develop a methodology for measuring officer job competence within the Army. The concept of a common set of generic competency skills that underlie successful performance of most complex officer tasks was presented, and generic skills were defined.

The generic skills identified as necessary for officer competence were those of problem solving, communication, critical inquiry, and valuing. Once identified, the generic skills were used in developing a generic skills test that could be administered to officers to determine their level of competence.

The specific methodology used in identifying generic skills or competencies is described in a study of Navy leadership and management competencies (Kemp, Munger, and Spencer, 1977). In this study, a procedure, job competency assessment, was used to identify what Navy leaders actually do in performing leadership and management tasks. Training programs were then developed based on the measurable characteristics found to differentiate between performance of superior Naval leaders and that of average Naval leaders. It was suggested that the job competency assessment approach is of value in yielding behaviorally derived competencies that identify attributes of the superior performer in effective job performance. It was contended that this procedure has an advantage over techniques limited to factor analysis or critical-incident analysis, both of which generally provide only descriptive accounts of average performance in routine situations.

In conducting the research, Kemp et al. (1977) interviewed 82 Naval personnel and analyzed the interviews using a "behavioral event analysis." Hypotheses were generated to explain performance differences between those rated as superior and those rated as average performers. From analysis of the data, 27 individual skills, characteristics, or abilities were identified. These were then grouped in clusters determined by prior theoretical and empirical research. The study was then repeated with another group of Naval personnel. The second group was interviewed, and the interviews were analyzed and cross-validated against the results of the first interviews.

The basis for the sample was ratings by commanders of whether the individual was an average or superior performer on the job. Comparisons of the content of interviews of superior and average performers were made to determine whether differences in skills could be identified. The behavioral event interview technique developed by McCelland and Burnham (1979) was used to gather the data about job performance. Based on the critical-incident technique described by Flanagan (1954), the McClelland method requires respondents to identify critical success and failure experiences that they have had in their job. They are asked to describe each incident in terms of:

1. the situation and what led to it;
2. who was involved;
3. their feelings, wants, or intentions in responding to the situation;
4. what was actually done;
5. the outcome of the action.

The interviews elicit subjects' thoughts, problem-solving techniques, evaluations of others, and other individual characteristics as well as behaviors.

Thematic content analysis of the critical incidents was conducted by the researchers. The transcripts of superior and average Navy leaders were examined to determine the characteristics that differentiated between superior performers and average performers and those that occurred with equal frequency in both groups.

Five clusters of competency categories were derived through factor analysis of 27 competency categories. The clusters included task achievement, skillful use of influence, management control, advising and counseling, and coercion.

Using a similar approach, Cullen, Kemp, and Rossini (1981) identified the critical knowledge, skills, abilities, and characteristics required of Organizational Effectiveness Staff Officers (OESOs) for successful job performance.

Ninety-two OESOs nominated peers considered to be outstanding in their jobs. Thirty-two OESOs were rated as either effective or less effective and served as the sample for in-depth interviews. As part of the interviews, subjects specified the major responsibilities and tasks of an OESO and the characteristics felt to be important for effective job performance. Interview data were content-analyzed by a panel of experts, and comparisons were made between responses of effective and less effective incumbents based on the tasks that they performed, their actual behavior, thoughts, and feelings, and the results of the job performance.

The procedures followed in conducting the study included several separate steps. In the initial procedure, the top-performing OESOs were identified, and less effective performers making up the rest of the sample were determined.

The next step involved a job task and performance characteristics analysis. A panel of experts was used to generate a list of tasks important for job performance of OESOs and a separate list of characteristics thought to be typical of outstanding OESOs. The lists of tasks and characteristics were then given to incumbent OESOs to rate. The tasks were rated according to:

1. importance to outstanding results.
2. required for routine performance.
3. most critical to performance of job.

The characteristics were rated according to:

1. whether they distinguish between superior and average performers.
2. whether marginal performers possess the characteristic.
3. which are most critical to consider for training and selection.
4. which are not found in the general OESO population.

The third step consisted of behavioral event interviews, which were nondirective in nature. These interviews focused on the respondent's accounts of behavioral incidents of effective and ineffective job performance and the behaviors or characteristics contributing to the outcomes.

Following the interviews, the data were subjected to content analysis to determine differences in behavioral patterns and themes between outstanding and average performances. This step provided behavioral definitions for the performance characteristics identified in the second step.

The OESO competency model developed from the interview data identified nine basic job competency clusters that distinguish the superior from the average OESO performer. The nine competency clusters include (1) functional knowledge, (2) strong self-concept, (3) professional self-image, (4) develops common understanding, (5) personal influence, (6) diagnostic skill, (7) tactical planning, (8) tactical flexibility, and (9) results orientation.

Subsumed under these nine clusters were 34 distinct knowledges, skills, and abilities found to distinguish between superior and average OESOs, which were defined in behavioral terms.

The job competency approach presented in the Cullen et al. (1981) and the Kemp et al. (1977) studies is based on the assumption that the best approach to use in identifying knowledges, skills, abilities, and other characteristics required of people within a given job or position is to identify the effective performers, study what they actually do on the job that distinguishes their performance from that of less effective job incumbents, and identify the knowledge, skills, abilities, or characteristics implied by those behaviors responsible for the difference in performance.

The attempt in both studies was to develop a criterion-based approach to determine the critical competency and skill requirements of effective performers. This approach is in contrast to a norm-referenced approach, which identifies only the knowledge and skills of the average performer. In addition, an attempt was made to identify a limited number of dimensions that could describe overall job performance requirements. These dimensions, derived from the underlying skills and knowledges, provided behaviorally based job descriptions that were used as a basis for training development, selection procedures, and promotion criteria.

Since these early studies, competency modeling has received considerable attention (McLagan, 1997; Mirabile, 1997; Brockbank, Ulrich, and Beatty, 1997; Laver and O'Connor, 2000). Although some researchers and practitioners have not embraced competency modeling, others, especially practitioners, have found the approach to be quite useful (Laver and O'Connor, 2000).

For this book, individual competencies have been labeled Individual Performance Elements (IPE).

Performance of Individuals

Here, our concern is not solely with whether required activities are performed but, in addition, with how well they are performed—the proficiency of an individual's performance. Proficiency is the capability to perform (i.e., how well an individual can perform).

Proficiency, at any given moment, is a function of (KSA × Motivation). A useful formula that takes into account all determining elements is:

Performance = f(KSA × Motivation + Situation).

In this formula it can be seen that proficiency (KSA × Motivation) can become confounded by elements in the situation that exert either positive or negative impacts.

Thus, the principal elements in the performance of individuals are:

1. Knowledges
2. Skills and abilities
3. Motivation
4. The situation

ELEMENTS IN PERFORMANCE

Here, the principal elements that influence the performance of individuals are identified and discussed briefly. Greater detail is provided in the next section. Each element is defined according to its relation to performance.

1. *Knowledge*—a cognitive requirement for effective performance. Knowledge is what and how much an individual must know in order to perform effectively. Two aspects of knowledge are included: (1) the kind of knowledge that is required and (2) the degree of knowledge that is required. The most common sources of knowledge are information, training, and experience.
2. *Skill*—a motor or verbal requirement for effective performance. Skills are capabilities of an individual to execute required activities. Sources of skills are training and experience.
3. *Motivation*—the degree of desire or inclination to perform. There are many aspects of motivation, some of which are very complex. For this discussion of performance, however, the above definition is most appropriate. Sources of motivation at any given time are (1) factors within the individual and (2) the impact of his or her existing situation.
4. *Situation*—the context of work, which includes all of the external factors that affect the individual at work. Sources are the climate within the entire organization, the leadership climate, and the group in which he or she works.

DETERMINANTS OF PERFORMANCE

The extent and quality of an individual's performance at any time may be determined by three broad elements that require consideration in any attempt to understand performance (Barnard, 1948). These are personal factors within an individual, personal factors within the leader or supervisor, and factors within the situation.

Factors within an Individual

Whether an action has the desired effect is partly determined by personal factors operating within each individual. In addition to such personal variables as attitudes, needs, and values, subordinates are influenced by their expectations of how their supervisor should act in relation to them. The supervisor may not agree with such expectations, but awareness that they exist makes him or her better able to predict which of his or her actions will enable subordinates to perform more effectively. Such factors as the following may require consideration:

1. *Needs to work independently.* People differ in the amount of control under which they can work most effectively. Do they possess relatively high needs for independence, or do they seem more comfortable under close control?
2. *Tolerance for ambiguity.* Can members tolerate ambiguous situations? Some people function best only under clear-cut directives; others can also perform well when problems are hazy and requirements are not clearly defined.
3. *Identification with mission.* Do people understand and closely identify with the mission and objectives of the organization?
4. *Knowledge and experience.* Do members have the necessary knowledge and experience to carry out their duties without strong guidance?

The abilities, experience, and general attitudes of individuals are likely to be major determinants in any situation. Whether a leader understands his or her subordinates relative to these factors partly determines the nature of his or her actions.

Factors within the Leaders or Supervisors

Leaders' behavior is influenced greatly by the many factors operating within their own personal makeup. They perceive their relationship problems on the basis of their background, knowledge, experiences, and personal characteristics. Among these factors having special relevance are the following:

1. *Leadership inclinations.* Some leaders function more comfortably and naturally in a team role where they work closely with subordinates. Others operate better as highly directive leaders, maintaining somewhat distant relationships with subordinates.
2. *Confidence in subordinates.* Leaders differ in the amount of confidence that they feel in other people's ability to perform effectively. A lack of confidence in others

is likely to result in a leader's giving more attention to detail and attempting to do the job himself or herself. On the other hand, confidence in subordinates can result in more delegation and less direct supervision.

3. *Feelings of insecurity in uncertain situations.* Some people have a greater need than others for predictability and stability in their environment. Low tolerance for ambiguity may result in efforts to obtain tighter control over the situation and over subordinates. Personal need for high predictability of outcomes can result in rigidity of action, which makes it difficult to react rapidly to unanticipated occurrences. Tolerance for uncertainty permits flexibility in coping with a variety of events.
4. *Value system.* What is the relative importance that the supervisor attaches to organizational efficiency, development of subordinates, and such factors as motivation and morale? How strongly does he or she feel that subordinates' ideas and opinions should be invited and considered in making decisions? How convinced is he or she that the leader should carry most of the burden of decision making and problem solving?

Awareness that these and other personal variables may be operating enables an observer to better judge the appropriateness of a contemplated action and to predict its potential effect.

Factors within the Work Situation

In addition to personal factors within the leader and his or her subordinates, certain characteristics of the general situation require consideration:

1. *Type of organization.* Like individuals, organizations differ considerably in terms of the kind of climate that exists. In each case, the type of organization and the way it is structured are of major importance in determining the effect on performance. Similarly, such variables as the size of the organization and its geographical dispersion also need to be considered.
2. *Experience and proficiency of the department.* Generally, groups that have experience in working together can be expected to cope with new tasks or problems more readily than inexperienced ones. However, this is not always true. Some organizations develop consistent histories of failure. In either case, past performance is also a factor for consideration.
3. *Nature of the mission.* Is the mission one in which the organization has experience? How difficult is it? What are the knowledge and skills required? Does the leader have knowledge about the mission that is not available to other members of the organization?
4. *The time perspective.* Here, the question involves the amount of pressure felt by people with respect to time for getting things done. When time pressures become intense, less carefully considered actions by both leader and subordinates may result.

5. *General conditions in the environment.* The way in which environmental conditions dictate the appropriateness of leader behavior can be illustrated by distinguishing between two extremes of what Barnard (1948) called "the conditions of leadership." The first extreme involves stable conditions. Such conditions are relatively free from violent changes, uncertainties of unusual character, and important hazards. Under stable conditions, the behavior of leaders can be calm, reflective, deliberate, and anticipatory of future contingencies. Their actions usually lack the dramatic characteristics often observed at the other extreme. Stable conditions may create difficulties because leadership must be exercised without the support of strong emotion or obvious necessity and must combat the indifference that frequently accompanies lack of stress and excitement. Stable conditions call for self-restraint and deliberation. The other extreme involves great instability, uncertainty, speed of decision and action, great risks, important stakes, and important issues. Here, leaders must exhibit physical and moral courage, decisiveness, inventiveness, and initiative.

Thus, a number of elements require consideration in predicting which actions and conditions most likely achieve maximum performance. The kinds of actions that may be effective differ widely depending upon the situation.

AN IMPACT MODEL OF PERFORMANCE

The importance of General Systems Theory and processes within organizations carries over to consideration of the performance of individuals. Viewed in this way, performance becomes more predictable and, therefore, more subject to improvement.

Clearly, the emphasis upon process has come more from theorists than from empirical researchers. This is understandable since processes are not as amenable to the classification and segmentation characteristic of most research efforts. In order to gain control over the phenomena under examination, many researchers are prone to break large problems into smaller parts that can be studied separately. Yet, the complex interactions between processes do not permit this to be accomplished readily.

Probably a more significant reason for the dearth of useful research concerned with organizational processes is that many of these processes are actually mediating variables between inputs and outputs. Situations involving mediating variables are more difficult to analyze than the simpler independent variable–dependent variable relationships typical of many studies.

The conventional study attempts to treat some single dimension, such as cohesiveness or leadership, as a predictor variable and then examines the relationship of this dimension to some single-factor criterion such as productivity, organizational performance, or employee satisfaction. Productivity, performance, and satisfaction are the dependent variables. Although most studies have been of this sort, findings have not been sufficiently consistent to demonstrate clear-cut relationships. The reason may be that the studies have been too simply conceived.

When the problem is broadened to include mediating variables, more facets become clear. In most organizations, three broad classes of variables must be studied simultaneously if useful knowledge is to be obtained. The classes are (1) impact variables, (2) mediating variables, and (3) dependent variables.

Impact variables are those factors that could be classed as input, predictor, or independent variables. They are those factors within the organization that can be changed or manipulated through management decision, training, or other actions of organizational representatives and thus impact upon or influence the other classes of variables.

Within the broad class of impact variables, there are two major types: (1) factors more or less related to one of the structures of the organization—formal, power, communications, status, and functional structures and (2) factors contributing to organizational climate. Climate consists of those factors that reflect the internal state and characteristic ways of working of organizations.

Mediating variables are those attitudes, perceptions, and motivations of personnel that affect performance and employee satisfaction. Included are personal, professional, and work attitudes and values, roles and role perceptions, performance goals, personal motivations, and organizational loyalties. Dependent variables are the various aspects of performance and job satisfaction, considered as two more or less independent factors.

Impact variables influence mediating variables, which, in turn, produce those results classed as dependent variables. Figure 6.1 shows each class of variables and their component factors.

The dependent variables (performance and satisfaction) are largely influenced by the mediating variables. Other things, such as ability and training, being equal, if the mediating variables are favorable, performance and satisfaction should be higher. Favorableness of the mediating variables, in turn, is affected by impact variables—structures and climate.

Genuine understanding of how organizational variables influence the performance and satisfactions of individuals requires simultaneous measurement of all of the factors shown in Figure 6.1. As demonstrated in the following discussion, this task is not as tremendous as it might appear at first. However, it is essential if the limitations of earlier research are to be avoided.

There are a number of possible ways for making systematic observations within organizations. One alternative is to conduct intensive, naturalistic observation of one or a few organizations (Argyris, 1958). Observation of actual, ongoing activities provides a researcher with a sensitive understanding of the particular organization under study and develops quite rich clin-

Figure 6.1
Variable Classes and Component Factors

Impact Variables	Mediating Variables	Dependent Variables
Structures	Role perceptions	Performance:
Formal	Norms	Quantity
Power	Attitudes	Quality
Communication	Motivation	Turnover
Status	Values	Absenteeism
Functional	Goal (performance)	
	Reference groups	
Climate:		Satisfaction:
Goals (organizational)		With work
Policies		With supervision
Leadership		With job
Autonomy		With other employees
Decision-making practices		With organization
Control		With potential for self-actualization
Emphasis (goal vs. task)		

ical insight. However, the practical expense in time and personnel, as well as the difficulty in pursuing such a study with a representative sample of organizations, usually precludes use of naturalistic observation, except perhaps as a short pilot investigation preliminary to a more comprehensive study.

One infrequently used method involves development of indices of objective properties of organizations through examinations of records, organization charts, and so on and comparing the organizations on the indices or correlating the indices with measures of other variables. Thus, it is possible to begin with an abstractly defined concept and develop indices that reflect that concept. As an example, hierarchy of authority can be measured by developing such indices as ratio of supervisory to nonsupervisory people or number of levels in the organization. In this way, objective measures of certain concepts can be developed and, if desired, dimensions can be constructed that enable either measurement of single concepts or derivation of a profile of the organization. Such indices are most objective in connection with formal structure.

A final method involves measurement of variables through questionnaire reports of the perceptions of organizational members (Likert, 1961). This method produces indirect measures of factors in that the responses are the perceptions of members. However, for climate and mediating variables, the perceptions of personnel are reality insofar as they influence performance and satisfaction. Accordingly, perceptual measures are the method of choice for measuring these variables.

Therefore, through one properly constructed questionnaire, administered to all or a representative sample of employees, simultaneous measures of all climate and mediating factors, some nonformal structural factors, and employee satisfaction can be obtained. Objective indices of formal structure and employee performance obtained from records would complete the requirements for data.

Pugh and his associates (1963, 1968) have described a procedure for developing dimensions whereby an organization can be placed on a scale (e.g., 10 points) with regard to any factor. It then becomes possible to develop profiles that provide a description of the organization. The derivation of scores on the dimensions makes it possible to perform multivariate correlational analyses. This statistical method provides indices of relationships between all factors (simple correlations), pure indices of the contribution of each factor or cluster of factors to criteria (partial correlations), and indices of best combinations of variables for predicting criteria.

In this way, a more complete understanding of the effects of organizational factors upon performance can be obtained.

UTILITY OF THE IMPACT MODEL

The impact model is useful because it demonstrates the interaction of the situation with the individual. It helps to clarify the importance of the interaction of impact and mediating variables upon performance. The model also permits derivation of competencies, which are behaviorally derived but encompass all elements of the model.

Some Competencies for Rank-and-File Personnel

Following are some competencies that were developed for rank-and-file employees by the Vanguard Research Group:

1. Contributing to teamwork
2. Showing motivation to perform
3. Emphasizing achievement
4. Demonstrating initiative
5. Showing self-discipline
6. Displaying professionalism
7. Showing and using mental ability
8. Emotional stability/performing under stress

9. Displaying personal responsibility
10. Demonstrating job knowledge and skills
11. Showing confidence to perform effectively
12. Communicating
13. Demonstrating social maturity
14. Competitive
15. Mastering job tasks (ability to learn to perform job requirements)
16. Solving job-related problems
17. Adaptability
18. Learning spontaneously
19. Tenacity under stress
20. Is patient
21. Tolerating monotony
22. Taking pride in self
23. Mental strength
24. Working well with others under stress
25. Maintaining good physical condition
26. Sustaining performance
27. Dependability
28. Dedication
29. Resourcefulness

As higher-order and generic skills, competencies may include both KSAs and motivation under a single concept. Accordingly, they indicate the individual's capability for performing and are highly useful in assessing performance. Competencies have been found relevant for both operating personnel and supervisors.

Chapter 7

Performance of Groups

An organization of any size is a complex system of relationships between individuals in which each person has much contact with a few people, a little contact with some, and practically no contact with most of the other members. These relationships constitute the bonds that hold an organization together; they develop wherever people are thrown into contact with one another, and they exert potent influences upon attitudes and performance.

The interaction that occurs is not usually a matter of random contacts. Much of it depends upon the logical division of work and responsibility. Relationships arise from the necessary division of personnel into small work units that become psychologically meaningful groups.

Much of the behavior of an individual in an organization is an expression of his or her place in the group to which he or she belongs. The formal structure typically establishes the basis for these affiliations by the way that it differentiates its work units. With all of the diligence and understanding that a manager can exert, differentiation across formal units and cohesion within each of them are the almost inevitable consequences of organizing for work.

From the foregoing discussion, a significant point emerges. An organization does not consist of an undifferentiated mass of people, all of whom have identical motives, attitudes, and loyalties. The very fact of organization means a network of smaller groups, each of which possesses its own values and standards of behavior. Because these groups have undergone certain common experiences as part of the larger organization, some of the values and behavioral standards are similar. However, they have also undergone unique experiences that result in the development of values and standards that differ between groups. Through such values and standards or norms, groups exert powerful influence upon their members and play an important role in the satisfaction and performance of all participants.

GROUP: A DEFINITION

It can be asked legitimately what distinguishes between a mere collectivity of people and a group. The answer is that a collectivity becomes a group when its members develop (1) common goals, (2) shared norms, (3) differentiated roles, and (4) some degree of cohesion. The leadership or management of groups must be devoted, at least minimally, to development of these attributes—if any level above minimum effectiveness is to be achieved. What defines effectiveness for this discussion is determined, in large part, by the fact that the groups under consideration exist in some sort of organization. Accordingly, the mission or goals assigned to a group by its organization dictate what constitutes effectiveness.

Development of the above four group attributes would be exceedingly haphazard and difficult except for the saving fact that the groups discussed here, of whatever type, occur in all organizations. Whatever their specific nature, all organizations possess certain common properties (see Chapter 2) that can be exploited, and, when a problem arises, its assessment in relation to basic organizational and group properties makes possible more insightful and lasting solutions.

The development of effective groups within organizations can be highly rewarding but sometimes difficult. Group relations and the norms that regulate them are not static. They do not stay put permanently. Successes, failures, deprivations, changed environmental conditions, personnel losses, new leaders—all tend to bring about changes in the norms, functional arrangements, and operations of groups. Accordingly, developing and sustaining a highly cohesive and effective group constitute a more or less constant maintenance activity for its leader.

EFFECTS OF COHESIVENESS

When people work together toward mutual goals and undergo meaningful common experiences, the resulting interaction produces changes in their perceptions, emotions, thinking, attitudes, and actions. The distinguishing feature of these changes is that the individual comes more and more to identify his or her feelings, thinking, attitudes, and actions with the group. Persisting personal relationships and values evolve and become stabilized, providing him or her with organized, enduring, and motivationally significant ties and rewarding experiences. These satisfactions may influence his or her attitudes toward other aspects of the work.

The opportunity for individuals to interact with other people has been found to be important. Thus, Kerr, Koppelmeier, and Sullivan (1951) found that departments having the highest turnover rates provided the least opportunity for interactions among workers; and Richards and Dobryns (1957) found that the morale of a group of workers in an insurance company was lowered when rearrangement of their office resulted in a restriction of opportunities for social interaction.

When individuals are able to interact with and thus maintain close relationships with members of a group in which they are highly accepted, their job satisfaction is usually higher (Van Zelst, 1951; Zaleznik, Christensen, and Roethlisberger, 1958). Similarly, workers are more satisfied when they belong to a group that they like and whose members like them. Greenbaum (1979) also found similar results in his study of small military units discussed earlier.

Central to an understanding of group relations and of their effects upon satisfaction and team performance is the concept of group cohesiveness or cohesion, discussed earlier. The term *cohesion refers to the feeling of group pride and solidarity that exists among members.* It has also been defined as "the extent to which group members share the same norms" (Coch and French, 1948, p. 530).

In individual terms, cohesiveness has been defined in a variety of ways. Thus, one popular definition (Festinger, Schacter, and Back, 1953) refers to cohesiveness as the attractiveness or valence of a group for its members or, in Lewinian terms, as the resultant of all of the forces acting on all of the members to remain in the group. Cartright and Zander (1960) described cohesiveness in terms of willingness of group members to work together toward a common goal, to overcome frustration or endure pain to accomplish that goal, and to readily defend the group against external criticism or attack. They have postulated that cohesiveness depends upon two categories or factors: (1) the properties of the group and (2) the needs of the members. Although the definitions in this paragraph can be made operational for research purposes, ease of discussion makes the definition of Sherif and Sherif (1956) preferable. Here, *cohesion is defined as group pride and solidarity.*

There have been numerous studies of both the effects of cohesiveness and conditions necessary for its development. Although some results have been mixed, there is almost unanimous agreement that cohesiveness is central to any understanding of groups, of teams, and of group influence.

In a large-scale industrial study, Seashore (1954) found that member morale was related to group cohesiveness and that group influences were related to standards of performance. He concluded that groups of small size are more likely to have a high degree of cohesiveness than groups of larger size and that the degree of cohesiveness that develops is significantly determined by managerial decisions concerning the size of work groups and the continuity of membership in the groups. Gross (1954), in a study of small work groups within the Air Force, found that satisfaction with the Air Force and personal commitment to group goals were directly related to group cohesiveness. These findings have been supported by a long series of studies, summarized by Kahn and Katz (1953) and Likert (1961), which show that cohesiveness tends to be positively correlated with productivity, although the relationships are not always high or consistent. On the other hand, studies by McCurdy and Lambert (1952), Albert (1953), Berkowitz and Levy (1956), Pepitone and Kleiner (1957), and Deutsch (1959) reported failures to find significant relationships between group cohesiveness and effectiveness.

Despite these mixed results, most findings favor cohesiveness as a major determinant of satisfaction and performance. At this point, an important distinction becomes necessary. After many years of research, it has become clear that no simple relationship exists between cohesiveness and group effectiveness. A group is not necessarily outstandingly productive simply because it is highly cohesive. An additional factor to consider is the norms held by the group. Cohesive groups usually have strong norms; however, the important question that must be asked is, "What are the norms?" It is possible for a highly cohesive group to possess strong norms for minimal productivity, in which case cohesiveness would not result in performance considered effective by the organization. On the other hand, if the norms of the group value high performance, effectiveness usually results.

As a result of a review of research on group effectiveness, Mills (1967) concluded that cohesive groups are more productive than less cohesive groups. Cohesiveness was manifested in the more effective groups through greater commitment to goals, more open communication, greater coordination, and more friendly interpersonal relations. However, of even more significance for training and team development, Mills found that a "circular relationship" exists between group effectiveness and solidarity. That is, as the group becomes more successful, it also becomes more cohesive. In short, experiences of success while a group is working together make the group more cohesive. Gill (1977) went even further by maintaining, on the basis of his research, that the predominant causal direction is from performance to cohesion, rather than vice versa. According to Gill, effective performance produces greater cohesion, rather than cohesion producing more effective performance.

Implications for Training

For training and development, the implication is clear. The provision to groups of success experiences should result in improved cohesion.

The conclusions from this discussion of group cohesion are important. As stated earlier, two factors appear to be essential for effective group performance, in addition to technical proficiency:

1. A group situation that is (1) attractive to the members and (2) that generates pride and solidarity (cohesion) and
2. Strong group norms that value high performance.

Occasionally, high cohesion develops spontaneously. Because of some fortuitous experience, usually dramatic, a group may suddenly evidence at least a temporary sense of unity where none existed previously. This sudden rise in cohesion may be nothing more than a sort of emotional upsurge that soon dissipates. If so, it serves little purpose except to provide the group with a temporary momentum. Under certain circumstances, such as entry into an extremely difficult situation—as for crisis management teams or military units—such momentum may be desirable. However, temporary unity of this nature cannot be expected to resist disruptive forces of any consequence, unless conditions favorable to the development of high cohesion already exist in the group.

Those properties that enable a group to resist both internal and external stress are most often the result of careful and calculated developmental efforts on the part of a patient leader carried out over a period of time. Cohesion developed under such conditions provides a substantial foundation both for the resistance of disruptive forces and for unified actions of a more routine nature.

Developing sound cohesion in a group cannot usually be accomplished overnight. Neither can it be achieved by exhortation or gimmicks, no matter how colorful. The development of sound bonds of unity and strength requires a fine sensitivity to the constantly shifting currents of feelings and attitudes among members, attention to details and occurrences that might cause a negative shift in attitudes if not corrected, alertness to every event that might be used to reinforce feelings of unity and solidarity, and, most of all, recognition of the frailty and fallibility of the human individuals who are attempting to cope with all of the complexities of existing in group environments.

CHARACTERISTICS OF AN IDEAL GROUP

There can be no doubt that the primary, face-to-face group can exert a powerful influence upon an individual. However, from the standpoint of an organization, the influence is not always positive. One of the strongest forms of cohesiveness occurs when members of a group coalesce in order to defend themselves against what they perceive to be an oppressive supervisor. Similarly, a very high level of cohesiveness can develop when members perceive their group to be threatened by actions of the larger organization. In either case, a cohesive group may have negative effects upon both the aims of its supervisor and the goals of the organization.

On the other hand, groups can play very positive roles as potent means for influencing the effectiveness of individual personnel. For most administrators and supervisors, the problem is to develop and control the processes and interactions within work groups so that they function constructively, and their activities are channeled by conscious design in directions most conducive to the achievement of organizational objectives.

Likert (1961) described some characteristics of the ideal work group, which have been adapted and condensed here to describe properties of work groups:

- *Knowledge and Skills.* All members are skilled in the technical requirements of their respective jobs and in the interpersonal and group functions required to serve as effective group members.
- *Attitudes.* All members like the group and are loyal to the other members, including the supervisor. The supervisor and all members have a high degree of confidence and trust in each other. They believe that each member of the group can perform competently. These expectations help each member to realize his or her highest potentialities.
- *Motivation.* The members of the group are highly motivated to meet group performance standards and to accomplish both group and organization objectives. Each member does all in his or her power to help the organization and the group achieve its objectives; expects every other member to do the same; is eager not to let the other members down; strives hard to do what he or she believes is expected of him or her; is ready to communicate fully all information that is relevant and of value to the group's work; and is genuinely interested in receiving relevant information that any other member of the group can provide. This information is welcomed and trusted as being honestly and sincerely given. The motivation and ability of the members of the group to communicate easily contribute to the flexibility and adaptability of the group.
- *Working Relationships.* Members of the group have developed well-established working relationships among themselves. The relationships are pleasant, and mutual assistance is the rule. When necessary, others give a member the assistance that he or she needs to accomplish his or her assignments successfully.
- *Atmosphere.* Problem-solving, decision-making, and goal-oriented activities of the group occur in an atmosphere that is stable, informal, comfortable, and relaxed. There are no obvious tensions; it is a working atmosphere in which people are interested and personally involved. Respect is shown for the point of view of others, both in the way that contributions are made and in the way that they are received. There may be real and important differences of opinion, but the focus is on arriving at sound solutions, not on aggravating the conflict. Individuals also feel secure in making independent decisions that seem appropriate for their respective roles because the atmosphere is one of clearly stipulated objectives and policies that provide each member with a solid basis for making decisions. This encourages initiative and pushes decisions down to the appropriate levels while maintaining a coordinated and directed effort.

Every group probably shows some of these characteristics at one time or another. More effective groups consistently demonstrate a preponderance of them.

In demonstrably effective groups, properties such as these can be readily observed. It is important to note that many of these properties are only remotely related to the adequacy of organizational techniques (i.e., techniques concerned with designing structures and developing operating policies and procedures). Good organizational techniques are essential for providing stability and channeling work activities. However, organizational techniques assume that people behave in accordance with the logic of the system, and this is not always the case. People do not always carry out their duties in accordance with the assumptions made by the formal, rational system. Therefore, strains may develop in the group, causing loss of effectiveness.

Groups often encounter difficulties because people have not learned, or perhaps are not motivated, to function well together. For example, it is possible for a new group composed entirely of experienced individuals to exhibit operational problems until common habits of functioning have evolved. It is possible for highly trained administrators with records of individual success to be unable to work together. It is even possible for a group with a long history of accomplishment to suddenly develop functional difficulties because of internal problems arising from changed circumstances within it.

Effective performance of a group is a matter not only of technical and organizational proficiency but also of such factors as its objectives, its level of morale, the state of motivation, and the degree of functional integration among its various individuals and subgroups. The group most likely to succeed is a tightly knit, efficiently functioning system of people and activities, composed of interlocking units effectively linked by capable leaders and served by an efficient communication system. The members are characterized by strong motivation and loyalty to the group, and there is mutual confidence and trust between them at all levels.

The attributes just described are characteristic of most effective groups. The problem is, how can leaders best determine what they need to do to adequately influence their groups so as to make them more effective?

Groups run a wide gamut of goals, sizes, missions, people, and geographical dispersion. The peculiar nature of each group determines to some extent the specific problems encountered. Usually this requires that managers be concerned with particular cases and with diagnosing problems and taking actions to improve unique situations.

The task of developing effectiveness within an organization is one of making a functioning, operational system out of the human and material resources available to it. Viewed as a part of a system, a group must be capable of performing more or better than all of the resources that constitute it. It must be a genuine whole, different from the sum of its parts, with its total performance more than the sum of its individual efforts. A group is not just a mechanical assemblage of resources. To make a functioning work unit from a collection of people, buildings, and equipment, it is not enough to put them together in some logical form and then to issue a directive for work to begin. What is needed is a transformation of the resources. This cannot come merely from a directive. It requires leadership of a high quality.

Not to recognize these requirements can lead to serious interference with group effectiveness by creating such problems as failure to meet performance goals; breakdowns in communication; conflict, strife, and competition between individuals or groups; low morale; and poor discipline. The sources of such problems are likely to be diffuse and quite complex and may be traced to any or all of an array of factors, including working conditions, superior–subordinate relationships, communication, operational inefficiency, or just about any other condition related to life within an organization.

All of these facts lead to a fundamental conclusion. The essence of leading a group is not solely a matter of solving individual problems. In addition, it involves achieving some measure of integration among the many elements constituting the group. Furthermore, leadership imposes a major responsibility for creative action. It cannot be just passive reaction to problems as they occur; it goes beyond merely fighting fires that arise within the group. This means taking action to make the desired results come to pass. A supervisor must take the necessary steps to shape his or her group and to plan, initiate, and carry through changes in it as required. He or she must constantly push back the limitations that human fallibility tends to place upon a group's capacity to perform more effectively.

Regardless of the type of organization or kind of group within an organization, a leader must make sure that objectives are established, plans are made, a structure is formed, people are assigned and trained, and policies and procedures are developed. Furthermore, the leader must establish areas of responsibility, set up mechanisms for coordination, delegate authority, direct subordinates, provide stimulation and inspiration for everyone, exercise control, maintain high levels of motivation and morale, and constantly adjust the activities of the group to broader changes in its programs and its environments. Fulfilling these and similar responsibilities is necessary regardless of the type of group being managed.

ORGANIZATIONS AS SYSTEMS OF GROUPS

It is helpful to view a group as part of a system. The basic idea of a system is that it is a set of interrelated parts. Also implicit in the concept is a degree of wholeness that makes the whole something different from, and more than, the individual units considered separately.

One of the most significant ways in which the system concept is useful to managers is the consideration of subordinate units as parts of the system. This includes divisions, departments, sections, groups, and so on that appear on the conventional organization chart. Also included are ad hoc committees, boards, and other groups that have official status but are frequently not shown on the chart.

Thinking of an organization as a system offers at least two benefits: (1) it focuses on the relatedness of activities carried on by different individuals and units; (2) it emphasizes the fact that, to meet the particular requirements for accomplishment of the organization's goals, each subunit must receive as careful attention in its development as does the overall organization. This is important because each part of a system affects, and is affected by, every other part.

A systems approach is especially useful in understanding the performance of people. For example, it is often customary to consider such factors as goals, motivation, or communication as independent factors, each contributing to performance on the basis of direct cause–effect relationships. A supervisor who pursues the cause–effect approach tries to find one or more factors that can be taken as causes of certain occurrences. He or she may conclude, for example, that a poor morale condition within a department is the cause of poor performance. Another manager might conclude that poor communication was the cause. Any number of such factors could be cited as causes, individually or in combination, of poor performance; yet, every presumed cause can be shown to have the given effect only under certain conditions and not under others.

A system view of organization recognizes the mutual dependence of various contributing factors. The formal structure affects, and is affected by, the objectives of the organization. Objectives affect, and are affected by, morale. Morale conditions affect, and are affected by, performance levels within the organization.

Thus, a change in a group's goals may be accompanied by changes in motivation and performance; a change introduced into morale is accompanied by changes in performance and, perhaps, in goals. Similarly, a change introduced into the formal structure has its effects upon goals, motivation, and performance. The interrelation of these elements constitutes the total pattern of organization, which is what a leader should attempt to influence.

Determinants of Effectiveness

In general, cohesiveness is increased by conditions that cause group members to develop common perceptions of problems, to evolve shared perspectives of themselves and their group, and to become consistently and harmoniously involved with the activities and goals of the group. On the other hand, cohesiveness is disrupted by conditions that encourage tendencies opposite to these. Following is a discussion of several general factors that may influence effectiveness.

Tasks and Organization

The kinds of tasks assigned to a group and the organization that results can exert a decided influence upon cohesiveness and effectiveness. Where a task requires the tightly coordinated efforts of everyone, with each individual's activity fitting closely into the total endeavor, higher cohesiveness is more likely to result. Where the task dictates independent actions by different individuals or where the individuals must be separated in space and type of activities, cohesiveness is more difficult to maintain.

Superordinate Goals

Superordinate goals are those objectives that are equally compelling for all and cannot be ignored but that cannot be achieved by the efforts and resources of one individual alone. They require the coordinated efforts and resources of all the individuals involved. This does not mean that every objective of every individual in every group must be identical. However, usually one or more goals are central within a group, and these weigh heavily in determining the kinds and quality of activities that result. Therefore, a maximum degree of compatibility should exist between those overall objectives that are important for the continued effectiveness of the group and the goals of individual group members. The goals and needs of individuals that have no relation to the activities and welfare of the group or the organization need not harmonize with these overall objectives.

Similarity of Personnel

Similarities among members have long been recognized as an important element in cohesiveness. When people perceive themselves to be alike in certain characteristics, a greater potential exists for mutual understanding, for the development of common attitudes, and, in general, for greater consensus on many matters that are of significance for the members. It is important to recognize that similarity can exist along many dimensions. For example, cohesiveness tends to be greater when members of a group are similar in level of experience. Individuals with like abilities are more attracted to each other than are people with widely divergent abilities. Similarly, uniformity of age and educational level is positively associated with cohesiveness. To generalize, high cohesiveness in a group is facilitated by perceived similarity or uniformity among its members. The conviction of similarity makes it possible for members to believe that they understand one another, and they are more attracted to other individuals and to the group. Homogeneity is not conducive to cohesiveness unless members are aware that similarities exist. Leaders can sometimes enhance cohesiveness by efforts to increase this awareness.

Common Experiences

Groups are held together by stable relationships (functional integration) and common attitudes (normative integration) among their members. Persisting relationships and common attitudes evolve and become stabilized only when people undergo significant experiences together. Shared experiences thus serve two important functions. First, they permit members to become familiar with one another, to learn each other's characteristic ways of behaving, and through this familiarization process to develop stable expectations relative to performance and ways of working. Second, shared experiences provide people with a common frame of reference. Because they have undergone the same experiences, members view things from similar perspectives. They are bound together by having experienced unique events to which others have not been exposed.

Success Experiences

Of particular significance here are experiences of success. Probably nothing contributes so greatly to cohesiveness as successful action. Success operates to confirm the validity of the group's ways of operating and gives the individual confidence in himself or herself and in the group. A long tradition of success appears to make for much greater cohesiveness. As a secondary effect, a tradition of success is likely to provide the group with greater prestige, thus encouraging more ready identification by members. Success is effective, however, only as it is experienced, and it is experienced only in relation to the objectives perceived by the members. An action by a group is deemed successful only if the members become aware that their efforts have actually resulted in achievement of the group's objectives. Administrative control of this factor is possible through such measures as setting realistically high objectives, ensuring clear recognition of them by everyone, and furnishing adequate evaluation of the results of group efforts.

Just as success tends to enhance cohesiveness, experiences that are perceived by members as failures of the group are disruptive. Severe or consistent failure usually results in loss of confidence, bickering, and recriminations. The amount of disruption that occurs depends upon both the level of cohesiveness reached prior to the failure and the severity of the failure. High prior cohesiveness, together with mild failure, may result in nothing more than minor loss of confidence, which may be rapidly recovered. At the other extreme, low prior cohesiveness and strong failure can result in severe disruption. It should be clear that failure alone does not necessarily result in disruption of cohesiveness. The critical factor appears to be whether failure causes personnel to lose confidence in their leaders, in the organization, or in themselves.

Organizational Stability

Cohesiveness requires sufficient organizational stability for emotional and social bonds to develop. Both integration of task functions and the development of strong norms require that people work together long enough for common perceptions and values to evolve. Neither can reach a very high level when there is a great deal of instability in the organization. Replacement and transfer policies that result in frequent movements into and out of groups are not conducive to high cohesiveness.

Communication

It should be self-evident that cohesiveness is related to communication. Those norms that give rise to cohesiveness are the products of interaction between people. These interactions must take the form of communication. Therefore, cohesiveness is strongly dependent upon communication. In general, the principle can be set forth that increased communication between members heightens cohesion—unless the communication is unpleasant, critical, hostile, or otherwise divisive. Any official communicative acts that emphasize membership in the group or focus attention upon group values and standards of conduct heighten cohesiveness. This especially applies to those communications of an informal and personal nature that emanate from a supervisor.

Anything that interferes with the communication process contributes to a disruption in cohesiveness. For example, blockages in the formal communications channels can lead to the opening of informal channels, which carry rumor, innuendo, and so on. These distortions create disruption because they tend to breed suspicion and hostility among group members. Cohesiveness may also be disrupted because of communication restrictions arising from the geographical dispersion of members. When members of a group are widely separated, the likelihood increases that only essential information is communicated. It becomes difficult for members to maintain identification with the group. Because of lack of information about the activities of other members, feelings of common effort and solidarity are absent. This, of course, is disastrous for cohesiveness.

Interpersonal Conflict

Particularly vicious kinds of disruption derive from conflicts that may develop between influential individuals within a work group. Conflicts between senior members, supervisors, or other individuals who occupy sensitive status positions may easily spread throughout the group. Cohesiveness is affected because of the tendency of people to take sides in such conflicts or because superiors may expect to be supported. The resultant cliques and splinter groups block unity and solidarity. When there are two or more strong or influential members competing and forcing other members to align themselves into cliques, the result is divided loyalties and discord. Such alignments often spread throughout a group. Conflicts of this sort sometimes arise because differential and preferential treatment by supervisors creates competition, jealousy, and rivalry. Regardless of the cause, conflicts between individuals who occupy influential positions carry with them the seeds of disruption of solidarity.

Cooperation and Competition

When members of a group engage in activities that are competitive and reciprocally frustrating, such that the achievement of a desired objective by one individual results in defeat or loss for other individuals, unfavorable attitudes develop that result in additional competition between them. As used here, *competition* refers to something more intense than friendly rivalry. It concerns a situation where important interests and/or welfare of an individual or group are at stake and where success by one results in a serious loss by another. The essence of a truly competitive situation is that one individual must win, and others must lose. When important stakes are involved, and the goal of each individual in a group is to win, the consequences for cohesiveness are disastrous. Personal reputations assume greater importance. Certain members, more aggressive than others or for whom the thought of victory carries particular appeal, may begin to try to exercise more weight in group affairs than has been previously customary. Actions may begin to be aimed more and more toward belittling the competitors' position. Members may develop more negative attitudes and express more hostility toward others. The negative attitudes thus generated usually intensify the conflict and further erode mutual respect and confidence within the group. When attitudes of this nature become predominant within a group, actions designed to protect self-interest and enhance personal aspirations are likely to take precedence over those that would contribute to the common objective.

On the other hand, when cooperation is the rule, members tend to view the group as a whole and other members individually in a favorable light. Members try to get along well in their interpersonal relations and tend to work with others in order that mutual objectives may be better accomplished. Communication is used to reduce conflict rather than aggravate it. When individuals pull together, favorable information about other members is seen in a positive light, and the probability of information being used effectively is enhanced. When members of a group are committed to cooperation, a manager or supervisor is in a position to take bolder steps toward bringing about understanding and mutually supportive actions. He or she can take concrete action to further cooperative endeavors and can more freely delegate responsibility, and decision processes can proceed more effectively. Decisions reached are more likely to receive wholehearted support from group members.

Reward System

Cooperation is most likely to develop when members can receive significant satisfactions from behaving cooperatively and when competitive behavior is not rewarded or is punished. Thus, the system of rewards is an important determinant of group effectiveness. The satisfactions available to members of a group are not limited to formal rewards such as promotions and salary increases, although these are highly useful devices for motivating people to behave cooperatively. The reward system in a group includes all of the means by which a member may receive satisfaction from behaving in a particular manner. This may be a word of approval by the supervisor, recognition from fellow members, or satisfaction from a job well done. The critical factor in determining cohesiveness is whether or not members can receive satisfaction of their personal needs only when they contribute to group effort. In a cooperatively organized group (one in which the more significant rewards are given for group effort), no individual can move toward his or her personal goals without also furthering the progress of other members and of the group, while the reverse is true of a competitively organized group (one in which rewards may be obtained for efforts that further individual interests without contributing particularly to group efforts). Formal group incentive plans have been found to be highly effective in this regard.

Administrative Practices

No matter how high the motivation to cooperate, effectiveness within a group does not result unless members' efforts are effectively channeled. Therefore, an additional requirement is efficient and effective administrative practices that provide the means through which activities of the group members can be integrated. The term "administrative practices" refers to those procedures and practices used to perform such functions as exercising direction, assigning responsibilities, exchanging information, making decisions, organizing, and coordinating within the group. They include formal policies and procedures but go beyond them to encompass the various means of a less formal nature by which the activities of members are integrated and coordinated. Effective group operations require administrative practices that ensure that, consistent with their goals, tasks, and responsibilities, members are provided with all the information, decisions, guidance, and assistance necessary to perform effectively and to contribute appropriately to the group effort. More specifically, the practices must function in such a manner that:

- Each member of the group is provided tasks and goals that he or she is motivated to accomplish and that, when accomplished, contribute to the goal of the group.

- The techniques, procedures, and plans developed by the group are such that members are motivated to use them to their maximum potentiality.
- The activities of group members fit together and are mutually supporting.
- Individuals who make decisions use fully and capably all information available within the group.
- Opportunity is provided for contacts between members sufficient for mutual trust and confidence to develop (Likert, 1959).

Effects of Group Size

Conceptually, the size of the basic work group should be one aspect of organizational configuration; however, it is of sufficient importance to be treated separately. Among all of the structural properties of organizations, work unit size stands out as one of the strongest influences upon job satisfaction, performance, absenteeism, and employee turnover.

There can be little doubt that work group size is significantly related to the attitudes of members. Consistently, workers in small groups have been found to display greater job satisfaction than those in larger groups. Higher satisfaction among members of small groups has also been suggested as the reason for less absenteeism and turnover. In general, larger work units have been found to have higher absence rates. Similar findings have been reported for turnover.

It is important to note that most of the studies were concerned with blue-collar workers and that there is some indication that size of work group may be less influential with white-collar workers (Porter and Lawler, 1965). This fact may have special relevance for the organization of paraprofessionals. If they can be said to be similar to blue-collar workers in their attitudes and preferences, placement in smaller units might enhance satisfaction and reduce turnover and absenteeism.

With regard to job performance, the evidence is not as clear-cut. Some studies have found that smaller work unit size leads to higher productivity (Katzell, Barrett, and Parker, 1961), while others have found tendencies for larger groups to be more productive (Argyle, Gardner, and Cioffi, 1958), and some have found that middle-sized groups produce better (Herbst, 1957). These mixed findings suggest that the kind of work in which the group is engaged and the way that the group is organized may be important modifiers of the effects of size. At least one study has found this differential effect in comparing work groups within different companies. Indik and Seashore (1961) found no relationship between size and productivity in automobile dealerships but did find that productivity was higher in small groups within a package-delivery organization. It begins to appear that, for some types of work, organization into smaller groups leads to improved performance; for other kinds of work, size of the group may be irrelevant for productivity. It can be conjectured that in highly structured, machine-dominant systems, the size of the work group may not be critical for productivity, although smaller groups are still important for job satisfaction, absenteeism, and turnover. On the other hand, in loosely structured, human-dominant systems, such as professional organizations, division into small work groups may be highly conducive to both performance and attitudes.

IMPLICATIONS

Why should small work groups be conducive to satisfaction and performance? The reason is clear. The most critical determinants of the attitudes and behavior of people in organizations are their experiences in their day-to-day work situations. Much of the situation is created by fellow workers. When people work together and undergo common experiences, the resulting interaction produces changes in their perceptions, emotions, attitudes, and actions. The distinguishing feature of these changes is that the individual comes more and more to identify his or her feelings, thinking, attitudes, and action with those of his or her fellow employees. Personal relationships and values evolve and become stabilized, providing each individual with organized, enduring, and motivationally significant ties with his or her primary group. In addition, he or she receives numerous satisfactions from interactions with the group, which exercise a strong influence upon his or her attitudes and behavior.

For this discussion, the critical point is that strong bonds are difficult to develop within a large work unit because interaction between more than a few members is impossible. Under such conditions, genuine group relationships that include all members cannot develop. This is the reason that small units are more satisfying and, when work permits interaction, frequently more productive.

The optimal size of a work unit has never been established and probably differs according to both type of work and other properties of the parent organization. Nevertheless, it is probably safe to say that the maximum should never be more than 20 members and that greater cohesion results from even smaller units, down to a minimum of six or seven individuals. It is also worth noting that, in work organizations, optimal group size must, in part, be determined by the number of people whom one supervisor can direct (span of control).

Group Competencies

Following are some group competencies adapted by the Vanguard Research Group from Likert's "Characteristics of an Ideal Group" (1961):

1. *Knowledges, Skills, and Proficiencies.* All members of the group possess the required knowledges and are skilled in the technical and role functions required to serve as effective members of the group.
2. *Attitudes.* All members like the group and the entire organization and are loyal to other members, including the supervisor. Furthermore, the supervisor and all group members have a high degree of mutual confidence and mutual trust.
3. *Motivation.* All members of the group are highly motivated to meet the performance standards and to accomplish the objectives of the group. Each member does all in his or her power to help the group achieve its objectives and expects every other member to do the same. Each team member is eager not to let other members down.
4. *Working Relationships.* Members of the group have developed well-established working relationships among themselves. The relationships are pleasant, and mutual assistance is the rule.
5. *Objectives and Standards.* The steadying influence of objectives and values held in common by all members provides a stabilizing factor in the group's activities. All members endeavor to have the objectives and performance standards of the group in harmony with those of the larger organization.
6. *Atmosphere.* Problem-solving and decision-making activities occur in an atmosphere that is stable, informal, comfortable, and relaxed. It is a working atmosphere in which people are interested and personally involved. The climate is sufficiently constructive for subordinates to accept readily any criticism that is offered.

   Because the climate is one of clearly stipulated objectives and policies, individuals feel secure in making independent decisions that seem appropriate for their work.
7. *Leadership Climate.* The group's supervisor or manager attempts to lead in a manner that seems most likely to create a constructive climate and cooperative, rather than competitive, relationships among members of the group. The leader tries to establish a workable balance between necessary compliance and excessive conformity on unessential matters.

Part III

Functionally Competent Oganizations: Application

Chapter 8

Integration in Organizations

The purpose of this chapter is to present a concise, general framework for addressing the development and maintenance of fully integrated organizations. Integration is essential for organizational competence. The concept of organization that is presented is anchored squarely in Open Systems Theory; however, it also has roots in the social psychology of organizations. This makes it possible to incorporate, in a meaningful way, elements from many sources when it makes sense to do so. The concept of organizational integration is derived mainly from small-group theory and research and is also anchored in Open Systems Theory.

BASIC CONCEPTS

Every human organization (referred to as *an organization*) exists in physical and social environments over time. Social environment refers to those elements external to the organization in which there are other people (e.g., higher levels, adjacent departments, other organizations). A human organization is a complex network of relationships among a number of people who are engaged in some activity for some purpose where the activity requires a division of effort and responsibility in such a manner as to make the members interdependent.

The people in the above definition are physical organisms and psychological processes. Relationships among people are states in which the activity and psychological state of one person is in a condition of mutual influence with that of another. A network of relationships is an abstraction of the relationships among a number of persons. The influence of a person is a function of his or her psychological properties (personality and current emotional state) and the properties of the coordinating and decision-making roles (rank, status, position) that he or she is assigned.

The boundary of an organization may be established by several means. Relative autonomy is one means of establishing boundaries. Another means is purpose and perceived membership.

Purpose is defined as the relationship of the organization to the external physical and social environments. The mode of organization is, in part, determined by the elements of purpose i.e., the mission dictates the method of distribution and execution of problem-solving, decision-making, and action functions (task organization). The distribution of the above functions and the assignment of authority and responsibility to go with them define the formal structure of the organization. The functions are arranged and systematized on the basis of ideas as to how they should be effectively performed and logically coordinated—on the basis of the "logics of organization" (see Chapter 2).

Organizational Effectiveness

Organizational effectiveness is the accomplishment of missions or the achievement of objectives. Whatever its mission, the effectiveness of an organization requires that it efficiently identify, assess, solve, and cope with events or problems that arise within its operational environments. These are the classical functions of all organizations, and performance of them has always been critical for organizational success.

It is now clear that functional proficiency and the integration of structure and function play important roles in the performance of all organizations (see Chapters 3 and 4). Two studies (Olmstead et al., 1973; Olmstead, Elder, and Forsyth, 1978) demonstrated conclusively the importance of Organizational Competence to the effectiveness of military ground tactical units. In two nationwide studies of city and county social welfare agencies (Olmstead and Christensen, 1973; Olmstead et al., 1975), organizational competence was found to be closely related to effectiveness in both large and small civilian organizations. For both studies of civilian organizations, Integration (cohesion) was found to be related to organizational effectiveness. Similar results have been found for business organizations.

In this regard, it is important to note that the above studies showed that Integration alone does not produce effectiveness. It only supports and sustains competence, which is qualitative proficiency in the performance of critical organizational functions.

On the other hand, competence without integration can be a very tenuous attribute, subject to dissolution by all of the tensions and pressures that may arise from highly turbulent and stressful environmental conditions. Both integration and competence are essential for maximum organizational effectiveness.

The development of Integration is discussed in this chapter. Development of organizational competence is discussed in Chapter 9.

ESSENTIAL ORGANIZATIONAL PROPERTIES

Organizations run a wide gamut with respect to size, mission, geographical dispersion, and personnel. The nature of the particular organization determines, in large part, the kinds of problems that are encountered by managers. Carried to the extreme, the specificity of problems would render hopeless any attempt to generalize about management, even at very broad levels. The saving factor is that the problems with which managers must be concerned all occur in organizations. Whatever their specific nature, all organizations possess certain common underlying properties that can be addressed by managers (see Chapter 2).

Regardless of the type of organization or kind of subunit within it, a manager must make sure that objectives are established, plans are made, a structure is formed, personnel are assigned and trained, and policies and procedures are developed. Furthermore, he or she must establish levels of responsibility, set up mechanisms for coordination, delegate authority, direct subordinates, provide stimulation and inspiration for everyone, exercise control, maintain high levels of motivation and morale, and constantly adjust the activities of his or her organization to broader changes in its programs and its environments. Fulfilling these and similar responsibilities is necessary regardless of the type of organization being managed.

In this regard, it is useful to view an organization as a system. The basic notion of a system is that it is a set of interrelated parts. Also implicit in the concept is a degree of "wholeness" that makes the whole something different from, and more than, the individual units considered separately.

One of the most significant ways in which the system concept is useful to managers is in the consideration of subordinate units as parts of the system. This includes divisions, departments, sections, and so on that appear on the conventional organization chart. Also included are ad hoc committees, boards, and other groups that have official status but are frequently not shown on the chart.

Thinking of an organization as a system offers at least two benefits to managers: (1) it focuses on the relatedness of activities carried on by different individuals and units, and (2) it emphasizes the fact that, to meet the particular requirements for accomplishment of the organization's goals, each subunit must receive as careful attention in its development as does the overall organization. This is important because each part of a system affects, and is affected by, every other part.

Therefore, the essence of the manager's job is not solely the solution of individual problems in specific areas but, rather, achieving some measure of integration among the many subsystems that form the organization. A manager must be constantly concerned with how things relate to each other. He or she must not only try to decide on and maintain the proper balance between the segments but also preserve harmony and cooperation among them.

A systems view is especially useful in approaching problems of performance. For example, it is often customary to consider such factors as goals, morale, or communications as independent factors, each contributing to performance on the basis of direct cause–effect relationships. Any number of such factors could be cited as causes, individually or in combination, of poor performance; yet, every presumed cause can be shown to have the given effect only under certain conditions and not under others.

On the other hand, a system view of organization recognizes the mutual dependence of various contributing factors. The interrelation of these elements constitutes the total pattern of organization, which is what a manager is attempting to influence.

DEVELOPING ORGANIZATIONS AS SYSTEMS

Probably the single most significant function of a manager is the development and maintenance of an organization as an integrated, viable, cohesive system of activities and relationships. One of the principal functions of management is to create those conditions within the organization that best enable the performance of required activities.

Few aspects of management are so important, yet so badly misunderstood, as the problem of organizational development. When the question of developing an organization arises, there is a tendency to think only in terms of clearly enunciated policies and procedures, well-defined responsibilities for individuals and units, and smoothly functioning channels of authority and communication. In short, there is a tendency to think solely in terms of the machinery of efficiency rather than the dynamics of effectiveness.

An organization needs a formal structure, with its concomitant procedures, in order to establish stability so that the activities of its personnel will be predictable. Most organizations are composed of members who occupy positions that are differentiated as to responsibility for various activities. Organization charts, procedures manuals, and directives give definition to these differentiated responsibilities and to the working relationships supposed to exist between members occupying different levels of accountability.

However, effective organizational performance is not made possible solely by definitions of authority and responsibility. Formal definitions and their accompanying procedures coordinate positions or specialized activities, not persons. The formal structure can never anticipate all the actions of individual members, and the relations outlined in an organization chart provide only a framework within which fuller and more spontaneous human behavior takes place. Limitations of ability, fluctuations in motivation, breakdowns in communication, personal conflicts, failures in coordination, and similar problems disrupt the ideal patterns of performance and relationships that are stipulated by organization charts and procedures.

Management has the job of transforming an engineered, technical arrangement of people and units into a functioning entity. A manager must know how to integrate this system of activities and relationships so that conditions are most conducive to effective performance.

Many people who are concerned with the performance of organizations consider effectiveness to be control over environment. Thus, an effective organization is a unified system equipped with the knowledge, skills, and resources to control its environments, while an ineffective organization, for the lack of such capabilities, remains subject to forces over which it can exert little control.

Not to recognize these requirements can lead to serious interference with oganizational competence and, therefore, organizational effectiveness by creating such problems as failures to set performance goals; breakdowns in communication; conflict, strife, and competition between individuals or groups; low morale; and poor work discipline. The sources of such problems are likely to be diffuse and quite complex and may be traced to any or all of an array of factors, including working conditions, superior–subordinate relationships, communication, operational inefficiency, or just about any other condition related to life within an organization. Any such conditions may ultimately be traced to inadequate leadership or management.

The Essence of Organizational Management

Several aspects of organizational management are especially important. First, *the work of a dynamic organization involves the continual identification and reformulation of problems.* Although activities may be planned to the smallest detail, they cannot be accomplished with absolute certainty because no one can ever be sure of all the factors that may become involved as an operation proceeds. Therefore, activities often have to be planned on the basis of less than complete information or in anticipation of many possible eventualities, some or all of which may never occur. Even to select the particular facts that are relevant from all the data that may be available is no easy matter. Much activity involves being alert to and exploring a wide range of data and ongoing events to find possible alternatives that will yield desirable consequences. *One important function of management is to guide this exploring process. By providing structure in the form of guidance and problem definition, the leader can keep ambiguity to a minimum.*

A second management function involves the provision of appropriate methodological assistance as needed by the organization. The manager must suggest relevant concepts and techniques that aid in handling operational problems. In addition, he or she must guide his or her subordinates along lines that provide a happy compromise between the procedural rigidity and flexibility that has been touched upon several times in this book. Failure to provide this methodological help may be a serious source of unsuccessful organizational functioning.

A third function of organizational management involves the identification and coordination of member resources. Attention must be paid to creating conditions that enable a person with the ability to fill an identified need to make a contribution. This function requires awareness of the different capabilities that people and units can bring to bear on tasks. It also requires defining members' assignments in each operation in such a way that the most suitable people and units can contribute the most. In this connection, leaders may encounter difficulty if they do not make themselves continually aware of the motivations and norms (behavioral standards) of their employees.

As stated in various ways throughout this book, for an organization to cope with its operational environments, it requires:

1. *Operational Proficiency*—the technical competence to successfully execute the tasks arising from the demands of the operational situation.
2. *The capability to assess reality*—the ability to search out, accurately perceive, and correctly interpret the attributes of the operational situation, including conditions both internal and external to the organization.
3. *Adaptability*—the capacity to solve problems and to react flexibly to changing demands of the operational situation.

To meet the above requirements, an organization must develop a number of identifiable characteristics. The characteristics are:

Operational Characteristics

1. The capacity to learn.
2. Open and efficient communication.
3. An organizational climate of confidence and trust.
4. Internal flexibility and innovative ability.
5. A state of functional integration among subordinate units.
6. Operational proficiency.

Human Resources

1. Members who possess the proficiencies necessary for mission accomplishment.

2. Commitment of members to organizational objectives.
3. A sense of unit identity among members.

Leader Resources

1. Leaders who are able to arrive at valid decisions speedily and efficiently.
2. Leaders skilled in identifying and using the full potential that is present among the members of the organization.
3. Leaders who are skilled in mobilizing and guiding the efforts of the organization's members.

In demonstrably effective organizations, characteristics such as those listed above can be frequently observed. For the most part, they either are associated with or derive from the activities of leaders.

Conditions Conducive to Performance

In many organizations, managers' attempts to improve effectiveness most often take the form of modifications of the structural framework—that is, reorganization—and of increased emphasis upon the more formalized organizational constraints, such as policies and procedures. Of course, attention to these aspects is important; however, overreliance upon them leads to organizational rigidity. Effectiveness under the complex conditions of today requires flexibility, a quality that has its principal source in the integrated functional processes discussed earlier.

It has sometimes been stated that the premier function of executives or leaders is to orchestrate the application of the skills and energies of their people to solutions of problems larger than any of them could handle separately. "Orchestrate" suggests many critical and coordinative activities; however, above all others, the term implies the necessity to provide conditions conducive to the effective performance of organizational members.

Some principal organizational conditions necessary for effective performance are listed in Chapter 5 and are included in the Competence Model (Chapter 5).

There are many specific things a leader can do to develop an effective organization. Some are simple, routine functions of administration. Others require rather complex leadership skills. In either case, most of the ways involve attending to matters that are related to the necessary organizational conditions listed in Chapter 5.

It might be possible to approach the development of competence and organizational effectiveness through random, on-the-job experiences; however, the most efficient and cost-effective way to ensure maximum effectiveness is to develop and systematically train an organization in a carefully planned cycle of developmental activities.

Developmental Activities

Training for competence is considered in Chapter 9. Here, the discussion is devoted to ways of developing an integrated organizational system through the enhancement of essential properties.

Organizational Properties

Briefly, those organizational properties necessary for the development of an integrated system are:

1. A clear role system.
2. Common superordinate goals.
3. Functional norms of performance and behavior.
4. A stable and efficient communication system.
5. Effective group relations.
6. A stable and efficient organization.

The above organizational properties are considered to be the minimum required for development of integration and competence. Attention to other aspects may help to enhance competence; however, the above properties should be considered essential for all developmental efforts.

A Clear Role System

The concept of role is a principal means for explaining individual behavior in organizations and for linking such behavior to the organizational process. Roles are at once the building blocks of organizational systems and the frameworks of requirements with which such systems control their members as individuals. Each person in an organization is linked to other members by the functional requirements of his or her role, which are implemented through the expectations that those members have of him or her. It is important to stress that roles are ideational (i.e., they are ideas about how behavior ought to occur, rather than being the actual behavior).

The functioning of organizational processes is determined, in large part, by the role perceptions of individuals in key positions—in this case, by members of management. The problem-solving, decision-making, and adapting processes are affected by the extent to which there are clear, accurate, and shared perceptions of role requirements by all members of the organization.

Roles of each organizational member should be clear to both role incumbents and all other members. This refers not just to written job descriptions but, rather, to all expectations, both formal and informal, held by leaders and all other members of the organization. Roles consist of all formal duties and responsibilities, plus informal expectations and norms that evolve through interaction between people. Especially with regard to teamwork, congruity of role perceptions between leaders and incumbents and among all organization members is vitally important. When people do not have common understandings about how the various roles should be performed, coordinative behavior is extremely difficult, if not impossible.

Role clarity is best achieved when (1) a leader makes explicit to personnel precisely what his or her expectations are with respect to each position and the group as a whole and (2) when members of a group have frequent opportunities to jointly examine performance and to clarify role expectations among the members.

An often neglected set of requirements in organizations and in teams includes those actions that are not specified by role prescriptions (job descriptions) but that facilitate the accomplishment of organizational objectives. Any organization's need for some actions of a relatively spontaneous sort is inevitable. Planning, standard procedures, and role prescriptions cannot foresee all contingencies and cannot anticipate all environmental changes that may occur. The resources of members for innovating and for spontaneous cooperation are thus vital to effective functioning. However, this spontaneous behavior requires some control to funnel it into organizationally approved channels. This control cannot be provided by the more formal role prescriptions. Norms serve this function.

Common Superordinate Goals

Organizations face the problem of adapting to environmental change without losing their basic character and distinctive capabilities. On the one hand, if the goals around which activities are mobilized are adhered to despite environmental change, there may be losses and inefficiencies or even threats to survival. On the other hand, if goals are changed too frequently, there is the risk of members' losing sight of the principal mission of the unit.

The importance of goals lies in the necessity for the efficient conduct of complex activities and for keeping activities on track. When goals are clear, operational, and shared and when people are emotionally committed to their accomplishment, misperceptions, conflicts, false starts, cross-purposes, and wasted effort are kept to a minimum. The overall (superordinate) objectives of the organization, the objectives of subordinate units, and the goals of individuals are in general harmony, and all aim toward accomplishing the mission of the organization. In turn, this should result in more efficient functioning of the organizational processes.

Organization members should be kept aware of objectives. Through both formal meetings and informal daily activities, the team-minded manager strives to keep both the objectives of the organization and the objectives of subordinate units constantly before the members of the organization. The problem for the manager and his or her subordinates is to establish and work toward the accomplishment of concrete objectives whose achievement results in execution of the basic mission. Objectives are the steppingstones to mission accomplishment. Effectiveness requires that all members keep these objectives constantly at the forefront of awareness. Accordingly, as he or she works with subordinates, the team-minded leader must use every opportunity to stress the current objectives and the means for their achievement. Through constant emphasis, the leader may be able to generate individual involvement with the common objectives of the organization.

Shared Norms of Performance and Behavior

Norms are attitudes and codes of behavior held in common by all or most of the members. When developed, this superstructure of customs, standards, and values regulates the behavior of members and provides them with the bases for assessing nonroutine situations and for governing their actions in such situations where no official guidance is available. It is evident that the patterned activities that make up the competence processes are so intrinsically cooperative and interrelated that the kinds of norms that develop must inevitably influence their functioning. *This influence is most likely in terms of the extent to which people execute the process functions above and beyond the minimal limits prescribed by formal role prescriptions.*

Agreement on appropriate standards of performance and behavior is intimately related to development of effectiveness because the system of standards in a group serves as a means of quality control. When individuals accept the norms (standards) of a group, they belong. When they belong, they coordinate their actions in accordance with the common needs.

Leaders can influence the development of common understandings by publicly and officially expressing the standards that they deem desirable and, even more important, by subjecting both their own performance and behavior and those of their subordinates to evaluation against these standards.

A Stable and Efficient Communications System

Viewed as a system, an organization is an elaborate network for gathering, evaluating, recombining, and disseminating information. For this reason, communication is the essence of organized activity and is the basic process out of which all other activities derive. The capacity of the organization to respond to changing situations and pressures, the motivation of people to contribute consistently and eagerly to the welfare of the organization, and the ability of managers to mobilize the vital human resources for accomplishment of objectives—these depend, in large part, upon the effectiveness of communication.

Effective Group Relations

Role structures, norms, and patterns of interaction develop when group members work together toward common objectives. These group attributes exert a lasting influence upon the ways that members go about their tasks, the levels of motivation that are achieved, and the extent to which a sense of identity develops within the group and the organization.

The cohesiveness or cohesion of a group refers to feelings of solidarity and pride among the members. Cohesiveness is essential to any undertaking to develop teamwork. An additional essential requirement involves strong norms that value high-quality performance or, in other terms, integration with organizational requirements and organizational structure and function.

A cooperative atmosphere must be developed within the organization. It is extremely important to develop genuinely cooperative relationships between leaders, groups, and members of the organization. It is impossible to impose true cooperation upon people. Therefore, the development of cooperation must be truly a matter of leadership by example. The leader must work at and rely upon his or her own team attitudes to filter gradually through the organization until, in time, individual members begin functioning more cooperatively, begin to communicate more among themselves, and gradually exchange dependence upon the leader for interdependence among all members, the leader included.

Control must be exercised on cooperative efforts within the organization. Organized groups with strong cohesion have been found to exhibit better teamwork and so disintegrate less rapidly under stress than unorganized groups. A part of organization is agreement (implicit or explicit) concerning the amount of control to be exercised by the various levels of authority, the degree of authority to be delegated, areas of assigned responsibility, and the limitations to be placed upon individual freedom to act.

The control exercised on cooperative effort is one of the functions most commonly associated with leadership. Whenever a leader undertakes to define, interpret, or clarify the freedoms extended to individual subordinates or the limitations imposed upon them, he or she is influencing the performance of the organization and is, at that time, giving leadership to its members.

Probably the most significant aspect of this leadership by control is the degree of discretion to be granted to subordinates, that is, the control of freedom of action or, more simply, the control of alternatives open to subordinates for making decisions. This particular point has long been a bone of contention in analyses of leadership. The positions have ranged from retention of complete and total control of all actions and decisions by a single leader, to the other extreme of wide diffusion of responsibility throughout a group of subordinates. However, neither of these extreme approaches has been found to be productive. Effective team performance results when subordinates are provided sufficient latitude to exercise responsibility at their own levels, while leaders simultaneously exercise the guidance and control necessary to coordinate those activities that contribute to the mission of the larger organization. This can be achieved through common understandings concerning areas of authority, responsibility, and freedom to act and through explicit policies that establish explicit criteria as to which decisions should be made at subordinate levels and which should be referred to higher levels.

Rewards must be distributed fairly and equitably within the organization. The distribution of rewards and other satisfactions can encourage teamwork, or it can splinter a group. Subordinates' perceptions of who gets the credit or their suspicion of exploitation—regardless of whether it actually exists—can be a serious problem. Because of the way function and responsibility are distributed in organizations, it is almost inevitable that some assignments seem to have more status than others, that some people have jobs more satisfying to them, that the contributions of everyone do not seem equally valuable and are not equally rewarded. Such reactions are especially subjective when the issue seems to be reward expressed in status or favor with leaders. Disgruntlement and competition arising from such perceptions can be especially destructive for cohesion. A leader must be constantly alert for such problems and must exercise extreme care that misperceptions in this area do not develop in his or her unit.

A Stable and Efficient Organizational System

In general, integration is enhanced through the existence of conditions that cause people to develop common perceptions of events and problems, to evolve shared perspectives of themselves and their unit (Identity), and to become consistently and harmoniously committed to the activities and objectives of the organization. These conditions can be achieved by a stable and efficient organizational system that provides effective operating procedures, efficient patterns of communication, and efficient, closely coordinated teamwork.

Effectiveness in organizations depends upon the performance of role-specific individual skills and team performance skills. Both types of skills are driven and controlled by integration; that is, *in addition to the proficiency of individuals, they depend upon cohesion.*

Stability is necessary to achieve integration in any organization. Stability in the relationships among members is essential for effective teamwork. Each member must be able to predict with assurance the behavior and actions of all other members. This required assurance results from familiarity and experience among all people. When relationships are stable, each member comes to know what is expected of him or her by others. Furthermore, he or she learns the roles of other people as well as their characteristic ways of acting. He or she knows what to expect from others, where other group members are weak, where they are strong, and so on. He or she also learns to depend upon other members, to work with them, and to support their efforts. This stability of roles and of performance expectations develops through frequent contacts among the members of a group and from experiences of success in working together. This stability cannot develop if there is constant turnover or other turbulence. It is one function of leadership to ensure that conditions exist within the unit sufficient for such stability to develop.

Teamwork requires an efficient organizational system that provides the means through which activities of members can be integrated. No matter how high the motivation to cooperate, teamwork does not result unless members' efforts can be effectively channeled. The term *organizational system* refers to those procedures and practices used to channel the efforts of people through such functions as exercising direction, assigning responsibilities, exchanging information, making decisions, organizing, coordinating, and so on. The system includes the formal organization and procedures but goes beyond them to also include the various informal means by which the activities are integrated and coordinated. These interdependent processes constitute an overall system that channels and guides the activities of the organization. For this reason, it is more appropriate to refer to the organizational system rather than merely to organization as a critical element.

Effective performance within a complex organizational context requires a system that ensures that, consistent with their objectives, missions, and responsibilities, members are provided with all the information, decisions, guidance, and assistance necessary to perform effectively and to contribute appropriately to overall organization effort. More specifically, the system must function in such a manner that:

1. Each member of the organization is provided missions and objectives that he or she is motivated to achieve and that when accomplished, contribute to the superordinate objectives of the organization.
2. The techniques, procedures, and plans developed by leaders are such that members are motivated to use them to their maximum potentiality.
3. The activities of organizational members fit together and are mutually supporting.
4. Opportunity is provided for contacts between members sufficient for mutual trust and confidence to develop.

Purposes Served by Properties

1. Clear superordinate objectives and a meaningful system of rewards focus efforts upon common aims and motivate members to cooperate and coordinate.

2. An efficient organizational system channels motivation to cooperate into effective actions.
3. A stable system provides continuity of personnel and the opportunity to develop shared experiences.
4. Shared experiences of success enhance a positive unit identity.
5. Shared norms of performance and behavior provide standards for action, especially in emergent situations.

REQUIRED MANAGER FUNCTIONS

Development and maintenance of an organization as a system calls for a number of closely related activities by a manager. Taken together, these activities contribute to creation of a climate that exerts positive effects upon both the performance and satisfaction of everyone. The activities are:

1. Formulating objectives and a role for the organization.
2. Developing core personnel.
3. Formulating ground rules for working.
4. Developing an effective communication system
5. Promoting a high level of motivation.
6. Setting standards of performance.

Formulating Objectives and Roles

The necessity for careful formulation of objectives and a role for an organization has long been a fundamental concern of managers. Indeed, the necessity for clear and unequivocal objectives is so much accepted these days that their very real utility as an instrument of leadership may sometimes be overlooked. This can be unfortunate because a manager who fails to use objectives effectively wastes a potent tool for influencing his or her organization.

Objectives serve the important functions of providing an organization with direction and of mobilizing efforts around common aims. It is impossible to effectively organize the activities of numbers of people unless they have a common target or set of targets toward which they can strive, around which they can focus their efforts, and against which they can evaluate their accomplishments. Furthermore, whenever members of an organization become attached to an objective because of its significance to them, the result is a prizing of that objective for its own sake. Therefore, it changes from an impersonal target to a valued source of satisfaction. In these ways, objectives serve both cognitive and motivational functions.

Objectives represent the specific things that an organization is trying to accomplish. They are usually fairly long-term and provide members with incentives for accomplishment. Since objectives give direction to the efforts of the organization, a manager must play a vital role in their formulation or, if they are assigned to him or her, in making them meaningful for his or her subordinates by interpreting these aims to everybody in such a way as to win support for them. Thus, the character of the organization is shaped and sensitized to ways of thinking and responding so that objectives become concrete operational targets toward which all efforts may be directed.

Objectives are statements of intent and usually say nothing about the mode of their achievement. Therefore, following from his or her objective-defining activities, a manager must also identify and make operational the role of his or her organization as indicated by the objectives.

As applied to organizations, role definition is, in effect, a decision by an organization or its leaders regarding how it ought to function. This involves estimates of its relationships with other organizations (including the demands to which it should respond), of the means to be used for achieving its objectives, and of its capabilities, potentialities, and limitations.

As conditions change, roles may shift. This necessitates periodic reevaluation by a manager. If reassessment is not carried out, changed conditions can result in the performance of activities that are no longer relevant or that, in the new situation, conflict with those of other elements in the organization.

Insofar as possible, roles should be prescribed when an organization is activated. When this can be done, the only problem remaining is to ensure that frequent reassessment occurs to adapt to changing conditions. When, however, organizations that are based on new concepts are activated, as happens frequently, roles must often be worked out on the basis of evolving experience, and leadership of a high quality is required.

Developing Core Personnel

An important activity in managing an organization as a system is the development of a core of people, homogeneous as to outlook, attitudes, and motivation, who occupy the key positions. This core group may include staff people, subordinate managers, and the occupants of critical positions at many levels. When developed properly, it serves as the nucleus around which the organization can be built. These individuals reflect the basic outlook of the organization and ensure that the development of derivative policies and practices is guided by a shared perspective.

The development of a core group may involve recruitment and certainly necessitates the selection of people who appear to meet both the technical and personal requirements of the particular organization. Of even more importance, however, are indoctrination of key people and definitions of the responsibilities, roles, and relationships that are supposed to exist between both individuals and units. This may be accomplished by formal statements, but it is more effective when developed by the sharing of experiences during which expectations can be communicated more clearly and less formally.

An important activity in both the development of core employees and the general promotion of organizational performance is training. The development of a high level of proficiency within an organization is ultimately a training process that involves two aspects.

The first involves the inculcation and perfection of technical skills, mainly accomplished through formal courses, on-the-job training, and the like. However, a competent, unified organization requires more than proficiency alone. Effective performance depends, to a considerable extent, on the attitudes and ways of thinking of all members, especially those who occupy key positions. Therefore, a second aspect of the development process involves shaping the attitudes of members in directions congruent with the objectives of the organization. The greatest opportunities that are available to a manager can be found in his or her daily interactions with his or her subordinates. At such times, he or she can interpret objectives and policies, transmit his or her views of appropriate actions and ways of functioning, and inculcate both general and specific perspectives relative to the proper role and character of the organization.

In this sense, training is a constant activity that requires recognition of the developmental opportunities that may be available and careful attention to the potential effects of day-to-day experiences upon long-term proficiency.

Formulating Ground Rules for Working

Organizational practices and ways of working are matters of legitimate concern for managers. The practices and the attitudes associated with them shape the character of the organization and thus contribute to performance. A part of the management function involves ensuring that each individual knows what the organization is supposed to accomplish, how his or her duties relate to the organization's objectives, and what constitutes the ground rules for performing his or her activities.

Ground rules are basic understandings that are supposed to be adhered to by all concerned. Many organizations are less than effective because basic ground rules have not been clearly set forth. If ways of working are not fully understood and agreed upon, departments spend their time competing against each other, line and staff people get into each other's hair, managers waste their energies fighting over cloudy jurisdictions, and it all ends by everyone's losing confidence in the organization.

Under certain conditions, such as the activation of a new organization or department, formal statements are useful for communicating policies about ways of working. However, the manager's greatest opportunities for leadership in this area arise in the course of daily work. It is here that he or she is best able to communicate desires and attitudes relative to ways that the organization should function.

Developing an Effective Communication System

The effectiveness of organizational communication rests upon fulfillment of several requirements. The first is that the formal communication system, which operates through the chain of authority, must function efficiently and according to its design. Therefore, most attention must be given to ensuring that everyone receive the information that he or she needs and that blockages do not develop within the system.

A second requirement involves obtaining uniform understanding and compliance with formal communications. This is a problem because each of the units within an organization has its own particular mission and certain unique objectives. Therefore, when a communication is sent to a number of subordinate units, each unit may extract a different meaning from the message depending upon its significance for that unit's mission and the things that it is striving to accomplish.

Accordingly, one task for a manager involves interpreting the purposes, intentions, and reasons for everything to everybody, especially reasons for changes that may exert drastic effects upon missions, roles, values, and the relationships among subordinate units. Interpretation means more than merely issuing a formal statement. The manager has to construe meanings to different units and individuals in such a manner as to obtain both understanding and support.

A third requirement involves regulation of the relationships that may affect the communication process. In organizations, people are structured into certain systems of relationships (e.g., those based on authority structures, functional [work] structures, or friendship structures). These systems of relationships both stimulate and inhibit effective communication. They facilitate communication because they provide stable expectations about who should communicate with whom about what and in what manner. However, uncertainty in these relationships can also inhibit communication. Personnel losses, transfers, promotions, replacements, and new policies and procedures can modify the relationships between people. When this occurs, communication can become less effective.

More than any other individual, a manager can govern these relationships and, by so doing, affect communication within his or her organization. By controlling and regulating relationships, he or she can stabilize the communications system, thus contributing to organizational performance.

Developing a High Level of Motivation

The power of organized activity depends upon the willingness of individuals to cooperate and to contribute their efforts to the work of the organization. In short, outstanding organizational performance requires that people be motivated.

It is characteristic of many organizations that motivational problems may be viewed as administrative ones. Thus, when such problems are identified, a manager may attempt to handle them through administrative fiat—through the issuance of new directives, the changing of policies, the correction of bad physical conditions, and so on. However, there is a significant distinction between these kinds of actions, which merely reduce already existing problems, and those aimed at developing and maintaining a positive state of attitude that can serve as an active force for achievement.

High motivational conditions require conscious and calculated efforts by leaders to develop and sustain them. A manager must use both his or her leadership skills and his or her organization's resources in order to create motivational conditions conducive to effective performance. The problem is that just about everything in an organization has effects upon motivation. This suggests that every decision and every action by a manager must be considered in the light of its possible consequences for motivation, as well as for its effect upon operations. This is not to say that decisions and actions that favor operations over motivation may not occasionally be required. However, it is one thing to make a decision favoring an objective while taking into account that motivation will likely suffer as a result. Such awareness permits a manager also to undertake appropriate measures to counter the anticipated drop in motivation. On the other hand, it is another matter to make such a decision with total disregard for its effects upon motivation.

Setting Standards of Performance

A final activity involves controlling the quality of performance through development and communication of standards of excellence and through inculcation of such standards into daily activities within the organization. Formal control devices are an essential tool in management. However, control is most effective when a manager develops explicit expectations relative to the quality and quantity of performance and communicates these expectations so that everyone has clear standards against which to gauge accomplishment.

Explicit standards of performance are not always easy to develop. However, everyone who directs the activities of other people uses some frame of reference for judging whether the work of his or her organization and subordinates is satisfactory. In certain instances, these standards are highly explicit; in other cases, the person making the judgments cannot himself or herself enunciate clearly the basis for his or her evaluations. But, regardless of whether his or her ideas are hazy or clear, every manager uses some guidelines for judging performance, and these standards should be a matter of record within the organization.

A MODEL FOR ORGANIZATIONAL INTEGRATION

In the conceptual framework for organizational effectiveness (Chapter 5), proficient role performance and integration were proposed as essential elements for developing and maintaining organizational competence. In Chapter 9, an operational model for competence is proposed. From results of research, it has been concluded that organizational competence (i.e., the caliber of critical functional processes) is an important determinant of organizational effectiveness. Effectiveness in performing the organizational processes results, in part, from proficiency in role performance.

In this chapter, that part of the conceptual framework pertaining to integration is reduced to an operational model. Necessary organizational conditions (properties) and developmental activities are set forth.

Assessment of Training and Development Models

Operational models serve utilitarian requirements. They are developed for the purpose of specifying for potential users the essential elements in complex concepts and the relationships between the elements. Although based upon and similar to a conceptual framework, a model is more utilitarian because it delineates the critical elements; shows their relationships; and most important, presents them in a form that makes the elements and their relationships subject to verification and manipulation for the particular purpose for which the model was designed.

Attributes of a Practical Training and Development Model

A useful model for training and development should possess the following attributes:

1. *The model should be parsimonious.* Like all scientific concepts, operational models should be parsimonious. They should explain the most relationships with the least feasible number of elements. The rule of parsimony also applies to training and development models.
2. *All elements should be manipulable.* Each element in the model should be capable of being changed (i.e., improved, in some fashion, either through training, development, or intervention). It serves no purpose to include elements that cannot be operationally defined and, thus, cannot be improved through systematic efforts of the organization.

3. *All elements should be capable of being measured.* This capability enables trainers and managers to assess the level of development of their organizations and to diagnose elements that may be especially strong or weak and to which special efforts should be directed.

The Integration Model presented here should be evaluated in terms of the above criteria.

CONCEPT OF INTEGRATION

Research (Chapter 4) has demonstrated the validity of an operational model of organizational competence. In particular, the relationships of competence and the processes of which it is composed to organizational effectiveness have been demonstrated.

In addition, it was shown that organizations differ in (1) their proficiencies in performing organizational processes and (2) their abilities to maintain such proficiency (organizational competence) under pressure. In this regard, two significant questions are, What determines the quality of performance of critical organizational processes? and Why, under equal stresses of operational pressures, do these critical organizational functions (processes) deteriorate in some organizations and not in others? The concept of integration is proposed as the answer to these questions.

An organization *is a role system driven and controlled by operational (task) demands and maintained by shared values and norms.* The roles of the system are the official positions occupied by individuals, together with both the formal duties and informal expectations associated with each position.

Members plan and carry out activities through performance of the several organizational functions or processes subsumed under the rubric of organizational competence. The persons in the system are conceived as having various motivations and attitudes and as performing certain activities (processes) in certain ways. The ways in which they perform the processes are, in part, determined by how they perceive the organization, other members, themselves, and their roles; in part, by their motivations; and, in part, by their skills in performing their roles and processes dictated by role and operational demands.

In short, organizational effectiveness is determined by:

1. The skills of each member in performing the various organizational processes dictated by operational and task demands.
2. Integration—the extent to which the roles, perceptions, motivations, and activities of all members are integrated into a unified whole.

Integration is the force that melds the activities of personnel, and it accomplishes this melding through norms and shared values of the members. Stated in more operational terms, *integration is the maintenance of structure and function under stress and a state of relations among subunits that ensures that coordination is maintained and that the various subunits do not work at cross-purposes.* Subunits may be either individuals or subordinate units of the organization.

It should be noted that both the maintenance of structure and function under stress and a state of relations among subunits can be measured and, therefore are manipulable (i.e., susceptible of development). Procedures for measurement are discussed.

Finally, *integration is a developmental process.* Integration *develops* within a group of people, starting from a mere collection of individuals with different perceptions, motivations, and attitudes and developing into a group with common goals, attitudes, and values. These attributes cannot be instilled with a single inoculation but, rather, must be propagated over time. The state of integration at any time is partly dependent upon what has occurred between the members in the past. Therefore, *integration is also a process*, occurring over time, with its state at any point determined by the unique history of the organization.

In summary, the essential factors necessary for effective organization performance are:

1. Proficiency in role and team skills by all members, both individually and collectively.
2. A continuing group situation that:
   a. Is attractive to members.
   b. Generates pride and solidarity (cohesion).
   c. Produces strong norms that value high performance (Integration).

THE INTEGRATION MODEL

Figure 8.1 shows a schematic of the Integration Model. Stated simply, integration should occur (1) when organizational conditions are conducive to cohesion and teamwork and (2) if developmental activities are designed to propagate high skill levels, stable team norms, and performance values. When these two components are combined, the result is an organizational state that encourages teamwork and provides a supportive climate that enhances member capabilities for resisting pressure and for maintaining proficiency under stress.

Necessary Organizational Properties

One requisite for the growth of integration involves organizational conditions that are conducive to cohesion and teamwork. Organizational prop-

Figure 8.1
The Integration Model

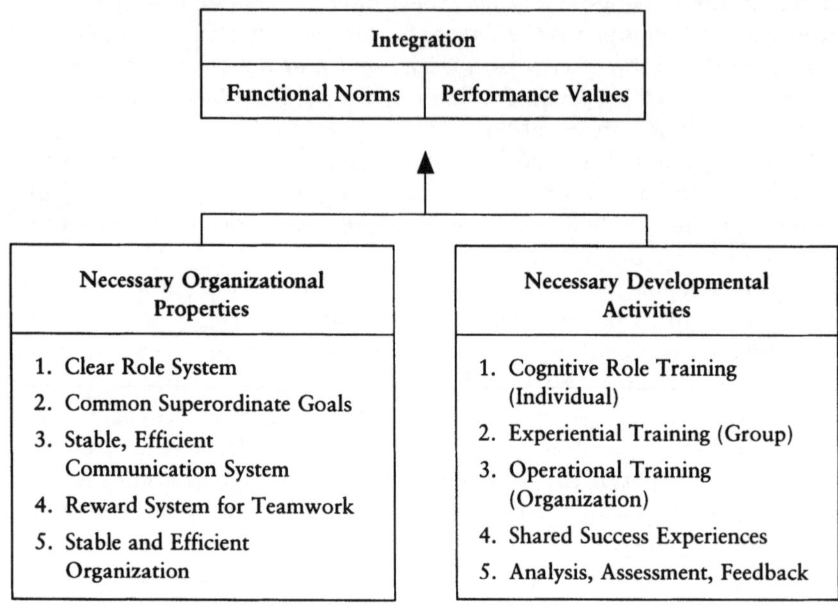

erties have their sources in the actions of the organization or its representatives, and they are important aspects of the organizational context within which people must perform.

The organizational context consists of those properties of an organization that reflect its internal state and characteristic ways of working. In recent years, the importance of organizational contexts has become increasingly apparent. For this discussion of integration, "necessary organizational properties" are those elements that have particular relevance for cohesion and teamwork and are deemed essential for the development of integration. Full rationales for the properties shown in Figure 8.1 are presented earlier in this chapter. The necessary organizational properties are:

1. *A clear system of roles within the organization.* Each member of the organization should know both his or her role and the roles of all other members. He or she should know clearly and accept the expectations that other members have of him or her as well as his or her expectations of the performance of other members.
2. *Common superordinate goals.* People should know and accept the objectives of the organization, and each should understand how his or her role contributes to the accomplishment of superordinate objectives. In addition, unit goals and superordinate goals should be held in common by everyone.

3. *A stable, efficient communication system.* Effective communication is the essential requirement for integration. This includes both the mechanics of communication and efforts to achieve understanding of what is communicated.
4. *A reward system for teamwork.* The system of rewards in a group is an important determinant of teamwork. Although intangible rewards may be received from highly cohesive groups for efforts that contribute to group welfare and success, cooperation is most likely to develop and become a way of life when members can receive formal rewards for behaving cooperatively and when competitive behavior is not rewarded. The most significant factor is whether leaders value and reward cooperative, team-centered behavior and whether all personnel know it.
5. *A stable and efficient organizational system.* Teamwork requires an efficient organizational system that provides a means through which activities of members can be integrated and coordinated. Also required is sufficient stability among people within the organization that common values and norms can evolve.

Each necessary property has its sources in actions of the organization or its representatives. That is, the condition develops as the result of some official action taken in the name of the organization or because of decisions or actions taken by organizational leaders. Roles are clear, understood, and accepted when a manager makes clear his or her expectations about how every role should be performed and ensures that all role occupants understand and accept his or her expectations. Similarly, clear superordinate goals require that leaders throughout the organization not only accept goals of the larger organization but, in addition, make the effort to ensure that everyone both understands and accepts the goals and their implications.

Reward systems usually result from actions of managers. They may develop because of conscious planning and concomitant actions by leaders, or they may develop informally and by accident. In either case, the kind of reward systems, if any, that develop derives from the philosophy and actions of the manager.

Finally, an efficient organizational system results from explicit management direction and emphasis, while a stable system results from (1) leader efforts to minimize turbulence and (2) continuity among people—which can result only from enlightened policies that retain them in units for periods that are sufficiently long for cohesion to develop.

It is clear that organizational conditions conducive to teamwork and cohesion are products of the organization and its leaders. Since the properties are the products of leadership, they can be changed through the efforts of leaders—they are manipulable. Furthermore, each condition can be measured. They can be assessed through the use of personnel surveys, questionnaires that target the conditions, or other devices that are designed to assess the perceptions and attitudes of members about existing teamwork, cohesion, and organizational conditions.

Necessary Developmental Activities

Organizational properties are part of the context within which people must perform. Necessary developmental activities are those training and development activities needed to equip members to function as members of a viable, role-proficient, and cohesive group.

The necessary developmental activities are:

1. *Cognitive role training (individual).* In this training, primary focus is upon providing all individuals with (1) full cognitive understanding of performance requirements for each role; (2) detailed understanding of organizational competence and the definitions and performance requirements of each organizational process; and, most important, (3) recognition and understanding of the organization as a team, together with requirements of teamwork.
2. *Experiential training (group).* This training follows cognitive role training and should be designed to provide practical experience under carefully controlled conditions. It is analogous to practical exercises and should be conducted as practical team training for groups. The training is characterized by objectives-based practical exercises, analyses of performance, and feedback of results.
3. *Operational training.* All training in operations should include observation, assessment, and feedback, especially with respect to organizational competence. In short, competence training should be an integral part of operational training.
4. *Shared success experiences.* An important requisite for the development of cohesion is shared experiences of success in matters of importance to the team. From the standpoint of planned organizational development, systematic provision of successful experiential and operational training experiences is the method of choice.

The recommended developmental activities have been selected to maximize role performance, centered around organizational competence processes, and group and individual competencies among members. When the developmental activities and other daily activities are conducted within an organizational context characterized by the conditions described above, it can be expected that integration and, therefore, organizational effectiveness are maximized.

Assessment Issues

Any proposed model should be tested in the context for which it is designed. The Integration Model has been tested in several types of organizations and can be accepted as valid. The Integration Model can be assessed in terms of the criteria for training and development models discussed at the beginning of this chapter. Together with parsimony, the two criteria for a useful model are set forth as manipulability and measurability.

Manipulability

First, the criterion of manipulability requires that each element in the model, as well as Integration itself, shall be susceptible to systematic change. Such change may be accomplished through development, training, or intervention.

It should be apparent that every element in the Integration Model meets the criterion of manipulability. Each organizational condition can be improved through managers' intervention and is likely to deteriorate when not given proper attention. As just one example, the first necessary organizational property—a clear role system—requires that someone, probably the manager, explicitly define expectations for each role and, equally important, inculcate these expectations so that all members perceive the various roles in the same way. This is manager intervention and, when used effectively, produces improved perceptions of his or her roles by everyone and contributes to integration. Thus, the element—a clear role system—is manipulable through manager intervention and meets the criterion for an element in a training and development model. Each necessary organizational condition meets the manipulability criterion in a similar fashion—all are subject to change through intervention.

The five necessary developmental activities are obviously manipulable because they involve training activities and, accordingly, can be easily changed by modifying training designs or methods. Each element can be enhanced by improved training design and methodology. In turn, enhancement of each developmental activity can be expected to contribute to both improved role performance and strengthened norms and values characteristic of heightened integration.

Measurability

Measurability is important because, for an effort to improve performance or any other condition, it is necessary first to determine the current status of the individual, group, or unit. When the current status has been ascertained, it is possible to plan efforts for change. Accordingly, measurability of the elements in a utilitarian model is essential to establish current status and to determine whether significant change has been achieved.

Viewed from another standpoint, everything that can be changed can be measured in some fashion. It is necessary to identify the units of change and then count the units to determine whether significant change has occurred.

Measurement of developmental activities is relatively simple. For cognitive role training, experiential training, and unit operational training, measurement involves conventional training evaluation procedures. Measurement of shared success experiences can be accomplished through survey techniques designed to measure members' perceptions of both training experiences and significant events in the daily activities of the unit. The four necessary organizational conditions can be assessed through questionnaire surveys of personnel. Similarly, norms and values, as well as an overall assessment of integration, can be accomplished with surveys.

Evaluation of the Integration Model

From the discussion in this chapter it should be clear that the Integration Model meets the general criteria for an operational model. The model is parsimonious, and all of its elements, as well as the overall concept of Integration, are both manipulable and measurable. Therefore, it can be concluded that the model is feasible for training and development purposes.

IMPLICATIONS

Until recently, systematic knowledge of the type most needed for the management of organizations has been limited by the traditional approaches in both sociology and psychology. In sociology, there has been a notable lack of interest in research in which organizational variables could be controlled and manipulated. On the other hand, psychology, with its more experimental approach, has generally neglected the formulation of systematic research problems in the broader setting of functioning organizations. It is only recently that a genuine hybrid—organizational psychology—has emerged (Schein, 1965). This new area is a true amalgamation of the sociology of organizations with industrial psychology and social psychology, including group dynamics. It possesses a conceptual vitality that offers great promise for understanding behavior within organizations. Most important, the concepts have significant practical implications.

Probably the greatest impact results from emphasis upon the interrelationships between structural and human aspects. As shown in the earlier discussion of theoretical approaches, there has been a decided tendency for theorists and researchers to stress either structure or people, usually while ignoring the other. Yet, in reality, neither can be safely ignored.

An organization is a number of persons performing some activity in relation to its external environment. The way that the persons are arranged in relation to each other and the task is the structure of the organization. However, formal structures and job definitions cannot consider differences between individual human beings. In the same way, formal structures cannot take account of the deviations introduced by the human variable, and formal control mechanisms break down if relied upon alone.

The existence of deviations forces a shift away from the purely formal structure as the principal determinant of effectiveness to a situation in which informal patterns of relationships and human motives exert a decided influence upon performance. These human factors must be considered in any reasonable consideration of organizational behavior.

Carried over to management, this suggests that the first thing of which a manager must become aware is that behavior in organizations is usually the result of many determinants, which may include both structural and human aspects operating together. To seize upon one or two factors as a basis for action and neglect the rest is usually a gross oversimplification. It can only cause the manager to misunderstand the problem and take the wrong course for its resolution.

Chapter 9

Competence Operationally Defined

In this chapter, the principal focus is upon developing or enhancing organizational effectiveness through the improvement of organizational competence. Effectiveness depends upon:

1. *Individual Role Skills*—the skills (both technical and process) of individuals in performing their respective roles.
2. *Individual Team Performance Skills*—the skills of individuals in coordinating their activities with those of other members and in contributing to the collective execution of group functions or team-related processes.
3. *Integration*—the force that melds the roles, attitudes, and activities of all members and strongly contributes to the maintenance of structure and function within the organization (see Chapter 8).

Of course, the elements are related. Each depends upon and also contributes to the other elements. These reciprocal relationships and activities that contribute to effectiveness are illustrated in Figure 10.1.

Organizational competence is the capability of an organization to perform the critical functions (processes) that lead to achievement of effectiveness (i.e., the ability to sense impacting events in both external and internal environments, to process information that is sensed, and to adapt operations so as to cope with sensed changes).

Competence should not be made ancillary to other performance elements. Rather, it should be one direct focus of training and should be a continuing concern during all day-to-day activities of the organization.

THE NATURE OF ORGANIZATIONAL COMPETENCE

Organizational competence is a concept. It is a way of classifying and systematizing organizational functions that must be performed and of making them more meaningful for everyday application. In reality, the processes that are the focus in competence are not new. They have always been a part of organizational activities and have always been performed, to one degree or another, wherever organizations have existed.

The problem has been that, all too often, the processes have been so commonplace that their importance has been ignored in favor of more goal-directed matters. As just one example, the execution of job requirements frequently is emphasized in training; however, the techniques (quality of processes) used to obtain decisions and to implement decisions are often given short shrift.

The fundamental premise of the concept is that an organization is a problem-solving, action-taking system that functions within environments that change constantly. For the organization to actively master its environments or to cope with events within them, adaptability is essential. According to Bennis (1966, p. 52), flexibility is the ability "to learn through experience, to change with changing internal and external circumstances."

In order for an organization to cope with its environments, it must be sufficiently flexible in its internal processes to enable it to modify operations so as to meet the demands of new problems arising in its environments, both internal and external. This is especially true for rapid-response organizations, where rigidity can be fatal.

In turn, adaptability relies upon the organization's capability for reality testing. According to Bennis, "if the conditions requisite for an organization are to be met, the organization must develop adequate techniques for determining the real properties of the field in which it exists" (1966, p. 51). Adequate reality testing refers to search and sensing processes sufficiently effective to provide the information that permits members to develop accurate perceptions of the environments within which the organization must function. In short, *a correct understanding of the problem is necessary before it can be solved and overcome. The search, sensing, and communication processes involved in reality testing help to provide that understanding.*

Organizational Attributes

As described in Chapters 3 and 4, extensive research has identified certain attributes that constitute the underpinnings for organizational effectiveness. In summary, to be successful, every organization needs three basic attributes, each of which encompasses several critical functions that must be performed well (components of competence).

1. *Reality Assessment*—the capability to accurately assess the reality of situations facing the organization—the ability of the organization to search out, accurately perceive, and correctly interpret the properties and characteristics of its environments (both external and internal), particularly those properties that have special relevance for the missions and operations of the organization.

   To survive and succeed, every organization must have structures and processes that enable it to assess the current reality demands of its particular environments.

   Critical functions—sensing; communicating information; feedback.

2. *Adaptability*—the capability for solving problems that arise from changing environmental demands and for acting with flexibility in response to the changing demands.

   To survive and succeed, every organization must have structures and processes that enable it to mobilize the necessary and appropriate resources for adapting to changes in the environments and to act so as to overcome such changes.

   Critical functions—decision making; communicating implementation; coping actions.

3. *Integration*—the maintenance of structure and functions under stress and maintenance of a state of relations among subunits that ensures that coordination is maintained and that the various subunits do not work at cross-purposes.

   Integration derives from a sense of identity, and, in order to develop and maintain integration, organizational members must possess knowledge, insight, and a reasonable consensus regarding organizational objectives, missions, and the functions necessary for the accomplishment of missions and objectives.

   Critical functions—stabilizing.

Concept of Organizational Competence

The concept of organizational competence is a key element in this approach to process development and training. It derives from recognition that one of the most critical factors in the effectiveness of any organization is its ability to sense impacting events in its external and internal environments, to process the information sensed, and to adapt its operations to cope with the sensed changes.

The ability of the organization to perform these critical functions is what is meant by organizational competence. It is further conceived that organizational competence is a major operational determinant of organizational effectiveness. Where effectiveness is the ultimate outcome (mission accomplishment, achievement of objectives, productivity, etc.), competence is the capability of the organization to perform the critical functions (processes) that lead to achievement of effectiveness.

IMPLEMENTING ORGANIZATIONAL COMPETENCE

Throughout this discussion, it is stressed that organizations function within constantly changing environments. Because of these constant changes, all organizational functions (processes) must be executed *in relation to* current conditions in the critical environments. The critical environments are all environments that can have an impact upon the organization and its operations.

Identifying Critical Environments

It is useful to speak of multiple environments, rather than one amorphous, large environment, because consideration of each separate impacting element as an environment makes it possible to better isolate each separate source of impact and to assess its potential impact upon the organization. Such environments may be the competition, with all of its ramifications; the economy; governments; climatic conditions; adjacent departments; higher organizational levels; or support organizations. Any element outside the organizational boundaries that may be relevant should be considered an environment and, accordingly, should be monitored for its potential impact.

Critical environments are those environments that can have important impacts upon the organization and its operations (i.e., all those environments to which the organization should be sensitive and about which all relevant information and intelligence should be obtained on a continual basis). At any given time, one or all environments may be critical, and the relative criticality of relevant environments can change during the course of an operation. Accordingly, *constant monitoring and assessment of relevant environments are an essential requirement for full effectiveness.*

At the beginning of an activity or training exercise and at periodic progress meetings, some responsible person should review with the staff the environments that may be critical, their main characteristics, and the types of impacts that each may exert. In planning an operation, study of potential environments and their possible impacts may be necessary before final identification of critical ones can be accomplished. The purpose is to ensure that people become alert to all elements that may possibly impact upon operations, so that an event occurring within an environment can be sensed at the earliest possible time and can receive the most comprehensive analysis of the situation that is possible.

Early identification of critical environments makes it possible to plan ways to conduct sensing activities (e.g., use of economic surveys or assigning a liaison person to higher headquarters to obtain early information about changes in plans or operations). Similarly, early identification of critical environments makes it possible to provide meaningful briefings to all workers about the kinds of events and information to which they should be alert and that should be reported.

Sensing

The execution of organizational processes must be *in relation to* the requirements of the operational situation. Accordingly, a process that is relevant and appropriate under one set of conditions may require modification or even elimination as conditions change. The problem is to identify changes in operational conditions and adapt activities to the changes.

Sensing is the initial process in the Adaptive-Coping Cycle. It is the process by which the organization acquires and interprets information about the external and internal environments. The specific character of required sensing activities may differ according to the mission and the particular environments that are critical for it. Whatever their specific nature, organizational sensing activities include the following:

1. *Search*—actively seeking information about critical environments.
2. *Acquisition of information*—acquisition through either active seeking or passive receipt of information.
3. *Processing*—collating, transforming, or otherwise organizing information for ready use.
4. *Storing*—keeping information in files and organization memory, in a form such that it can be retrieved and used.
5. *Interpreting*—attaching meaning, either speculative or confirmed, to information that has been acquired.

Sensing activities are those through which an organization obtains as accurate an understanding as possible about the environments that affect it and the events that occur within those environments. Sensing is a responsibility of every member of an organization. However, the very shape of an organization—a pyramid—and the separation of roles mean that sensing responsibilities may be greater for some individuals than others.

Search and Acquisition

Most initial sensing responsibilities fall upon individuals who are in contact with environments that are critical. Thus, considerable sensing responsibility rests with those people who are at points of contact with impacting elements in the environment, have opportunities to observe, or have designated responsibilities for acquiring information.

Responsibility for the acquisition of information may fall upon any member of an organization, depending upon his or her circumstances and access to the information. However, certain positions have more opportunities to conduct sensing activities. In fact, information collection may be a stipulated part of some job descriptions.

It is important to note that, in sensing, the acquisition of information may be either passive or active or both. Passive sensing is merely the receipt of information without actively seeking it. This might include many of the materials transmitted by a headquarters staff, which are provided without solicitation or actively seeking them, as well as all other information that is not actively sought but is received.

On the other hand, active sensing occurs when the organization or its individual members actively seek information about anything that may affect it. These search activities are initiated within the organization, may be formal or informal, and involve active efforts to obtain needed information.

Effective organizations engage in many more active sensing activities than do those that are less effective. It has become clear that, in the present and future, units of any size cannot rely for all critically needed information solely upon sources outside their own boundaries. This applies especially to personnel or units that are geographically dispersed. To be effective, such units must be fully aware of both current and contingent events that affect them. This awareness can be achieved only through continual, active searches for information.

The acquisition (seeking and obtaining) of information is probably the most important aspect of sensing. However, other types of activities are also involved in sensing. These are processing, storing, and interpreting information that has been acquired.

Processing

In a modern organization, information can be derived from many sources and in numerous forms. Furthermore, information continues to be acquired throughout daily operations. Accordingly, an important aspect of organizational sensing involves processing acquired information so that it is available in a form that (1) is meaningful and useful to everyone and (2) permits storage in the unit memory so that it can be easily retrieved for later use.

As a part of Sensing, the processing of information includes:

1. Collating related information that is acquired from various sources, so that it can be integrated into a meaningful whole.
2. Transforming acquired information into forms that are most useful.
3. Organizing sensed information so that it will be most meaningful and relevant for potential users.

Storing

In a modern organization, the availability of information can be critical. Accordingly, storing of information so that it is readily available for use becomes highly important.

A major problem noted in many observations of both training simulations and actual operating organizations is that information that has been acquired is frequently not posted or logged so that it is readily available. On the other hand, frequently, information that is stored is not used by planners and decision makers. The use of computers is making systematic storing of large quantities of information more feasible than formerly.

Interpreting

Often, information may be acquired only to have the wrong interpretation placed upon it, thereby making the information useless or even erroneous. Interpretation is attaching meaning, relevance, or significance to information that has been acquired.

Next to acquisition, interpretation is probably the most important aspect of sensing. Information that is totally complete and fully valid is useless unless the correct meaning is attached to it at all levels.

The special danger is that, before the sensing process is fully complete, information that is acquired at the boundaries of an organization may be handled and processed at several levels, with opportunity for faulty interpretation and erroneous transmission at every level. *For this reason, training in interpreting information should be provided to all levels in the organization that may have access to information.*

Quality Requirements

The essential requirement of organizational competence is quality—how well the processes are performed. The following are some general questions that should be addressed about Sensing (specific criteria are presented later in this chapter):

1. Was all information that could be available to the organization obtained by it?
2. Were attempts to obtain information both relevant and effective?
3. Was acquired information processed, integrated, recorded, and stored so as to have maximum utility?
4. Was correct interpretation placed upon information that was obtained?
5. In view of the information obtained, was a correct assessment made of it?
6. Was sensing performed effectively at all levels?

Communicating Information

This process is concerned with those activities whereby sensed information is transmitted to those who must make decisions about it or otherwise act upon it. It is the function whereby acquired information is transmitted to points where it may be needed; but it especially applies to the transmittal of information from points where it is sensed to those who must make decisions about it. *This process does not include the transmittal of decisions, orders, instructions, or requirements for implementing them.*

Communicating information includes the following:

1. The initial transmittal of information by those who have sensed it.
2. Relaying of information by intervening levels.
3. Dissemination of information or intelligence throughout the organization.
4. Discussion and interpretation—those communicative acts through which members attempt to clarify information and its meaning or to discuss implications of the information.

Studies have shown clearly that communicating information is one of the most important processes in the system. Effective performance in it is highly correlated with effectiveness, and this process contributes one of the highest weights to Effectiveness ratings.

When communicating information is recognized as a function of the entire organization, its importance is easy to understand. At every organizational level, decisions must be made as to what to communicate, what not to transmit, how much to communicate, when to do it, to whom it should be sent, and how to transmit it. These problems are difficult when communication is between two levels. In a multilevel organization, the potentials for error and distortion increase greatly.

There are a considerable paradox and conflict here between the need for complete information, the need for communications discipline and security, and the need to avoid overload of communication channels. The optimum solution is difficult to discern, and the answer probably depends upon the situation of the moment. However, the position taken here is that more is better; too much information is better than not enough. Within limits, everyone should be provided all information that permits good and valid decisions and actions.

Quality Requirements

Some general questions about Communicating Information are:

1. Was information that was sensed by the organization communicated to all who needed it when they needed it?
2. Was communication of information complete, accurate, and timely?
3. Was communication of information efficient?

Decision Making

This process is concerned with the quality of decisions made at all levels of the organization. Decision making is the deliberative acts of one or more persons that lead to a conclusion that some action should be taken or should not be taken by the organization. It is important to note that the decision-making process is not limited to those major decisions made by an executive but, rather, includes all decisions, however large or small, made by any member. It is also important to note that decisions may be made that lead to sensing actions, stabilizing actions, coping actions, or feedback actions.

Although decision making is usually considered to be the most critical determinant of organizational success, the training and exercise of people in decision making, especially group decision making, seem to be in short supply as well as very unsystematic.

Aside from decisions that are simply erroneous—wrong or mistaken—the greatest problems arise from decisions that are made without coordination with other people. Additional problems may occur when the activities of other units or impacts of contemplated actions upon other elements are not taken into account during the process of making decisions. The importance of coordination and of coordinative decision making can be imbued only through repeated emphasis during both training and ongoing operations.

Quality Requirements

Some *general* questions for decision making are:

1. Was all relevant available information used in decision making?
2. Were the decisions made at each level correct in view of information available to decision makers?
3. Were decisions timely?

Stabilizing

Stabilizing is the process of adjusting internal operations or internal conditions or of otherwise taking action to maintain stability and functional integration within a unit. The process involves actions taken to forestall potential disruption that might result either from events in the environment or from actions taken within the unit. Thus, Stabilizing decisions and actions are frequently made simultaneously and in connection with major decisions. A division director may make a major operational decision and, at the same time, decide to make adjustments within the organization to counter the turbulence that could be generated by the operational decision and the resulting actions.

Keeping in mind that Integration involves teamwork, Stabilizing includes actions intended to maintain integration and, thus, coordination and teamwork.

Stabilizing is one of the more nebulous, yet one of the more important, processes in the Adaptive-Coping Cycle. It involves most of those activities that usually fall under the rubric of leadership. Whereas the other competence processes are devoted mainly to task or mission-related actions, Stabilizing is concerned with those maintenance activities needed to keep the organization strong, stable, and integrated and, thus, capable of executing and sustaining required operations. Put in the terms of Benne and Sheats (1948), whereas most of the processes are concerned with *task functions*, stabilizing is devoted to *maintenance functions* of the organization.

The premise behind the inclusion of stabilizing as a fundamental organizational function is that, when a system faces and attempts to cope with disrupting events in its environments, internal adjustments may be needed in order to maintain stability and integration within the system. Thus, when a combat unit acts to deal with occurrences on the battlefield, adjustments in internal functioning or internal conditions may also be necessary to preserve unit stability and integrity. Stabilizing is the process by which stability and integration are maintained by the leaders or managers.

Findings in military research and observations in many Army field training exercises suggest that performance of the Stabilizing process may be a major determinant of combat effectiveness. As stated earlier, the activities involved in stabilizing encompass most leadership. However, it appears that, in the heat of an operation, leaders may fail to provide the maintenance functions that might be performed routinely under less stressful conditions. Yet, the maintenance of functional integration may be critical under emergency conditions. The continuance of Stabilizing functions under stressful conditions may be the mark of more effective leaders. The importance of stabilizing is equally notable in corporations and other civilian organizations.

Especially common failures in this area are:

1. Failure to consider the impact of a change in one subsystem upon another subsystem. Because the various parts of an organization tend to be linked, a proposed change in one part should be carefully assessed to ascertain its probable impact upon other parts.
2. Failure to achieve stable change. Where the effects of proposed task-related changes have been assessed, stabilizing actions should be initiated simultaneously with the change in order to avoid negative impacts upon other subsystem and to restabilize relationships between subsystems.

Quality Requirements

Following are some general questions:

1. When decisions were made, were their potential effects upon the organization taken into account, and were actions taken to counter any negative effects or to prevent excessive turbulence in the organization?

2. Were internal operations or organizational arrangements adjusted appropriately to accommodate new decisions, developments, and requirements?
3. Were procedures and practices sufficiently flexible to enable the organization to adjust its activities easily to changed conditions and situations?

Communicating Implementation

This process includes those activities through which decisions and the requirements resulting from decisions are communicated to those individuals or units that must implement the decisions. It is important to note that the process includes the full chain of communication from the original decision maker and planner to units or individuals who must carry out the action.

It goes without saying that initiators of implementing communications should ensure clarity and completeness in their directives, orders, and instructions. In addition, however, the activities of linking individuals are of particular importance in the process. Linking individuals are those individuals at intervening levels who relay instructions between the original decision maker and the people who must ultimately implement the decision. It is incumbent upon these linking individuals to ensure that the intent and sense of the original communication are maintained throughout passage along the entire chain of authority. *The communication links served by intervening organizational levels are hazardous in their potential for distortion and error; however, they are also necessary for the maintenance of coordination and the supervision of operations.*

In addition to the straightforward transmission of directives, orders, and instructions, communicating implementation also includes discussion and interpretation—those communicative acts through which clarification of requirements is achieved and implications for action are discussed. This includes both requests for clarification and responses to such requests, as well as inquiries and responses about implications and consequences of planned activities.

Aborted Decisions

There is considerable evidence that errors, distortions, selective omissions, and outright breakdowns in communications as messages pass down the chain of authority are major causes of failures to implement executive decisions. In one study of military combat units (Olmstead et al., 1973), it was estimated that at least 50 percent of the aborted decisions found for low effectiveness groups were caused by errors, delays, or breakdowns in Communicating Implementation (aborted decisions were those command decisions made but never implemented by subordinate units).

Aborted decisions may occur for either of two reasons. The first arises when there is error, distortion, or breakdown in the communication chain, as discussed above. The second reason for an aborted decision is simple failure to carry out the action by individuals or units at the end of the chain. Such failures to execute may be justified or not; however, the fact remains that, in some organizations, many aborted decisions occur, and such failures to execute required operations contribute heavily to low effectiveness.

Quality Requirements

Some general questions concerning Communicating Implementation are:

1. After decisions, was communication about implementation requirements complete, accurate, and timely?
2. Did all communication links between decision makers and executing personnel function effectively and efficiently?
3. Was everyone informed who should have been informed about implementation decisions and requirements?

Coping Actions

This process is concerned with execution and with how actions are carried out against target environments. The process is primarily concerned with the actual execution of actions at points of contact with the target environments. Although heavily oriented toward the environment, coping actions also include responses to higher-level queries, requests, and requirements, as well as actions or recommendations addressed to higher levels when intended to cope with higher-level requirements or when attempting to obtain some change in a higher-level environment.

Analysis and assessments of organizational competence are always approached from the standpoint of the organizational being analyzed (i.e., from inside the unit under scrutiny). Accordingly, coping actions very often include actions taken in relation to the higher-level environments of the unit (e.g., in the case of task forces, action in response to some request, inquiry, directive, or other action by a Task Force Director). On occasion, such coping actions may be as critical for success as those concerned with contacts with the external world. In all cases, the ability of a unit to cope with the requirements and actions of higher levels may be extremely important to its welfare and its future.

The main consideration in assessing coping actions is execution. How well was the action performed? Was it executed according to the original plan or in accordance with approved modifications to the original directive? What were the effects of changed circumstances on the environment? Was the use of discretion permitted to leaders at the points of contact? Did leaders use discretion? Was the discretion appropriate to the circumstances of the moment? What were the effects of the executed coping action? Were results (including successes, failures, delays) communicated promptly to higher levels?

Questions such as those above get to the heart of some important considerations in the assessment of coping actions, as well as in after-action reviews of training exercises. The problem is that there may be considerable deviation between the formulation of a plan and its execution, and, under some circumstances, deviation may be justified. Mission-type orders are designed to permit reasonable latitude to leaders at the point of action. How much latitude should be permitted, and what circumstances make deviation acceptable? All of the above considerations are important aspects of coping actions and their evaluations.

Quality Requirements

Following are some general questions about Coping Actions:

1. Was execution of actions correct and effective?
2. Were the actions executed in accordance with the intent of the decisions and plans from which they derived?
3. Were all actions leading from decisions actually carried out (i.e., were there any aborted decisions)?
4. What were the effects of distorted or aborted decisions and plans?

Feedback

According to Bennis (1966), for an organization to actively master constantly changing environments, adaptability is an essential attribute. In turn, adaptability depends upon the organization's flexibility, which is "the ability of the organization to learn through experience, to change with changing internal and external circumstances" (p. 52).

Feedback is the process that enables an organization to obtain information about actions taken, their outcomes, and the reasons for them. It is the process whereby an organization evaluates actions taken and learns from them so that changes in its activities can be made and performance may be thus improved.

More specifically, feedback includes those activities that assist the organization to evaluate the results of its actions and provide information about such results to be used in future planning and decision making. They include the process of obtaining feedback about actions taken, but they also include internal efforts to evaluate such actions so that the organization can learn from its successes and mistakes and actions to adjust future activities accordingly.

The essence of the feedback process is conscious and planned efforts to systematically obtain knowledge of results and to use such data as bases for learning to improve operations. There is now considerable evidence that planned, systematic efforts to obtain and use feedback are important elements in organizational improvement.

Thus, the planning of feedback is critical and should be accomplished more or less simultaneously with, or immediately after, the formal planning of operations. Determination of the proper methods for obtaining feedback in a particular exercise or operation may be a critical aspect of feedback planning. Accordingly, special knowledge of feedback techniques may be required.

Like all other processes, feedback is part of a repetitive cycle. Accordingly, feedback activities should be more or less continual efforts that become integral parts of routine activities.

Quality Requirements

Following are some general questions to be asked in considering feedback:

1. Was action taken to obtain information about the outcome of decisions and actions?
2. Was the information that was obtained in follow-up or feedback actions later used to modify operations or to make new plans or decisions?

CRITERIA OF QUALITY

Competence is concerned with the quality of process performance within an organization. Although each process must be performed at least to a minimal degree, the frequency with which the processes are performed does not correlate with effectiveness. The critical requirement is quality (i.e., *how well the processes are performed*). The following specific criteria indicate the qualitative requirements of each process.

1. *Sensing*
   a. Accurate detection of all available information, including active seeking of information from higher and lower levels as well as all other available sources of information.
   b. Correct interpretation of all detected information.
   c. Accurate discrimination between relevant and irrelevant information.
   d. Relevance to mission, task, or problem of all attempts to obtain information.
   e. Accurate and relevant processing of acquired information.
2. *Communicating information*
   a. Accurate transmission of relevant information.
   b. Sufficient completeness in transmission to achieve full and adequate understanding by recipient.

   c. Timely transmission of information.
   d. Correct determination of whether information should be transmitted.
   e. Transmission to appropriate recipients.
3. *Decision Making*
   a. Timeliness of decisions in view of available information.
   b. Correctness of decisions in view of circumstances and available information.
   c. Consideration in the decision process of all contingencies, alternatives, and possibilities.
4. *Communicating implementation*
   a. Accurate transmission of directives, orders, and instructions.
   b. Transmission to appropriate recipients.
   c. Sufficient completeness to communicate adequate and full understanding of actions required.
   d. Timely transmission of directives, orders, and instructions, in view of both available information and the action requirements of recipients.
5. *Actions: Stabilizing, coping, and feedback*
   a. Correctness of action in view of both the operational circumstances and the decision or directive from which the action derives.
   b. Timeliness of the action in view of both the current circumstances and the decision or order from which the action derives.
   c. Correctness of choice of target for the action.
   d. Adequacy of execution of the action.

IMPLICATIONS

Competence depends upon the skills of individuals in acquiring and interpreting information; making choices concerning to whom acquired information is to be communicated, accurately and completely; making decisions concerning ways to cope with unusual or unanticipated situations; and executing actions deriving from such decisions—all performed at high levels of proficiency and coordination.

Of equal importance, the performance of organizational processes is a team product, and much of the quality of process performance depends upon teamwork and the coordination of separate responsibilities and activities. Accordingly, equal to the skills of individuals is what is termed here the integration of structure and function (Chapter 8). This means that the positions, roles, and functions that make up an organizational system must fit together and support each other in their respective activities. Where the integration of structure and function does not occur, there may result missed signals, aborted decisions, overlooked information, and activities at cross-purposes. In the extreme, loss of integration may produce a collapse of essential functions, which can threaten survival of the organization.

For any particular problem, event, or situation, the seven processes that constitute competence are conceived to occur in the sequence that is called the Adaptive-Coping Cycle. Thus, when a problem arises or a change occurs in the environment, the organization first must sense the problem or change, followed by communication of the sensed information, the making of decisions concerning how to cope with the problem or change, and so on through the cycle.

Of course, in actual practice, the cycle is not always so clear-cut or straightforward. It tends to operate erratically, with much redundancy and backtracking at many points. Nevertheless, there is considerable evidence that processes that occur later in the cycle are dependent upon the quality of those that occur earlier (e.g., the quality of decisions depends upon the amount and quality of information available to decision makers, upon the amount and quality of information that has been sensed by various elements of the organization and communicated to decision makers). Similarly, the quality of actions taken to cope with the environment depends upon the character of earlier decisions and the communication used to obtain implementation. This leads to the obvious conclusion that maximum effectiveness requires that all processes be performed equally well. It also means that the correction of dysfunctional processes results in improvement in overall process performance and, therefore, contributes to improved effectiveness.

Chapter 10

A Model for Organizational Effectiveness

An organization is a system of roles, driven and controlled by operational (task) demands and maintained by shared values and norms. To be fully effective, an organization must perform as a unified system that executes competently all of the functions (processes) needed to enable it to adapt to and cope with every condition presented by its environments. Maximally effective performance requires full integration of members' roles, attitudes, and activities.

Each element depends upon and also contributes to the other elements. These reciprocal relationships and activities that contribute to effectiveness are illustrated in Figure 10.1.

Figure 10.1 also shows conditions and activities that are necessary for the development and maintenance of organizational competence and integration. Overall, the figure illustrates the developmental requirements for organizational effectiveness.

AN ORGANIZATIONAL EFFECTIVENESS MODEL

To develop an organization that is fully effective, leadership and training efforts should be addressed to the above elements and relationships. Figure 10.1 shows an Organizational Effectiveness Model that includes both the developmental sequences and the relationships between the elements that appeared in both the Competence Model and the Integration Model discussed in Chapters 8 and 9, respectively.

Organization members plan, supervise, and execute its operations through performance of the several functions (processes) included in the concept of organizational competence. The people in the system have var-

Figure 10.1
Organizational Effectiveness Model

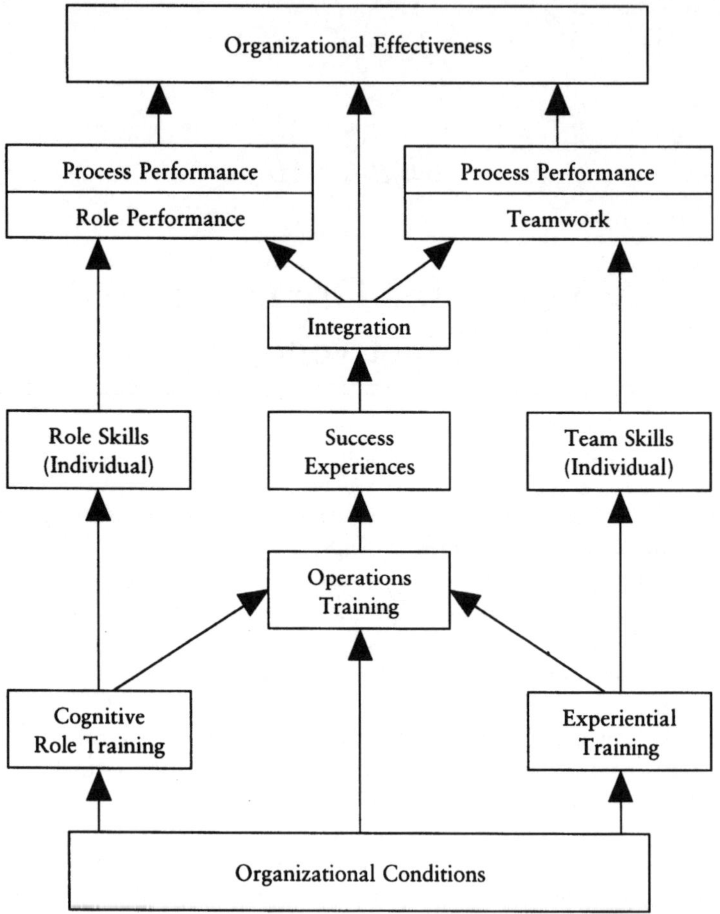

ious motivations and attitudes and perform certain activities (processes) in certain ways. The ways that members perform the processes are, in part, determined by how they perceive the organization, other members, themselves, and their roles; in part, by their motivations; and, in part, by their skills in performing their roles and the processes dictated by role and operational demands.

Organizational Conditions

In Figure 10.1, organizational conditions are shown as the foundation upon which all developmental efforts rest. The sociopsychological conditions within an organization constitute the fundamental context within which all people perform their duties and functions. They sometimes have been called leadership conditions because it is assumed that leaders create and are responsible for the state of such conditions within their organizations.

Regardless of the label given to them, sociopsychological conditions within an organization have been found to exert significant effects upon role performance, integration, and teamwork. Sound and healthy organizational conditions provide a solid underpinning for all efforts to develop and maintain effectiveness. If conditions are not sound and healthy, the likelihood of effectiveness is reduced considerably.

The several critical organizational conditions are discussed in detail elsewhere in this book. Here, it suffices to mention the more essential conditions. The required organizational conditions are:

1. Clearly defined roles for member personnel.
2. Goals that are clear, well defined, and relevant.
3. Norms that are solidified around excellence and organizational pride.
4. Group relations that are amiable, cohesive, rewarding, and cooperative—leading to teamwork.
5. A stable and efficient organizational system.
6. Shared success experiences.

Training Activities

In the Organizational Effectiveness Model depicted in Figure 10.1 organizational conditions are shown to impact upon cognitive role training, experiential training, and operations training, as well as upon performance of the skills that should be produced by such training.

Cognitive Role Training

This type of training involves straightforward instruction designed to inform participants about the requirements and duties of all individuals and roles and, most important, to provide intensive instruction about organizational competence, the organizational processes, and their performance requirements.

As depicted in Figure 10.1, cognitive role training produces the fundamental skills needed by individuals to perform their respective roles. In turn, individual role skills determine the Effectiveness with which each member executes his or her role, including his or her process performance.

Cognitive role training also feeds into operations training by influencing the performance of members' roles during operations training.

Experiential Training

The several kinds of experiential training (practical exercises, simulations, etc.) are designed to provide individuals with practical experience in role performance and in working in team contexts. The products of such training should be reinforced role skills and individual coordinative and team skills. The resultant team skills contribute to teamwork and team process performance.

In addition, the team skills developed by individuals in experiential training should feed into operations training, where team and individual role skills are brought together and practiced.

Operations Training

Here, operations training refers to all types of training in which an organization functions, exercises, and practices *as a unit*, either separately from or together with the remainder of the organization. In such programs, opportunities are provided for practice of role and team skills and, through these common experiences, for the natural development of integration.

Integration

Through the exercise of role and team skills within common settings and through the reinforcement that comes from group success experiences, operations training, when conducted properly, can produce the team norms and values that are essential for the development of Integration. When norms and values for teamwork are highly developed, they serve as melding forces for the integration of structure, function, and roles. They exert strong influences upon the ways that people perform their roles and practice teamwork.

Since Integration derives from the team norms and values held by members, it should be apparent that both individual role performance and team work can be influenced by Integration. Team-oriented values guide the actions of members toward coordinative behavior as they go about performing their respective roles. On the other hand, norms that have developed may serve as behavioral standards for determining when teamwork is required and for enforcing team-oriented behavior.

Role/Process Performance

Figure 10.1 shows that role performance results from individual role skills and integration. Role performance is the execution of the duties and requirements of the several positions that make up a unit. As indicated in Figure 10.1, the extent to which each role is performed is determined by

(1) the skills of the individuals who occupy the several positions and (2) the amount of integration in the organization.

Role performance is manifested, in large part, through performance of the processes that constitute organizational competence. This relationship is shown in Figure 10.1, with process performance leading to organizational effectiveness.

Teamwork/Process Performance

Figure 10.1 shows that teamwork results from (1) the team skills of individuals and (2) the integration existing within the organization. Team skills provide the capabilities, and Integration enhances motivation for teamwork.

As with role performance, teamwork is most often manifested through execution of the processes that constitute organizational competence. *Thus, effectiveness results from (1) performance of organizational processes based upon individual role performance and teamwork and (2) organizational integration.*

Utility of the Model

In summary, Figure 10.1 shows that organizational effectiveness depends upon the following elements:

1. Role skills of individuals—the skills (both technical and process) of individual members in performing their respective roles.
2. Team performance skills of individuals—the skills of individual members in coordinating their activities with those of other members and in contributing to the collective execution of team functions or team-related processes.
3. Integration—the force that melds the roles, attitudes, and activities of personnel and strongly contributes to the maintenance of structure and function within the organization.

It should be apparent that the elements are related. Each depends upon and also contributes to the other elements. These reciprocal relationships and activities that contribute to effectiveness are illustrated in Figure 10.1.

Figure 10.1 also shows conditions and activities required for the development and maintenance of competence and integration. It should be apparent that what is contemplated is a carefully planned and systematic approach to the enhancement of organizational functioning.

Such a functional approach is required because the way in which an organization functions is one of the more important aspects of its capability for survival. Organizational functioning (competence) is the foundation upon which all planning, strategies, and use of resources are built. If an organization does not function well, plans, strategies, and expenditure of resources are futile. Accordingly, organizational functioning is equal to planning, strategies, and use of resources as a critical determinant of effectiveness and survivability. Because of this importance, it is essential that integration and competence be given the same emphasis during training as that for other performance elements.

During training, competence should not be made ancillary to other performance elements. Rather, organizational functioning (competence) should be one direct focus of training and should be a continuing concern during all day-to-day activities of the organization.

Potential Uses

The organizational processes that have been discussed constitute a basic framework for analyzing some of the more intangible but exceedingly important aspects of organizational performance. Use of the framework makes it possible to:

1. Assess the quality of performance of organizations and their subunits;
2. Identify processes that are dysfunctional or poorly performed;
3. Identify strengths and weaknesses in process performance and determine sources of deficiencies;
4. Identify individuals, groups, or units in which process performance requires improvement;
5. In general, assess performance in a manner that produces sound and credible bases for feedback or training;
6. Provides a credible basis for clarifying performance evaluation and developing teamwork within organizations.

IMPROVING COMPETENCE IN EXISTING ORGANIZATIONS

Organizational competence is a concept. It is a way of classifying and systematizing organizational functions that must be performed and of making them more meaningful for everyday application.

The Adaptive-Coping Cycle

It is important to remember that for any particular problem, event, or situation, the seven processes of organizational competence are conceived to occur in the sequence that was described earlier as the Adaptive-Coping Cycle. When a problem arises or a change occurs, the organization must first sense the problem or change, followed by communication of the sensed information, making decisions concerning how to cope with the problem or change, and so on through the cycle.

Analyzing and Assessing Organizational Performance

The analysis and assessment of organizational performance include:

1. Observation of an organization under operational or simulated operational conditions;
2. Identification of trends, consistencies, and critical events in the performance of organizational processes;
3. Making judgments about how well the processes are performed;
4. Identification of reasons and sources of such performance, with special emphasis upon dysfunctional performance.

A General Framework for Analysis

The essential questions to be answered in the analysis of organizational competence are:

1. Overall, in relation to established assessment criteria, how well was each process performed?
2. What were significant instances of dysfunctional performance?
3. What processes, if any, were consistently inadequate? Why?
4. What impact did any noted dysfunctional processes have upon operations and outcomes?
5. Was consistently dysfunctional performance centered in any particular positions or levels in the organization?

To make such judgments, an assessor requires a general framework of questions for addressing what he or she is observing and some specific criteria for evaluating observed processes. Questions to be asked about each process appear as quality requirements in an earlier chapter and are also listed below.

Questions about Organizational Competence

Following are general questions that may be asked about performance of each organizational process.

Sensing

1. Was all information that was available to the organization obtained by it?
2. Were attempts to obtain information relevant and effective?

3. Was acquired information processed, integrated, recorded, and stored so as to have maximum utility?
4. Was correct interpretation placed upon information that was obtained?
5. In view of the information available to the organization, was a correct assessment made of it?
6. Was sensing performed effectively at all levels?

Communicating Information

1. Was information sensed by the organization communicated to all who needed it when they needed it?
2. Was communication of information complete, accurate, and timely?
3. Was communication of information efficient?

Decision Making

1. Was all relevant available information used in decision making?
2. Were the decisions made at each level correct in view of information available to decision makers?
3. Were decisions timely?

Stabilizing

1. When decisions were made, were their potential effects upon the organization taken into account, and were actions taken to counter any negative effects or to prevent excessive turbulence?
2. Were internal operations or organizational arrangements adjusted appropriately to accommodate new decisions, developments, or requirements?
3. Were procedures and practices sufficiently flexible to enable the organization to adjust its activities easily to changed conditions and situations?

Communicating Implementation

1. After decisions, was communication about implementation requirements complete, accurate, and timely?
2. Did all communication links between decision makers and executing personnel function effectively and efficiently?
3. Was everyone informed who should have been informed about implementation decisions and requirements?

Coping Actions

1. Was execution of actions correct and effective?
2. Were the actions executed in accord with the intent of the decisions and plans from which they derived?

3. Were all actions leading from decisions actually carried out (i.e., were there any aborted decisions)?
4. What were the effects of aborted decisions and plans?

Feedback

1. Was action taken to obtain information about the outcomes of decisions or actions?
2. Was information obtained in follow-ups used to modify activities or make new plans or decisions?

Define the Organization

The first step in preparing to make process observations is to identify and define the organization whose processes will be assessed. This is necessary because operational definition of the seven organizational processes requires specific knowledge of the boundaries of the organization to be observed. For example, as an organization, an Army battalion would include all levels, personnel, and units normally included in the entire table of organization, and it would be feasible to conduct a process analysis of the entire unit from highest to lowest grades—if sufficient observers were available. However, much more frequently, process analysis is made of constricted organizations, such as a battle staff (battalion commander, executive officer, staff, and company commanders) or a command group (battalion commander and staff). For the purposes of process assessment, these smaller segments would constitute the organization and the points of interaction between these groups, and higher, lower, and adjacent levels would be the boundaries of the organization to be observed.

Similarly, for civilian organizations, it is possible to analyze an entire complex organization or only smaller segments of it. Naturally, increased size and complexity make assessment more difficult. It is extremely important to carefully define the organization that will be observed and to identify the boundaries of the observed organization. Observations and assessments of processes should be made only within or at the boundaries of the identified organization.

After defining the boundaries of the organization to be observed, *identify all key elements within the organization.* Key elements are positions, people, or units that are focal points in the flow of information, decisions, and actions during operations. Advance identification of probable key elements enables observers to station themselves strategically so as to be more likely to observe critical events and to trace the evolution of processes through the organization.

Identifying the Processes

In order to assess process performance within contexts of actual operations, an observer must be able to see and identify processes as they are occurring. The most difficult problem in assessment is to identify, accurately classify, and judge organizational processes as they occur. This requires translation of the general process definitions that appeared earlier to specific actions relevant for both actual and simulated operations and the ability to discriminate between the different processes.

ASSESSING ORGANIZATIONAL COMPETENCE

In order to assess the competence of an organization, it is necessary for observers or evaluators to make systematic judgments about how well people perform the organizational processes needed to make the unit effective. This assessment provides a manager with important information that is useful in both development and guidance of his or her organization. Operational definitions and criteria are available for use in evaluating the seven processes. However, the only means of becoming highly proficient is practice in observing and assessing actual organizations engaged in real or simulator training. Criteria for assessing process performance follow.

Sensing

1. Accurate detection of all available information.
2. Correct interpretation (attachment of correct meaning) of all detected information, to include appropriate weighting of its importance.
3. Accurate discrimination between relevant and irrelevant information.
4. Attempts to obtain information are relevant to mission, task, or problem.
5. Sensing activities are timely in relation to information requirements and the operational situation of the moment.
6. Internal processing and recording of information provide ready availability to users.

Communicating Information

1. Accuracy of transmission of available information.
2. Sufficiently complete to transmit full and accurate understanding to receivers of communications.
3. Timeliness appropriate to organizational requirements.
4. Correct choice of recipients; everyone who needs information receives it.
5. Whether the message should have been communicated.

Decision Making

1. Adequacy—Was the decision adequately correct in view of circumstances and information available to the decision maker?

2. Appropriateness—Was the decision timely in view of the information available to the decision maker?
3. Completeness—Did the decision take into account all or most contingencies, alternatives, and possibilities?

Stabilizing

1. Adequacy—Action is correct in view of the operational situation and conditions that the action is intended to change or overcome.
2. Appropriateness—Timing is appropriate in view of the situation, conditions, and intended effects. Choice of target of the action is appropriate.
3. Completeness—Action fully meets the requirements of the situation.

Communicating Implementation

1. Accuracy of transmission of instructions.
2. Sufficient completeness to transmit adequate and full understanding of actions required.
3. Timely transmission in view of both available information and the action requirements of the participants.
4. Transmission to appropriate recipients.
5. Discussion and interpretation are efficient and relevant and achieve their purpose.
6. Whether the message should have been communicated.

Coping Actions

1. Correctness of actions in view of both the current operational circumstances and the decision or order from which the action derives.
2. Timeliness of the action in view of both operational circumstances and the decision or order from which the action derives.
3. Correctness of choice of target of the action.
4. Adequacy of execution of action.

Feedback

1. Correctness of the decision and action to obtain feedback in view of operational circumstances, the preceding actions whose results are being evaluated, and current information.
2. Timeliness of the feedback decision and action.
3. Correctness of choice of target(s) of the action.
4. Appropriate use of feedback information in new actions, decisions, and plans.

Qualitative Assessment

Assessment may be either *qualitative* or *quantitative* or both. In assessment that is solely qualitative, observers make judgments about areas of strength or dysfunction, and these analyses are used in after-action reviews and as diagnostic points to be used in planning future training. No numbers are attached to the judgments, and no quantitative comparisons are made. Some examples are, "No efforts were made by any member of the staff to obtain on-the-ground information (Sensing) after receipt of the first directive and prior to initiation of the planned activity, resulting in unwarranted losses because of the lack of knowledge about recent changes in the size and strategy of the competition" or "After the opening of the marketing campaign, notification of decisions made by the director, although appropriate to circumstances, was delayed beyond the time frame within which they would have been maximally effective (timeliness of decision making)" or "The Southeastern Sales Manager failed to stay in contact with Marketing Headquarters (communicating information)."

Quantitative Assessment

In quantitative assessment, observers assign numerical values (scores) to performance on the various processes. Both Process scores and Competence scores (combined process scores) can be derived.

Use of quantitative assessment permits diagnostic comparisons between units or repeated measures of a single unit at different times. Repeated measurement of performance makes it possible to gauge improvements or degradations in performance and helps to keep track of changes or improvements in identified areas of deficiency.

Public Comparisons of Scores between Units Are Not Recommended

Such comparisons may generate unhealthy competition, thus damaging cohesion within the organization. Furthermore, quantitative scores of organizational competence should not be used for evaluation of personnel under any circumstances. Such evaluations would be too threatening and thus destructive to organizational integration.

Under no circumstances should assessment be used for corrective or punitive purposes. Assessment is conceived to be solely a device for development of competence within an organization. An additional use is for pooling the judgments of multiple observers.

An Alternative Procedure

Where observers are not available or where it is desirable to compare members' assessments with observers', an alternative procedure is to obtain members' own assessments. This procedure may be used as an alternative to observer assessment; however, it should be clearly understood that it may not be as accurate as the judgments of trained observers because it represents the personal viewpoints of participants.

The use of pooled (mean) member assessments can be especially useful as the basis for member group discussions of process performance, the discussions to be part of after-action reviews. Data (means) from Member Competence Evaluations can serve as the starting point for group discussions and analyses of ways of improving process performance. Handled properly, the discussion should also enhance integration. In this way, the procedure can serve a highly useful developmental function within an organization.

The Organizational Effectiveness Model shown in Figure 10.1 depicts both relationships and the sequencing of the various elements required for the development of effectiveness. It might be possible to approach effectiveness through simple, random, on-the-job experience; however, the most efficient and most cost-effective way to ensure maximum effectiveness is to develop and train all people in a carefully planned sequence such as that shown in Figure 10.1.

DEVELOPMENTAL ACTIVITIES

Figure 10.1 shows the relationship between necessary organizational conditions and developmental activities and between both and process performance. Here, the discussion is devoted to ways of developing an integrated organization through the enhancement of these two classes of elements: (1) required organizational conditions and (2) required developmental activities.

Developing Favorable Conditions

A full discussion is in Chapter 8. Briefly, those organizational conditions required for effective training and the development of Integration and teamwork are:

1. A clear role system.
2. Shared norms of performance and behavior.
3. Superordinate goals held in common.

4. A reward system for teamwork.
5. A stable and efficient organizational system.
6. Shared success experiences.

These six conditions should be considered the minimum required for development of integration within an organization. Attention to other organizational conditions may help to enhance integration; however, the above six conditions should be considered essential for all developmental efforts.

Teamwork in organizations depends upon the effective performance of role-specific individual skills and team performance skills. Both types of skills are driven and controlled by integration. *That is, in addition to the proficiency of individuals, they depend upon cohesion and coordination.*

Purposes Served by Conditions

1. Clear, superordinate objectives and a meaningful system of rewards focus efforts upon common aims and motivate members to cooperate and coordinate.
2. An efficient organizational system channels motivation to cooperate into effective actions.
3. A stable system provides continuity of participation and, hence, the opportunity to develop shared experiences.
4. Shared experiences of success enhance a positive organization identity.
5. Shared norms of performance and behavior provide standards for action in emergent situations.

Importance of Leadership

In developing an organization, the leader's goals should be the transmission of knowledge, the inculcation of skills, and the cultivation of teamwork. This involves training managers in their respective role requirements while, at the same time, teaching them to concentrate upon solving mutual problems rather than protecting private jurisdictions.

TRAINING ACTIVITIES

The training activities shown in Figure 10.1 serve two purposes. They are used to develop the role-specific skills of individuals and, in addition, they provide the common experiences that are necessary for integration and for teamwork to develop among the members. Accordingly, developmental activities contribute to both organizational competence and integration.

With respect to organizational competence, developmental activities provide straightforward instruction about competence, its elements, and its performance requirements, as well as hands-on practice in process performance. With respect to integration, the developmental activities provide practice in performing within team contexts, common experiences that enhance team identification, and success in performing together as a unit.

The following discussion of the several developmental activities recommended for maximizing organizational effectiveness applies to the development of both organizational competence and integration. It is anticipated that all of the following developmental activities are conducted within an organization as part of its internal training activities.

Special Role Training

This is formal classroom training and should be designed to provide:

1. Knowledge about the framework and functions of the organization.
2. Knowledge about organizational competence, its rationale, and its essential components.
3. Knowledge about each organizational process, its definition, and its general criteria of effectiveness.
4. Knowledge about each role or position, its relation to organizational competence, the processes most likely to be performed in the position, and how they should be performed.
5. Knowledge about teamwork requirements and the organization's expectations about performance as a team.

The preferred method of instruction is lecture-discussion, with the overall objective of providing working knowledge of the real organization and its roles and of organizational competence, its processes, and its effects upon organizational performance. Training to mastery can be accomplished within approximately 15 hours of classroom instruction.

Experiential Training

This type of training is intended to provide practice, feedback, and critique to participants in the performance of their respective roles within a team context. Through such experiences, knowledge obtained in special role training is reinforced and converted to individual role-specific competencies—those skills required by individual members in order for them to contribute effectively to the collective execution of team functions or team processes.

Experiential training should follow special role training and should consist of (1) controlled practical exercises, (2) open-ended practical exercises, and (3) simulations, in that sequence. All experiential training exercises should be designed to accomplish specific instructional objectives. At a minimum, the training plan for each exercise should include:

1. Statement of instructional objectives.
2. Scenario for practical exercise or simulation.
3. Plan for after-action analysis, feedback, and critique.

At a minimum, at least three exercises of each type of experiential training should be administered. Ideally, experiential training should be conducted to mastery of the following instructional objectives:

Each trainee should:

1. Know and be able to perform satisfactorily all role requirements for his or her own position.
2. Know the general role requirements for all other positions in the unit.
3. Be able to perform satisfactorily all coordinative requirements of his or her role.
4. Be able to execute satisfactorily all seven organizational processes, as appropriate for his or her own position.
5. In coordination with all other positions in his or her unit, be able to perform and adapt to requirements of varying task situations as required.

Preferably, experiential training should be conducted in a team context for all members of an operational unit (section, department, division) simultaneously.

Operations Training

The rubric "operations training" is used here to include all types of training in which a unit functions, exercises, practices, and gains experience under realistic conditions *as a unit*, either separately from or together with the remainder of the organization. Thus, operations training may include short exercises, large training exercises, management staff or full unit simulations, and other programs that are designed to provide practice and experience in extended operations. Such programs provide opportunities both for practice of role-specific and team skills and, through common experiences, for the natural development of integration within the organization.

Although some degree of cohesion can develop merely through casual, uncontrolled participation in routine daily operations, maximum integration occurs only when training is carefully planned to emphasize and challenge teamwork and to encourage team identification and cooperative efforts through positive reinforcement of team successes.

Effective operations training should include the following training management activities:

1. Planning Training
   a. Plan operational problems and scenarios that:
      (1) Teach and challenge proficiency.
      (2) Teach and challenge proficiency in organizational competence.
      (3) Challenge and maximize team efforts and teamwork.
   b. Plan systematic procedures for observing individuals and units in operation.
   c. Develop and plan after-action review with feedback and analyses of proficiency, organizational competence, and integration.
2. Conduct Training

   Effective operations training must consist of two activities, and *neither can be effective without the other*:
   a. Conduct of the operation or training exercise.
   b. Systematic observation of focused activities (i.e., of execution, leadership, team effectiveness, process performance, etc.).
3. Conduct feedback and critique based on systematic observation of performance.

   Feedback and critique should be designed and conducted in noncoercive terms to accomplish constructive learning.

IMPROVING COMPETENCE

Although some effectiveness can be achieved solely from training individuals to perform their separate roles (individual, role-specific training) and inculcating requirements of performance as a team member (individual team performance training), the ultimate payoff in integration and effectiveness can be achieved only through experience and practice in performing together under conditions that are conducive to learning. Such conditions include:

1. Opportunities to experience realistically the changing demands of the environment—as they occur (operations training).
2. Opportunities to practice, under realistic and safe conditions, the role and team skills needed to meet the changing demands of the real-life operations (operations training). Realistic conditions are those that generate behavior most like that in the real world. Safe conditions are those in which there is freedom to try new or different behaviors and to make mistakes without fear of punishment.
3. Systematic observation and assessment of performance by personnel who are trained and experienced in the analysis of organizational competence and performance.

4. Learning-oriented, after-action reviews based on observation and assessment, to include noncoercive and nonthreatening feedback, critique, and team analyses of critical events and their implications.

To achieve maximum organizational effectiveness, it is necessary for all members to make the several critical processes fully operational and fully effective. Accordingly, participants must become proficient in performing the processes as required by the mission, the objectives, and the venue in which activities occur.

To make the processes fully operational, it is necessary to determine how each process in the Adaptive-Coping Cycle can be most effective, that is:

1. How each process should be performed,
2. When it should be performed, and
3. Who should perform it.

IMPLICATIONS

The development of an effective organization cannot be accomplished overnight. Organizational integration and competence are developmental processes. They occur over time and most often result from systematic efforts to produce the competence skills and teamwork necessary to function in a unified system.

Organizational competence and integration are not static. They do not "stay put" permanently. New leaders, personnel losses, successes, failures, and changed situations—all tend to bring about changes in daily practices and in the norms and functional relationships that hold an organization together. Accordingly, developing and maintaining a strong organization must be a constant leadership endeavor.

It is important to recognize that competence, to include the processes discussed here, is an attribute of an organization, not of roles or of individuals. This fact is important because it governs how one views an organization and whether performance is analyzed, assessed, and developed as an attribute of individuals, groups, or entire units. On the one hand, if a leader views process performance as an attribute of individuals or of particular roles (positions), he or she may devote all of his or her efforts to individual training. On the other hand, if he or she recognizes that performance of processes is an attribute of organizations, he or she will devote his or her efforts to development of a unified system.

Organizational competence represents capability of the organization and is different from individual capabilities. Although most often performed by single individuals, processes involve organizational responses, and the quality of any single response event is determined by the entire network of antecedent relationships and responses. Thus, competence and integration can best be improved by efforts that focus upon developing the organization to function as a system.

What is contemplated here is a full-scale development and training program spread over several years with intermittent training episodes and continuous developmental activities. It is important to acknowledge the complexity of the activities recommended in this chapter and to recognize the administrative difficulties in implementing them. However, the value of such a program makes the effort and cost worthwhile.

Chapter 11

Elements of Organizational Effectiveness

THE CONTEXT OF WORK

In recent years, the importance of the environment within which people work has become increasingly apparent. More and more, one finds in literature concerning organizations such terms as "organizational culture," "company personality," and "psychological climate" to describe the overall context within which people work; and, more and more, research has demonstrated that the work environment exerts a major impact upon the performance, attitudes, and motivations of people who are employed in organizations.

The individual's environment includes his or her job, which may be either stultifying or stimulating; fellow workers, whose acceptance he or she is likely to strongly desire; the immediate supervisor, who may either watch him or her closely or trust him or her to get things done on his or her own; financial administrators, who may think of him or her either as an independent economic person working solely for money or as a more complex creature with social as well as financial needs; and top managers, who may unknowingly be guided by numerous preconceived notions about what he or she is like and wants. The whole complex of factors impinges on the individual at every moment, shaping his or her actions and attitudes and the motivations that he or she may carry with him or her throughout his or her career (Senn and Childress, 1999; Harris and Moran, 2000).

The individual is not altogether a victim of this environment but is able to exert some control on how it affects him or her. However, a major finding of those who have been studying the impact of work contexts is that all too often the environment does dominate a person by blocking his or her motivations and driving him or her into a sort of stubborn, foot-dragging negativism. This result does not always occur by intent or even by default of organizational managers. For example, it has been found that actions taken to simplify management controls or to improve efficiency have often been accompanied by a drop in motivation among employees. Thus, management actions that are not at all intended to affect motivation do, in fact, have a definite motivational impact. Frequently, it is a negative impact.

Of course, many conventional administrative practices may exert a positive impact on an individual's desire to handle his or her job properly. Sound salary and benefit programs, sensitive and appropriate supervisory methods, two-way communication systems, and procedures for recognition and promotion are all examples of traditional ways of motivating employees that can be quite effective. It is clear that factors in the work environment can have either positive or negative impacts upon performance and attitudes.

Through its effects upon the perceptions and motivations of people, the work context especially influences such aspects as job performance of individuals and groups, attitudes toward the organization, interdepartmental relationships, communication practices, decision-making processes, and ability of the organization to function flexibly in response to rapidly changing work requirements.

Components of the Work Context

The importance of the work context to both individual and organizational effectiveness can no longer be denied. Although the abilities and personal characteristics of individuals contribute significantly to performance, more and more evidence indicates that the conditions surrounding these individuals frequently make a difference. Accordingly, it is important to understand the components of the work context and the ways in which it both derives from and impacts upon the functioning of an organization.

The overriding concept of organization escapes any precise or all-inclusive definition. To many people, "organization" means something that is drawn on charts and recorded in manuals and that describes jobs or specific responsibilities. Viewed in this way, "organization" takes on the aspect of a series of orderly cubicles contrived according to some rational logic. Such a view is useful for clarifying duties and responsibilities but, taken alone, is not sufficient for fully understanding a living, functioning entity that we call an organization.

For this book, the term *organization* refers to the complex network of relationships among a number of people who are engaged in some activity for some reason, where the activity requires a division of work and responsibility in such a manner as to make the members interdependent. The clumsiness of this definition is only partly a matter of syntax. The fact is that only such a general statement can possibly embrace the varied forms of organizations encountered in the real world.

Two aspects of the definition warrant particular emphasis: an organization engages in activities for some reason—that is, it has goals that must be attained; the pursuit of these goals establishes relationships between individuals and subunits that give the organization its bonds of identity and interdependence.

These aspects coincide with Barnard's (1938) important distinction between effectiveness (goal achievement) and efficiency (internal working relationships). The rational, formal, task-centered aspect is mainly concerned with what is loosely called the structure of an organization—that framework of roles resulting from the allocation of authority, responsibility, and duties as usually depicted in an organization chart and reflecting the formal bonds that tie the organization together. Closely related to structure are certain processes that function through it and make it viable, namely, authority and influence. Since structure is the principal mechanism for channeling the activities of members in the direction required by the organization, it is a critical component of the work context.

The relationship, motivational, maintenance aspect is concerned with the climate of an organization—the atmosphere that is peculiar to it and that reflects and determines its internal state and characteristic ways of working. Factors contributing to climate are such things as goals, policies, constraints, cohesion, relationships within and between work groups, leadership, and communication practices.

Taken together, structure and climate constitute the environment within which the work of an organization is accomplished. They play essential roles in channeling activities and mobilizing the efforts of the members.

Developing Favorable Work Contexts

The preceding definition of organization suggests that the rational, formal, procedural, task-centered aspect of organization must be reconciled with the relationship, motivational, maintenance aspect. Only by giving equal attention to both aspects is it possible to gain control over all of the factors that contribute to effective organizational performance.

Structural Aspects

Attention to structural aspects is necessary for at least two reasons. First, an effective structure, including concomitant processes of authority and control, is essential for operational efficiency. When circumstances or inclination dictates a disregard for structural considerations, chaos is the usual result. Second, a poorly designed system tends to create frustration and conflict. Excessive interference with work activities because of breakdowns in the system can be as devastating to motivation as inadequate working conditions or poor personnel policies. This is important because of its multiplying effects upon attitudes. People get frustrated and angry with one another when they have difficulties in doing their jobs.

Climate

The necessity for attention to climate is even more obvious. Climate is the atmosphere within an organization that results from customary ways of working. It pervades every aspect of an organization and exerts some astounding effects upon the motivations, satisfactions, and performance of its members. Stated very generally, climate is the motivational aspect of organization and, because motivation is critical, the elements that contribute to climate can be disregarded only at severe risk.

In many organizations, the most common attempts to improve Effectiveness take the form of modifications of the structural framework—that is, reorganization—and of increased emphasis upon the more formalized organizational constraints, such as policies and procedures. Attention to these aspects is important; however, overreliance upon them leads to organizational rigidity. Effectiveness under the complex conditions of today requires flexibility, a quality that has its principal source in the relationships, motivations, commitments, and loyalties of people. These aspects are mainly determined by the climate within the organization.

Emphasis upon both structure and climate is required, with maintenance of a reasonable balance between the two. Achieving balance between the two aspects is not easy. However, many executives find ways of reconciling the conflict between them and of developing practices that incorporate both.

Conditions Conducive to Performance

It has sometimes been said that the proper function of an executive is to orchestrate the application of the skills and energies of his or her people to solutions of problems larger than any of them could handle separately. "Orchestrate" suggests many critical activities; however, above all others, the term implies the necessity to provide conditions conducive to effective performance of organizational members. Some principal conditions necessary for effective performance were listed in Chapter 8. They are repeated here because of their special relevance for this discussion:

Factors that enhance proficiency

- Effective structure and job design.
- Efficient procedures and practices.
- Excellent training for both personnel and leaders.

- Communication practices that supply each individual with information and knowledge necessary for intelligent performance of duties.

Factors that enhance motivation

- A system that makes careful provision for incentives, reward, and approval of good performance.
- Procedures that make information about individual and group progress available to personnel.
- Opportunity for individuals and groups to experience success in performance of tasks.
- Opportunities for challenge and growth for each individual.
- Opportunities for optimum independence in the performance of jobs.

Factors that promote a common desire to belong to the organization and identify with it

- Good administrative, supervisory, and leadership practices at all levels.
- Good working conditions and good equipment.
- Opportunity for each individual to perform as a conscious member of a larger whole.
- Means of providing occasional explicit acknowledgment of organizational progress to all members and of recognition of the shared responsibility of such progress.
- Opportunities for people to influence decisions about matters that affect them.

Implementation Requirements

Careful scrutiny of these conditions reveals that they encompass a wide range of elements. These varied elements must be brought together in such a manner that the result contributes to, and does not impede, organizational effectiveness. The problem of developing effectiveness in an organization is one of making a functioning, operational system out of available human and material resources. Viewed as a system, an organization must be capable of performing more or better than all of the resources that constitute it. It must be a genuine whole, greater than the sum of its parts, with its total performance more than the sum of its individual efforts.

FACTORS THAT CONTROL PERFORMANCE

An organization is not just a mechanical assemblage of resources. To make a functioning entity from a collection of people, buildings, and equipment, it is not enough to put them together in some logical form and then to issue a directive for work to begin. What is needed is a transformation of the resources. This cannot come merely from a directive. It requires large doses of leadership of the highest quality.

Effective Use of Human Resources

The only resources within an organization capable of transformation are human resources. Money and materials are depleted. Equipment is subject to the laws of mechanics; it can be used well or badly but can never perform more efficiently than it was originally designed to do. Only humans can grow and develop. Therefore, it is essential that this resource be used as fully and as effectively as possible.

Effective utilization requires the organization of duties and functions so that they are the most suitable for the capabilities of people in the light of organizational goals and requires the mobilization of everyone so as to elicit the most productive and effective performance from them. It requires recognition of the organization's members as a resource, that is, as having properties and limitations that require the same amount of maintenance and attention as any other resource. It also requires recognition that the human resource, unlike other resources, consists of people who possess citizenship, legal status, personalities, emotions, and control over how much and how well they perform. Therefore, they require incentives, rewards, satisfactions, stimulation, inspiration, and consideration.

Not to recognize these requirements can lead to serious interference with organizational effectiveness by creating such problems as failures to set performance goals; breakdowns in communication; conflict, strife, and competition between individuals or groups; low morale; and poor discipline. The sources of such problems are likely to be diffuse and quite complex and may be traced to any or all of an array of factors, including working conditions, superior–subordinate relationships, communication, operational inefficiency, or just about any other condition related to life within an organization. The major point of this discussion is that many such problems have their sources in the failures of organizational leaders to provide work-context conditions that are most conducive to effective performance. Furthermore, if one examines the above-listed conditions closely, it becomes apparent that all are dependent upon three general factors that control performance in every organization: effective management, effective leadership, and effective training.

Effective Management

Management is the development and application of the proper procedures for allocating and using the resources, both human and physical, of the organization.

Management encompasses all of the efforts required to mobilize the energies of an organization toward attainment of its goals. It involves those planning, decision-making, guiding, controlling, and implementing activities necessary to gather, integrate, and coordinate resources of the organization (Drucker, 1999, 2001).

Organizations run a wide gamut of goals, sizes, activities, personnel, and geographical dispersion. The peculiar nature of each organization determines to some extent the specific problems encountered. Usually, this requires that managers be concerned with particular cases and with diagnosing problems and taking actions to improve unique situations.

Carried to the extreme, an insistence on the specificity of problems would render hopeless any attempt to obtain a prior understanding of factors that affect organizational functioning. The saving element is that the problems all occur *in organizations*. Whatever their specific nature, all organizations possess certain common properties that can be manipulated, and, when problems arise, their identification in relation to basic organizational properties makes possible more insightful and lasting solutions (see Chapter 2).

Differences between organizations occur because of variations in the form and degree of these properties and in the specific configurations that evolve because of particular goals, tasks, and circumstances. However, every organization possesses the properties in some form and to some degree. Taken together, they constitute a foundation upon which developmental efforts can be based.

This fact leads to a fundamental conclusion. The essence of administering an organization is not so much a matter of solving individual problems as of achieving some measure of integration among its many elements. Furthermore, management of an organization imposes a major responsibility for creative action. It cannot be just passive reaction to problems as they occur; it goes beyond merely fighting fires that arise within the organization. This means taking action to make the desired results come to pass. An executive must take the necessary steps to shape his or her organization; to plan, initiate, and carry through changes in its structure and climate; and to constantly push back the limitations that human fallibility tends to place upon its capacity to perform more effectively.

Regardless of the type and size of an organization, the chief executive must make sure that goals are established, plans are made, policies are developed, and people are recruited, assigned, and trained. He or she must establish levels of responsibility, set up mechanisms of coordination, delegate authority, direct subordinates, provide stimulation and inspiration to everyone, exercise control, develop high levels of motivation and morale, and adjust the plans and activities of his or her organization to broader changes in government, the society, and the community.

If these activities are not performed well, the organization does not function effectively. Any organization is built from the top down. The thinking, ideas, and behavior of the chief executive spread out to include his or her close subordinates and are translated into a variety of specific actions and patterns of behavior throughout the organization. If the original ideas or actions of the manager are unsound, the trends in thinking and action that permeate the organization are likely to be wrong. If the basic thinking is sound, this is reflected throughout the organization.

In particular, some broad decisions—or lack of such decisions—concerning the way the organization is operated have significant effects upon the behavior patterns that develop at lower levels. The executive who decides to operate his or her organization along mechanical principles—through stress upon regulations, standardization, and procedures—produces communication patterns, administrative attitudes, and supervisory behavior that reflect this attitude. If he or she places stress upon people and relationships to get the job done, rather than upon the mechanics of operations, this emphasis is reflected throughout the organization. He or she consequently develops in his or her organization a totally different approach to work, to subordinates, and to customers or clients.

Much of this book has stressed the importance of human factors in organizational effectiveness. Recognition of the importance of human factors leads to the conclusion that top management has a responsibility for doing certain things that ensure the effectiveness of the organization's human resources. Some of the specific conditions that lead to effectiveness were listed in the preceding section. However, above all of the requirements is one overriding premise: What attracts people most strongly to any organization and maintains their feeling of well-being while working in it are their faith in the common purpose, faith in the leadership, and faith in each other.

Faith in the purposes and leadership of an organization depends upon the integrity of decisions that managers make about goals, operations, and the internal human affairs of the organization. The human affairs aspect requires that managers be chosen with due regard for both their ability and their character, particularly from the standpoint of human values. It also requires that the top management, in its policies and practices, be concerned with personnel matters and make decisions supportive of members, thus confirming in this broad way its concern for the welfare of individuals associated with the organization.

It is an advantage to have people who are well motivated and generally satisfied with the organization. It is desirable from the standpoint of the organization that the experiences of people on their jobs and in their work environment be good, not bad. It is only realistic to recognize that neither all experiences nor all aspects of a work environment are always exactly as every employee would prefer them. However, it is important for employees that their lives at work make sense in terms of their own interests and abilities, because people's attitudes and motivations are largely shaped by the meaning that they get from their experiences and the experiences of their friends and acquaintances.

This suggests that personnel administration and leadership must be considered integral and important aspects of general management. The successful incorporation of the human factor into management at all levels seems to be desired by employees, many managements, and society at large. It also suggests that managers have a responsibility to wisely handle the human, as well as the operational, aspects of their roles. This realization is becoming more widespread, although there seems to be continuing confusion in many organizations as to precisely what this means and how to accomplish it.

One far from satisfactory answer must be that there does not appear to be any one formula or set of formulas that provides ready-made solutions to the problem of developing a constructive work context. A constructive work context is usually the result of careful and calculated developmental efforts by an enlightened management over a considerable period. Someone has said that the essential difference between an effective manager and an ineffective one is that the effective manager thinks of today's actions in terms of tomorrow's objectives, while the ineffective manager takes each event as it comes without concern for tomorrow. Nowhere is this statement more relevant than with regard to development of a constructive work context.

Effective Leadership

Without a doubt, the quality of leadership available at all levels determines the character of the work context of an organization. Leadership is an influence process, and the influence exerted by leaders may have either constructive or destructive effects upon the environment of work.

An important step for a manager is recognition that both job satisfaction and motivation depend primarily and almost entirely upon the leadership in the organization. The leaders at all levels control conditions that make for good or poor motivation and satisfaction. As one example, a key element in a climate of good human affairs is the same degree of integrity in small, day-to-day actions concerning any single employee anywhere in the organization as in top-level decisions about large programs that affect many employees.

The fact that leaders at all levels control the work context suggests the necessity for a top manager to develop high-quality subordinates and to insist upon good leadership practices at each and every level from the lowest supervisor up to, and including, the chief executive. He or she must demand the same degree of competence and integrity in lower-level actions as in his or her own behavior.

Directives and training programs that emphasize good leadership are valuable for communicating the importance placed upon it by a chief executive. However, they alone are not sufficient to produce it throughout an organization. If good leadership practices are to be attained, the reward system in the organization must be geared to this goal. High-quality leadership develops when high-quality leaders are the ones who are rewarded. Building a reward system is a basic step toward establishing a climate conducive to motivation and satisfaction.

Of at least equal importance is what is done by top managers themselves in creating a climate favorable to good leadership practices. There is overwhelming evidence that the kinds of supervisory practices in an organization are likely to follow closely the pattern set by those individuals in higher levels of management. The supervisor tends to offer his or her people the style of leadership that he or she experiences from his or her own superiors. This applies equally to all levels in organization. Through his or her own leadership practices and those that he or she emphasizes throughout the organization, the top executive can influence those low-level leaders who exercise the most potent effects upon satisfaction, motivation, and performance.

At any level, sound leadership is not just a matter of hunch or native skill; its fundamentals can be analyzed, organized systematically, and learned by most individuals with normal abilities. Yet, taken alone, no amount of knowledge improves insight and judgment or increases ability to act wisely under conditions of responsibility.

This raises a series of questions about the abilities needed in order to function effectively as a leader. For example, how aware is a leader of the emotional and motivational conditions of the various groups and individuals—conditions that he or she must take into account in making decisions? Is he or she able to gather relevant and accurate information about the internal conditions of the organization? How competent is he or she in observing, talking with, and listening to the people with, and through whom, he or she must work? Is he or she able to translate his or her ideas for leading the organization into actions consistent with these ideas? How sensitive is he or she in determining whether to intervene in activities of the organization? Is he or she skillful in providing the necessary guidance to subordinates in such a manner that motivation and performance are not damaged? How well can he or she pick out the essential elements in leadership problems and then supply actions appropriate to the demands of the situation?

Answers to questions such as these have an important bearing upon leader performance. One would hope for a set of rules that equip an executive or supervisor to cope with the complex leadership problems that he or she faces. Unfortunately, no such rules exist because human behavior occurs in specific situations that have endless variety. Each situation is new, requiring imagination, understanding, and skillful actions.

A leader must be concerned with assessing events and finding appropriate courses of action. What is needed is not a set of rules but good skills both in diagnosing situations and in acting appropriately within them. If a leader has a framework of ideas in mind as a working guide, diagnosis shows him or her where the limits lie. He or she can then take the appropriate actions.

As one noted writer on administration has put it (Urwick, 1957), effectiveness is control over environment. An effective organization is a unified system equipped with the knowledge and skills to control its environment, while an ineffective organization, for the lack of such capabilities, remains subject to forces over which it can exert little control. Similarly, an effective leader understands the organization of which he or she is a part and the forces by which it is moved, while the ineffective leader is the plaything of arbitrary and capricious powers acting beyond the range of his or her limited understanding.

Thus, understanding appears to be one vital key. Executives and supervisors become effective leaders by understanding what is required of them, and how, in any organization, human forces such as those discussed in this book may be combined, balanced, and directed toward the ultimate goals.

Effective Training

A third element that contributes to the proficiency of an organization is effective training. A variety of terms has been used to describe efforts designed to upgrade proficiency. However, for this discussion, the term *training* is preferred in order to emphasize a point to be mentioned here and elaborated later. What appears to be needed at all levels in most organizations are systematically provided experiences specifically designed to develop hard skills related to actual job requirements—in short, training.

It is important to distinguish between the concept of *training* and the concept of *education* (McClelland and Lyons, 1968). Both terms are often wrongly applied to the process of human learning with little differentiation. Training is any set of more or less formally organized learning experiences designed to prepare an individual to perform certain acts specifiable in advance. If these acts cannot be specified, for whatever reason, a set of similarly organized learning experiences is called "education." In the case of training, learning can be sharply focused on later job behaviors. In the case of education, the learning experience must be devoted to providing an individual with a background of general knowledge and attitudes relevant to broad requirements that may be imposed following learning.

What is advocated here is training—the development of concrete skills designed specifically to upgrade proficiency in jobs relevant to the mission of the organization. In many organizations, training is not given much attention; in others it is not very effective. In many small organizations, where it is usually needed most, no training is conducted at all.

Most often, the state of training within an organization is almost solely determined by the amount of emphasis placed upon it by the chief executive. If the top manager values high-quality training, he or she usually finds ways of getting it accomplished. If training is regarded as merely another item of overhead, to be conducted in spare time as an added duty for some already overburdened functionary, poor results are likely to be obtained.

Unfortunately, all too often training is viewed as undesirable overhead and is the first activity to be dropped when funds are low. De-emphasis on training as a means of cost reduction is especially shortsighted because it is at precisely the point when funds are short that the productivity of employees needs to be raised. Training is one of the few ways in which this can be readily accomplished.

Efficient and effective training can contribute to organizational effectiveness in at least the following ways:

- Reducing overhead and direct costs by decreasing the time necessary to perform operations effectively and the time required to bring inexperienced employees to full productivity.
- Reducing the costs of personnel administration by creating a climate that orients employees toward high performance.
- Reducing the costs of administration as reflected in turnover, absenteeism, grievances, and complaints.
- Reducing costs by improving the flow of work.
- Decreasing the costs of administration by reducing need for low supervisor–worker ratios through increasing the proficiency of workers.
- Upgrading the quality of products or services by increasing the proficiency of workers.

To be fully effective, the training program of an organization should be a full-time responsibility for at least one fully qualified individual and should cover the full spectrum of jobs. Effective training cannot be achieved through part-time efforts or when training positions are viewed either as sinecures for worn-out employees or dead-end jobs for members who have failed elsewhere. Training is a complex endeavor that requires a high level of specialized knowledge and sophistication to be effectively managed and conducted.

In many organizations, training specifically designed to develop knowledges and skills concerned with supervision and leadership is especially needed. Many managers are professionally educated, but the courses that they take are not noted for their emphasis upon leadership. What is more, all of the accumulated knowledge about human behavior and social processes is not sufficient to equip an individual to be a good supervisor. He or she needs excellent training specifically designed to develop hard supervisory and leadership skills that have been scientifically confirmed as relevant for effective performance in real-life situations.

The implications for organizational effectiveness are clear. Employees need the skills to perform their jobs proficiently, and they also need good leadership. Both of these requirements can be met through effective training. In company with management and leadership, excellent training is one of the most important contributors to development of a constructive work context and, therefore, to organizational effectiveness.

IMPLICATIONS

It has become axiomatic that human factors must receive full recognition in any reasonable consideration of organizational effectiveness. However, in attempts to do something about the human element, the most common approach is to focus upon the characteristics, skills, and deficiencies of individuals. This approach most often leads to emphasis upon selection procedures, performance evaluations, interviews, remedial training, and so forth. These and other such activities that focus upon individuals are important and, indeed, essential for upgrading or maintaining the proficiency of an organization.

On the other hand, it is unreasonable to consider people without recognizing the impact of their environment upon them. People function within situational contexts, and these contexts define and limit behavior. An organization is a very important context and, accordingly, produces potent forces that circumscribe and channel the activities, attitudes, and motivations of people. For this reason, both individual behavior and group behavior within an organization are simply not the same outside it. This fact can never be safely ignored.

The importance of the work context to effectiveness cannot be overemphasized. The environment within which people work has come to be recognized as probably the single most critical determinant of performance. Although the abilities and personal characteristics of individuals contribute significantly to their performance, more and more evidence indicates that the conditions surrounding these individuals frequently make the difference. It is universally acknowledged that elements that compose the work context warrant the critical attention of responsible administrators, whatever the nature of their organizations.

Chapter 12

Summary and Conclusions

In this book we attempt to accomplish three purposes:

1. To set forth a sound, research-based conceptual framework for understanding and addressing organizational functioning and its relation to organizational effectiveness. After a review of relevant literature in Chapter 3, a conceptual model centered around the rubric *organizational competence* is evolved, and tests of it are reported (Chapter 4). Findings are conclusive that processes identified in the model are strongly related to the effectiveness of organizations.
2. To develop a concept embracing the maintenance of both structure and function under heavy stress. Together with organizational competence, this melding of structure and function constitutes Integration. A model for Integration is derived and evaluated.
3. To provide practitioners (managers, leaders, trainers, and performance analysts) with guidance for developing and directing effective organizations. Chapter 5 presents a practical rationale for understanding organizational functioning. Models outline the various elements that should be taken into account and controlled in order to improve performance (Chapters 6, 8, 10).

This final chapter presents a concise general framework for addressing problems of organizational performance and a summary of the elements involved in effectiveness. The concept of organization that is presented is anchored squarely in Open Systems Theory; however, it also has roots in the social psychology of organizations. This makes it possible to incorporate in a meaningful way elements from many sources—when it makes sense do so. The concept of Integration is derived mainly from small-group theory and research and is also anchored in Open Systems Theory.

SOME BASIC CONCEPTS

A main unit of analysis is a human organization (referred to as "an organization") existing in physical and social environments over time. Social environment refers to those elements external to the organization in which there are other people (e.g., higher levels, adjacent units, competition). A human organization is a complex network of relationships among a number of people who are engaged in some activity for some purpose where the activity requires a division of effort and responsibility in such a manner as to make the members interdependent.

The people in the above definition are physical organisms and psychological processes. Relationships among people are states in which the activity state and psychological state of one person are in a condition of mutual influence with those of another person. A network of relationships is an abstraction of the relationships among a number of persons. The influence of a person is a function of his or her psychological properties (personality) and the properties of the coordinating and decision-making roles (rank, position) that he or she is assigned.

The boundary of an organization may be established by several means. Relative autonomy is one means of establishing boundaries. Another means is purpose and perceived membership. For military units, the existence of a commanding officer may be considered to define an independent organizational unit.

Purpose is defined as the relationship of the organization to the external physical and social environment. The assignment of a mission or objectives may be considered to indicate the existence of a purpose.

The mode of organization is, in part, determined by the elements of purpose; that is, the mission dictates the method of distribution and execution of problem-solving, decision-making, and action functions (task organization). The distribution of the above functions and the assignment of authority and responsibility to go with them define the formal structure of the organization. The functions are arranged and systematized on the basis of ideas as to how they should be effectively performed and logically coordinated—on the basis of the logics of organization.

Organizational Effectiveness

Organizational effectiveness is the accomplishment of missions or the achievement of objectives. Whatever its mission, the effectiveness of an organization requires that it efficiently identify, assess, solve, and cope with events or problems that arise within its operational environments. These are the classical functions of all organizations, and performance of them has always been critical for organizational success.

It is now clear that functional proficiency and the integration of structural and functional systems play important roles in the performance of all organizations. Three separate research studies (Olmstead and Elder, 1980; Olmstead, Elder, and Forsythe, 1978; Olmstead et al., 1973) demonstrated conclusively the importance of Battle Staff Competence to the effectiveness of military ground tactical units. In two nationwide studies of city and county social welfare agencies (Olmstead and Christensen, 1973; Olmstead et al., 1975), organizational competence was found to be closely related to effectiveness in both large and small civilian organizations. For both studies of civilian organizations, Integration (cohesion) was found to be related to organizational effectiveness.

In this regard, it is important to note that the above studies showed that Integration alone does not produce effectiveness. It only supports and sustains competence, which is qualitative proficiency in the performance of critical organizational functions.

On the other hand, competence without Integration can be a very tenuous attribute, subject to dissolution by all of the tensions and pressures that may arise from highly turbulent and stressful environmental conditions. Both competence and integration are essential for maximum organizational effectiveness.

Organizations as Open Systems

It is useful to consider an organization as an open system. The basic notion of a system is that it is a set of interrelated parts. Implicit in the concept is a degree of wholeness that makes the whole something different from, and more than, the several parts considered individually and summatively.

One of the most significant ways in which the systems concept is useful is in the consideration of subordinate units as the parts of a system. This includes such units as departments, sections, divisions, crews, and teams that appear on the conventional organization chart. Also included are staff sections, ad hoc committees, boards, and other groups that may have official or semiofficial status but are frequently not shown on the chart.

Thinking of an organization as a system offers many benefits. Two, in particular, have special relevance. First, it focuses on the relatedness of activities carried on by different individuals and units, and it emphasizes the fact that, to meet the specific requirements of a particular mission, each of the subunits of an organization must receive as careful attention in its preparation and during its operations as does the overall organization. This is important because each part of a system affects and is affected by every other part.

Second, thinking of an organization as an open system focuses attention upon its interaction with its environments and, more important, upon the processes involved in adapting to and coping with changes in the environments. When made operational, such processes provide a powerful means for using systems concepts to assess and improve organizational performance.

Systems Theory embraces a much more comprehensive set of concepts than is possible to cover here; however, a brief review of Bennis's abbreviated approach (Chapter 5) provides insight into the application of Systems Theory to any organization. According to Bennis (1966), successful organizations need three basic attributes:

1. *Reality testing*—the capacity to test the reality of situations facing the organization—the ability of the organization to search out, accurately perceive, and correctly interpret the properties and characteristics of its environments (both external and internal), particularly those properties that have special relevance for the operations of the organization. In short, every organization must have the capability for accurately determining the real conditions within its important environments. Reality refers to the way conditions are, not how they are supposed to be or how they are desired to be.
   To survive, every organization must have structures and processes that enable it to assess the reality demands of its particular environments.
   Reality Testing involves the Competence processes of Sensing, Communicating Information, and Feedback.
2. *Adaptability*—the capability for solving problems arising from changing environmental demands and to act with flexibility in response to the changing demands. *Each organization must have structures and processes that enable it to mobilize the necessary and appropriate resources for adapting to and overcoming changes in its environments. Adaptability involves the competence processes of decision making, Communicating Implementation, and coping (executing).*
3. *Sense of identity*—knowledge, insight, and a reasonable consensus on the part of organizational members regarding organizational objectives, missions, and the functions necessary for accomplishment of objectives and missions. In terms of the models proposed in this book, this concept leads to Integration, which is defined as the maintenance of structure and function under stress and a state of relations among subunits that ensures that coordination is maintained and that the various subunits do not work at cross-purposes. *Integration derives from a sense of identity. During operations, integration involves the competence process of stabilizing but is mainly developed from experiences occurring during training and from previous success experiences.*

Bennis's concepts above can be applied to any organization, regardless of type. These concepts, together with the processes derived from them, can be the starting point for understanding and improving the functioning of an organization.

Organizational Competence

The concept of *organizational competence* is a key element in this book. The concept derives from the analysis of Open Systems Theory and concepts in Chapter 5, especially those of Bennis (1966) and Schein (1965, 1970). It also derives from recognition that one of the most critical factors in the effectiveness of any organization is to sense impacting events in its external and internal environments, to process the information sensed, and to adapt its operations to cope with the sensed changes.

The ability of an organization to perform these critical functions is what is meant by organizational competence. It is the capability of an organization to cope with the continuously changing demands of its critical environments.

It is further conceived that organizational competence is the major operational determinant of organizational effectiveness. Where effectiveness is the ultimate outcome (mission accomplishment, achievement of objectives, productivity, etc.), Competence is the capability of the organization to perform the critical functions (processes) that lead to achievement of effectiveness.

Competence as Flexibility

By now, it should be apparent that what is being discussed throughout this book is organizational flexibility. The crux of organizational competence is adaptability—and adaptability depends upon the capability of the organization to readily modify its operations as required by changes in its objectives, its missions, and its environments, (i.e., its flexibility).

Many organizations are so bound by plans or procedures that they cannot efficiently or effectively modify activities to meet changed operational requirements. Efficient and effective performance of the processes subsumed under organizational competence makes it possible for an organization to readily adapt to changed or new requirements.

The turbulent and unpredictable environments that are characteristic of the present and anticipated for the future place a premium upon the capability of organizations to respond flexibly to a more or less constant flow of situations of uncertainty. Under such conditions, organizations must possess capabilities for searching out, accurately identifying, and correctly interpreting the properties of operational situations as they develop. They must also have capabilities for solving problems within the context of rapidly changing situational demands, for generating flexible decisions to cope with these situations, and for reacting to shifting situational requirements with precise appropriateness.

This emphasis upon organizational responses to problem situations points up the role of the organization as problem solver, decision maker, and action taker. Although individual members actually perform the decision-making and action-taking activities, the necessity for global organizational responses makes it useful to think of the organization as a single entity engaged in these activities.

The overall function of an organization is to take directed, unified action in an environment that presents a continuous flow of uncertainties. Its method is to coordinate the activities of its members so that all contribute to the ultimate mission.

The principal device for maintaining this effort is the chain of authority, which runs through the heart of the organization from the topmost level to the lowest point of oversight. The various levels in the chain of authority, together with staff roles designated to assist certain positions, strive to control and coordinate information, decisions, and actions so that unified action results.

The interaction whereby information, decisions, and actions are brought into conjunction involves a complex interplay between and among levels in the chain of authority. *The constant interplay that occurs is the essence of organizational functioning.*

Management and control of the functioning are two of the more important responsibilities of management or leader personnel. Although the overall responsibilities of a leader, his or her staff, and subordinates is to manage a unit, it is also a responsibility to ensure that it and all units and individuals function as needed to enable the organization to bring all of its parts together and to perform as a united whole. *The seven processes constituting organizational competence have been identified as functions that are crucial for implementing planned activities.*

The stability of the organization through time is obtained through a sufficient coincidence of the psychological fields of all of its members. However, in this regard, the shared perspectives of members of management are especially critical. When an organization is viewed as an open system, members of management at all levels are the gatekeepers, controllers, and directors of the organizational processes previously discussed as critical to the effectiveness of all units.

Accordingly, the stability of the organization in relation to its mission, its objectives, and the performance of critical processes is obtained through a sufficient coincidence of the psychological fields of the members of management. For an organization to be maximally effective, shared understandings are essential. A common means of communication, a common acceptance of purposes and subpurposes, a common acceptance of the distribution of duties and responsibilities, and a common motivation to do whatever is needed are required for effective performance.

Integration

It is apparent that numerous factors play a part in determining whether the system processes are performed effectively and whether they are resistant to disruption under pressure. Knowledge, experience, and skills of people, especially those of members of management, influence functioning of the processes. Furthermore, standard operating procedures and contingency plans reduce the potentiality of disruption. However, there is a vital aspect of organizational experience that cannot be understood as codified procedures, routine functions, personal characteristics, or formal organizational relationships. This aspect involves more than simple activity. Rather, it involves the interaction of individuals and groups that results in shared understandings and common perspectives. In this interaction, such as occurs between members of a well-functioning team, there is no simple, one-to-one relation between an isolated cause and effect. Instead, there is a more or less continuous process of action and reaction. Over time, the product of this interaction is a condition that is critical for the maximally effective functioning of organizational processes. For this book, the condition has been termed *Integration.*

FACTORS AFFECTING INTEGRATION

Following are brief discussions of the major factors that influence integration and performance.

Roles

The concept of role is a principal means for explaining individual behavior in organizations and for linking such behavior to the organizational processes. Roles are at once the building blocks of organizational systems and the frameworks of requirements with which such systems control their members as individuals. Each person in an organization is linked to other members by the functional requirements of his or her role, which are implemented through the expectations that those members have of him or her. It is important to stress that roles are ideational (i.e., they are ideas about how behavior ought to occur, rather than being the actual behavior).

The functioning of organizational processes is determined in large part by the role perceptions of individuals in key positions—in this case, by members of management at all levels. The problem-solving, decision-making, and adapting processes are affected by the extent to which there are clear, accurate, and shared perceptions of role requirements by all members of the organization.

Goals

Organizations face the problem of adapting to environmental change without losing their basic character and distinctive capabilities. On the one hand, if the goals around which activities are mobilized are adhered to despite environmental change, there may be losses and inefficiencies or even threats to survival. On the other hand, if goals are changed too frequently, there is the risk of members' losing sight of the principal mission.

The importance of goals lies in the necessity for the efficient conduct of complex activities and for keeping activities on track. When goals are clear, operational, and shared, and when people are emotionally committed to their accomplishment, misperceptions, conflicts, false starts, cross-purposes, and wasted effort are kept to a minimum. The overall (superordinate) objectives of the organization, the objectives of subordinate units, and the goals of the management are in general harmony, and all aim toward accomplishing the mission of the organization. In turn, this should result in more efficient functioning of the organizational processes.

Norms

An often neglected set of requirements in organizations and in teams includes those actions that are not specified by role prescriptions (job descriptions) but that facilitate the accomplishment of organizational objectives. An organization's need for some actions of a relatively spontaneous sort is inevitable. Planning, standard procedures, and role prescriptions cannot foresee all contingencies and cannot anticipate all environmental changes that may occur. The resources of people for innovating and for spontaneous cooperation are thus vital to effective functioning. However, this spontaneous behavior requires some control to funnel it into organizationally approved channels. This control cannot be provided by the more formal role prescriptions. Norms serve this function.

Norms are attitudes and codes of behavior held in common by all or most of the members. When well developed, this superstructure of customs, standards, and values regulates the behavior of members and provides them with the bases for assessing nonroutine situations and for governing their actions in such situations, where no official guidance is available.

It is evident that the patterned activities that make up the organizational processes are so intrinsically cooperative and interrelated that the kinds of norms that develop must inevitably influence their functioning. *This influence is most likely in terms of the extent to which members execute the process functions above and beyond the minimal limits prescribed by formal role prescriptions.*

Group Relations

When people work together toward common objectives over time, role structures, norms, and patterns of interaction develop. These group attributes exert a lasting influence upon the ways that members go about their tasks, the levels of motivation that are achieved, and the extent to which a sense of identity develops within the team and the organization. A sense of identity is Bennis's third ingredient of organizational health, and, when highly developed, it contributes to the evolution of integration within an organization.

Group relations influence the performance of organizational processes in at least two ways. First, group relations determine the extent to which personnel develop shared perspectives concerning organizational problems and practices. Second, group relationships influence the motivation of members to perform the activities related to organizational processes.

Cohesion is the major element in determining the impact of group relations upon the development of norms, values, and stable role structures and upon group performance. The cohesiveness or cohesion of a group refers to feelings of solidarity and pride that exist among the members. Cohesiveness is central to any undertaking to develop teamwork; however, the relationship between cohesiveness and group effectiveness is not simple. A group is not necessarily effective from the organization's viewpoint merely because it is highly cohesive. An additional essential requirement involves strong norms that value high-quality performance or, in other terms, integration with organizational requirements and organizational structure and function.

In general, Integration is enhanced through the existence of conditions that cause people to develop common perceptions of events and problems, to evolve shared perspectives of themselves and their group (identity), and to become consistently and harmoniously committed to the activities and objectives of the organization. Such conditions are specified below.

Teamwork

Teamwork in organizations depends upon the effective performance of role-specific individual skills and team performance (coordinative) skills. Both types of skills are driven and controlled by organizational integration. *That is, in addition to the proficiency of individuals, they depend upon cohesion.*

The general conditions necessary for the development of cohesion and teamwork in organizations are:

1. Superordinate objectives that are meaningful, clear, and desired by all (i.e., *common objectives conducive to cooperation*).

2. *A stable and efficient organizational system* that provides effective operating procedures, efficient patterns of communication, and efficient, closely coordinated teamwork.
3. *A system of potential rewards* for contribution to collective efforts.
4. *Shared norms* of performance and behavior.
5. *Shared experiences of success.*

The purposes served by the above conditions are:

1. Clear, superordinate objectives and a meaningful system of rewards focus efforts upon common aims and motivate members to cooperate and coordinate.
2. An efficient organizational system channels motivation to cooperate into effective actions.
3. A stable system provides continuity of personnel and, hence, the opportunity to develop shared experiences.
4. Shared experiences of success enhance a positive unit identity.
5. Shared norms of performance and behavior provide standards for action in emergent situations.

Taken together, these elements combine to provide a supportive climate within an organization (Griffith, 1988, 1989) that enhances the members' capabilities for resisting pressure and for performing proficiently under stress. Integration is the overriding force that melds the roles, norms, and activities and, therefore, exercises overall influence over cooperative and coordinative activities within the organization. Furthermore, integration provides organizations with the internal strength to resist forces destructive to the effective performance of essential organizational functions (processes).

TRAINING AND DEVELOPMENT

It is important to recognize that organizational competence, to include the processes discussed here, is an attribute of an organization, not of roles or of individuals. This fact is important because it governs how one views an organization and whether performance is analyzed, assessed, and developed as a attribute of individuals, groups, and entire organizations. On the one hand, managers who view process performance as an attribute of individuals or of particular roles (positions) devote all of their efforts to individual training. On the other hand, if they recognize that performance of processes is an attribute of organizations, they devote their efforts to development of the organization as a unified whole.

Organizational competence represents the capability of the organization and is different from individual capabilities. Although most often performed by single individuals, processes involve organizational responses, and the quality of any single response event is determined by the entire network of antecedent relationships and responses. Thus, Organizational competence and integration can best be improved by efforts that focus upon developing the organization to function as a system.

Procedures for analysis and development of competence and integration are set forth in Chapters 6, 8, 9, and 10.

CONCLUSION

It has become axiomatic that human factors must receive full recognition in any reasonable consideration of organizational effectiveness. However, in attempts to do something about the human element, the most common approach is to focus upon the characteristics, skills, and deficiencies of individuals. This approach most often leads to emphasis upon selection procedures, performance evaluations and interviews, remedial training, and so forth. These and other such activities that focus upon individuals are important and, indeed, essential for upgrading or maintaining the proficiency of an organization.

On the other hand, it is unreasonable to consider people without recognizing the impact of their environment upon them. People function within situational contexts, and these contexts define and limit behavior. An organization is a very important context and, accordingly, produces potent forces that circumscribe and channel the activities, attitudes, and motivations of people. For this reason, both individual behavior and group behavior within an organization are simply not the same outside it. This fact can never be safely ignored.

Carried over to management or leadership, this suggests that the first thing of which a leader must become aware is that behavior in organizations is usually the resultant of numerous determinants, many of which have their source in the work context. To neglect context factors can only cause a manager to misunderstand the problem and take the wrong course for its resolution.

The work context is indeed a most potent factor in individual and organizational effectiveness. This is fortunate because the work context is one thing that can be greatly influenced and controlled by managers.

RELEVANCE FOR RAPID-RESPONSE ORGANIZATIONS

Army and Marine tactical units are examples par excellence of rapid-response organizations. Rapid-response units are organizations that must identify and adapt effectively to events that occur in fast-changing and uncertain environmental conditions. Other examples of military rapid-response organizations are Navy fire-direction and fire-control centers and Air Force tactical control centers.

In civilian contexts, examples of rapid-response organizations are civil-disaster organizations and police, fire, and forest-fire command centers. All such units are organizations that must collectively and continually adapt to uncertain, hostile, and fast-changing conditions.

In both military and civilian rapid-response organizations, each unit is governed by a command and control group closely resembling a battle staff. Furthermore, effectiveness is, in large part, determined by the execution of processes quite similar to those discussed in Chapter 5.

The conceptual models described in this book are applicable to all types of rapid-response organizations. Similarly, the development and training procedures described in Chapters 8 and 9 are appropriate for most such organizations with only minor modifications.

RELEVANCE FOR OTHER ORGANIZATIONS

Upon careful examination of Bennis's concepts, it is apparent that they can be applied to any organization, regardless of type. These concepts (reality testing, adaptability, identity), together with the seven processes derived from them, can be the starting point for understanding and improving the functioning of any organization. The seven processes include all of the essential general functions performed by all organizations. Aside from the types of environments encountered, the kinds of activities in which they engage, and the particular stresses that arise from the dangers and pressures of combat, the greatest difference between tactical units and other organizations, both military and civilian, is in the time frames within which problems occur and must be solved.

In contrast to rapid-response units, the time spans for operations and problems in more conventional organizations may extend over weeks, months, or even years, and problems may overlap so that it is difficult to know where one begins and another ends. In rapid-response operations, situations are usually more clearly demarcated and shorter in duration. These differences make processes in nonemergency organizations somewhat more ambiguous, often complex, and sometimes difficult to trace.

Nevertheless, the seven processes that constitute competence include all of the essential functions performed by any organization, and, with care, they can be identified and traced. Accordingly, attention to competence warrants major effort in any program intended to improve organizational effectiveness.

Attention to competence appears to be especially important in civilian organizations because of increasing needs to adapt to changing conditions in civilian life. The increasing rapidity with which change is occurring in modern society makes it essential for most types of organizations to learn to adapt flexibly to continuously fluid conditions. Such adaptation should occur with minimal internal turbulence. Notable examples are requirements for the military establishment to adapt to changed or reduced threat to national security, to changed sources of its recruits from draft to volunteer, and the new values in society. Similar are requirements for aerospace firms to remain viable despite reduced services required by military and space agencies.

Almost every industrial firm is faced with the necessity of accommodating to rapidly shifting markets, increased competition, fast-changing technology, and heightened public concern about pollution, ecology, and damage to the environment. Governments must stay abreast of their citizens' needs and desires. Even educational institutions must constantly modify goals and operations to meet the demands of constantly shifting constituencies.

Under such conditions, the survival of an organization requires fine sensitivity to the often subtle cues provided by critical environments, the ability to read such cues promptly and interpret them accurately, and the capacity for rapid but efficient modification of internal operations so that new developments can be met and mastered as they arise. Inadequacy in these capabilities can result in failure or destruction of the organization.

Annotated Bibliography

Abrahamson, E. 1996. "Management Fashion." *Academy of Management Review*, 21, 254–285. A discussion of varying views of management.

Albert, R.S. 1953. "Comments on the Scientific Function of the Concept of Cohesiveness." *American Journal of Psychology*, 59, 231–234. A brief report of a study in which only a small correlation was found between a measure of group cohesiveness and judged group effectiveness.

Allport, F.H. 1962. "A Structuronomic Conception of Behavior: Individual and Collective. I. Structural Theory and the Master Problem of Social Psychology." *Journal of Abnormal and Social Psychology*, 64, 3–30. The author is one of the early critics of behaviorism in psychology, and his structuronomic theory closely resembles Open Systems Theory. It is similar to General Systems Theory, and he discusses a cycle of events that closely resemble processes characteristic of open systems.

Allport, G.W. 1941. "The Nature of Democratic Morale." In G. Watson (ed.), *Civilian Morale*. Boston: Houghton Mifflin. A theoretical analysis of morale, with particular emphasis upon civilian morale. The article makes a useful distinction between "democratic" and "totalitarian" morale and lists the characteristics of "democratic" morale.

Altman, I. 1966. "The Small Group Field: Implications for Research on Behavior in Organizations." In R. V. Bowers (ed.), *Studies on Behavior and Organizations: A Research Symposium*. Athens: University of Georgia Press. In this incisive analysis of the state of small-group research in 1966, the author makes a strong case for opening the "black box" of small groups and of organizations and for examining the internal processes through which system outputs are accomplished. Such analyses would permit better management of critical factors that impact upon ultimate effectiveness.

Anderson, D., and Anderson, L.A. 2001. *Beyond Change Management: Advanced Strategies for Today's Transformational Leaders*. San Francisco: Wiley-

Pfeiffer. The authors combine personal observations and some sharp insights to produce a work that could be significant for understanding leadership and organizational development. The book is specifically about the interaction of leadership style, mind-set, and the change process.

Argyle, M., Gardner, G., and Cioffi, I. 1958. "Supervisory Methods Related to Productivity, Absenteeism, and Turnover." *Human Relations*, 11, 23–40. An interesting report about supervision and its effects upon personnel. In addition, there are some interesting findings about group size, performance, and attitudes.

Argyris, C. 1954. "Human Problems with Budgets." *Harvard Business Review*, 31 (1), 97–110. An analysis of budgets as one type of pressure device for increasing efficiency. The effects of pressure upon performance are examined, the opposing factors affecting performance are analyzed, and a method for improving performance without pressure is suggested.

Argyris, C. 1957. *Personality and Organization: The Conflict between System and the Individual.* New York: Harper & Brothers. This is a well-known and controversial analysis of the effects of formal organization and organizational practices upon the performance and attitudes of industrial personnel. Although concerned with industrial practices, this book contains many provocative ideas about leadership and organizations in general.

Argyris, C. 1958. "Some Problems in Conceptualizing Organizational Climate: A Case Study of a Bank." *Administrative Science Quarterly*, 2, 501–520. This is a case study of the organizational climate within a bank. It identifies many of the problems of conceptualizing climate and also some of the results of climate and their impacts upon performance. It also discusses some of the ramifications of change in organizational theory.

Argyris, C. 1962. *Interpersonal Competence and Organizational Effectiveness.* Homewood, IL: Irwin–Dorsey Press. This book analyzes interpersonal Competence as a major determinant of effectiveness in high-level executive groups. It presents a model for diagnosing high-level effectiveness. It also attempts to show the impact of values held by executives about "effective human relations" upon their interpersonal relationships and administrative competence. Explanation is offered of how these values, in turn, influence organizational defensiveness, organizational structure, interdepartmental conflict and cooperation, rational decision making, and policy formulation and execution.

Barnard, C.I. 1938. *The Functions of the Executive.* Cambridge, MA: Harvard University Press. This book is the classic in the field of organizational theory. Although written in terms of a business organization, the theory is actually a sociological analysis and is generally applicable with only slight modification to all types of organizations, including military units. Although the concepts presented are sometimes hazy and highly abstract, the book provides valuable insights into the elements of formal organization, the relation to them of the "executive" function (i.e., functions of control, management, leadership, and administration), and the place of these functions in the survival of an organization. Most present-day theories of organization owe credit to this book.

Barnard, C.I. 1948. "The Nature of Leadership." In C.I. Barnard (ed.), *Organiza-*

tion and Management. Cambridge, MA: Harvard University Press. This article discusses leadership as a function of three complex variables: the leader, the followers, and the conditions. The discussion includes a general description of what leaders have to do in four sectors of leadership behavior, thoughts concerning certain differences of conditions of leadership, remarks about the active personal qualities of leaders, notes on the problem of the deportment of leaders, and observations about the selection of leaders.

Bavelas, A., and Barrett, D. 1951. "An Experimental Approach to Organizational Communication." *Personnel*, 27, 367–371. This is a summary and general discussion of findings from a number of experiments concerned with the effects of different communication patterns upon performance in small groups and organizations.

Benne, K.D. 1961. "Case Methods in the Training of Administrators." In W.G. Bennis, K.D. Benne, and R. Chin (eds.), 1961. *The Planning of Change: Readings in the Applied Behavioral Sciences*. New York: Holt, Rinehart and Winston. A critique of methods for training leaders of organizations. It includes a discussion of the skills required to lead an organization. It advocates training methods that confront trainees with concrete, complex behavioral situations to be diagnosed and acted upon.

Benne, K.D., and Sheats, P.D. 1948. "Functional Roles of Group Members." *Journal of Social Issues*, 4(2), 41–49. This article defines and describes the various functional roles that a person may perform in a group. The actions of members are categorized into three broad classes: those that facilitate the accomplishment of a group's task, those that help build or maintain the group, and those that are concerned solely with satisfying the needs of the individual. The article is one of the earliest formulations of the concept of "task" and "maintenance" functions in groups and organizations.

Bennis, W.G. 1959. "Leadership Theory and Administrative Behavior: The Problem of Authority." *Administrative Science Quarterly*, 4, 259–301. This is an excellent review of the state of leadership theory in 1959, including a discussion of the philosophies, ideologies, and practices that identify the major conflicting movements in the field of leadership. The author also presents his explanation of leadership in terms of certain propositions based on a priori criteria of organizational effectiveness.

Bennis, W.G. 1966. *Changing Organizations: Essays on the Development and Evolution of Human Organizations*. New York: McGraw-Hill Book Co. This short book is a collection of addresses, articles, and essays by Warren Bennis, probably the most articulate writer on leadership, psychology, and organizations in the late twentieth century. He analyzes, in a very readable way, the evolution of organizational and management theory, the current state of leadership theory, and the emergence of systems concepts in relation to organizations. Very elegant but pleasurable writing about subjects that can be difficult to absorb.

Bennis, W.G., Benne, K.D., and Chin, R. (eds.). 1961. *The Planning of Change: Readings in the Applied Behavioral Sciences*. New York: Holt, Rinehart, and Winston. This book is a comprehensive collection of articles concerned with both theoretical and applied aspects of achieving change within organizations. It is written for the professional psychologist, sociologist, and educator. Although difficult in parts, the book contains many helpful hints for achieving organizational change.

Berkowitz, L., and Levy, B.I. 1956. "Pride in Group Performance and Group-Task Motivation." *Journal of Abnormal and Social Psychology*. 53, 300–306. This article is a conventional experimental study of group cohesiveness and group task motivation upon the extent to which people were motivated to perform a task. It illustrates some of the early experimental methods, which have later been improved.

Blake, R.R., and Bradford, L.P. 1953. "Decisions . . . Decisions . . . Decisions!" *Adult Leadership*. 2(7), 23–24, 33. This is a practical discussion of the psychological difficulties encountered in decision making by groups. Also discussed are ways of overcoming the difficulties. This article is a helpful guide for leaders of committees, project teams, staffs, and problem-solving groups.

Blake, R.R., and Mouton, J.S. 1962. "The Intergroup Dynamics of Win-Lose Conflict and Problem-Solving Collaboration in Union-Management Relations." In M. Sherif (ed.), *Intergroup Relations and Leadership: Approaches and Research in Industrial, Ethnic, Cultural, and Political Areas*. New York: John Wiley & Sons. The authors develop a comprehensive theory of conflict and collaboration between groups, validated through experimental work. Although the theory is discussed in terms of union–management conflict, it is applicable to all types of intergroup situations.

Blake, R.R., and Mouton, J.S. 1964. *The Managerial Grid*. Houston, TX: Gulf Publishing Co. This book presents the authors' well-known managerial grid approach to leadership. The approach stresses the importance of leadership as the main integrating factor upon personnel and contends that if leaders see their organizations as organic rather than mechanistic—as adaptable rather than controlled by rigid structure—emphasis within the organizations will shift from arbitration to problem solving, from delegated to shared responsibility, and from centralized to decentralized authority.

Blau, P.M., and Scott, W.R. 1962. *Formal Organizations: A Comparative Approach*. San Francisco: Chandler Publishing Company. This book is a sociological analysis of formal organizations. It examines the nature and types of formal organizations, the connections between them, the larger social context of which they are a part, and various aspects of their internal structure, such as peer group and hierarchical relations, processes of communication, authority, leadership, and impersonal mechanisms of control.

Bolger, D.P. 1986. *Dragons at War: 2–34 Infantry in the Mojave*. Novato, CA: Presidio Press. In this book, the experiences are described of an infantry battalion in a desert training center in California, in which the troops go through several training exercises. While it is mainly concerned with military exercises and experience in training, it illustrates some of the problems in organizational functioning that may arise under pressure and stressful conditions.

Bonner, H. 1959. *Group Dynamics: Principles and Applications*. New York: The Ronald Press. This is a textbook for college students and for professional readers. It is a comprehensive survey of the dynamics of small groups. The analysis includes group structure, group cohesiveness, intergroup tensions, group learning, group problem solving, and group leadership. Application is made to the areas of business, community relations, political behavior, group psychotherapy, and education.

Bouwen, R., and Hosking, D.M. (eds.). 2000. *Organizational Learning.* Philadelphia: Psychology Press. The author describes some of the ways in which organizations learn and identifies some of the requirements and conditions for effective learning by organizations.

Bovard, E.W., Jr. 1951. "Group Structure and Perception." *Journal of Abnormal and Social Psychology,* 46, 398–405. This article describes the results of an experiment designed to study the effects of leadership and group structure upon how members perceive external situations, other members, and the group as a whole. The principal conclusion is that the methods that a leader uses to encourage or to control interaction between group members and between him and group members exert material influence upon members' perceptions.

Bowers, R.V. (ed.). 1962. *Studies in Organizational Effectiveness: Contributions to Military Sociology.* Washington, DC: Air Force Office of Scientific Research (Office of Aerospace Research). This book contains reports of five studies of Air Force units dealing with significant factors in Organizational Effectiveness. Among the areas covered are role conflict, role ambiguity, leadership and morale, and the effects of changes in leaders upon an organization.

Brayfield, A.H., and Crockett, W.H. 1955. "Employee Performance." *Psychological Bulletin,* 52, 396–424. This rather extensive article is an analysis of performance and job satisfaction. It is concluded that job satisfaction and productivity are not necessarily complementary; that is, in some cases, they may be highly correlated, and in other cases they are not necessarily highly correlated. This is one of the first studies in which the discrepancy between job satisfaction and productivity was noted.

Brockbank, W., Ulrich, D., and Beatty, R.W. 1997. "HR Professional Development: Creating the Future Creators at the University of Michigan Business School." *Human Resources Management,* 51, 73–77. This article sets out some useful pointers for developing more creative managers. The authors examine the present state of professional training.

Burns, T., and Stalker, G.M. 1961. *The Management of Innovation.* London: Tavistock Publications. An interesting book by two of the "organizational neostructuralists," whose approach is important because they recognize that, for an organization to function effectively, both structure and functional behavior requirements must be considered.

Campbell, A. 1953. "Administering Research Organizations." *The American Psychologist,* 8, 225–230. This is a discussion of the role of a research administrator; however, it contains practical insights useful to leaders of all types of organizations.

Cannon-Bowers, J., Salas, E., Tanenbaum, S.T., and Mathiew, J.V. 1995. "Toward Theoretically Based Principles of Training Effectiveness: A Model and Empirical Investigation." *Military Psychology,* 3, 141–164. This article describes an investigation of factors that may influence the effectiveness of training. It includes a comprehensive model of training effectiveness and description of a large-scale data collection effort.

Carlisle, H.A. 1973. *Situational Management: A Contingency Approach to Lead-*

ership. New York: AMACOM. This is an excellent book published by the American Management Association. It presents a new methodology called "Structural Analysis and Systems Theory."

Cartwright, D. 1951. "Achieving Change in People." *Human Relations*, 4, 381–392. Starting from the premise that the behavior, attitudes, beliefs, and values of the individual are grounded in the groups to which he or she belongs, the author discusses ways that group factors can be used to change people. This article includes a number of principles for achieving change in people.

Cartwright, D. 1959. "Power: A Neglected Variable in Social Psychology." In D. Cartwright, (ed.), *Studies in Social Power*. Ann Arbor: The Institute for Social Research, University of Michigan, pp. 235–251. This book is a collection of technical studies concerned with "social power," the ability of one person to influence another. In his introduction to the book, Cartwright comes out strongly for recognition of power as an important variable in groups and organizations. He contends that many small group and human relations theorists have been soft on power as a significant influence.

Cartwright, D., and Zander, A. (eds.). 1953, 1960. *Group Dynamics: Research and Theory* (1st and 2nd eds.). Evanston, IL: Row, Peterson, and Company. These two editions of one of the definitive books on the dynamics of small groups contain selections of significant research papers in the field. Areas covered in separate sections are (1) group cohesiveness, (2) group pressures and standards, (3) individual motives and group goals, (4) leadership and group performance, and (5) the structural properties of groups. Each section includes an introduction that analyzes both practical and theoretical issues in the area under consideration.

Charters, W.W., Jr., and Newcomb, T.M. 1952. "Some Attitudinal Effects of Experimentally Increased Salience of a Membership Group." In G.E. Swanson, T.M. Newcomb, and E.L. Hartley (eds.), *Readings in Social Psychology* (rev. ed.). New York: Henry Holt and Company. This article reports a study demonstrating that an individual's favorable attitudes toward a group and his or her agreement with the official values of the group are heightened as his or her conscious awareness of membership in that group is increased.

Coch, L., and French, J.P.R., Jr. 1948. "Overcoming Resistance to Change." *Human Relations*, 1, 512–532. This is the classical study concerned with overcoming resistance to change. It examined resistance to changes in operations in a manufacturing company and describes methods that were successful in reducing resistance to change and in obtaining acceptance of changed work procedures.

Cullen, B.S., Kemp, G.O., and Rossini, L.A. 1981. *Competencies of Organizational Effectiveness Consultants in the U.S. Army* (L&M TA 81-1). Boston: McBer & Co. In this study, researchers identified competencies required by organizational effectiveness staff officers in the U.S. Army. The competencies were then used to design training programs for these officers and to determine what kinds of competencies and skills are needed for the job. This is one of the first studies of competencies on record.

Cyert, R.M., and March, T.G. 1964. "The Behavioral Theory of the Firm: A Behavioral Science-Economics Amalgram." In W.W. Cooper, H.J. Leavitt, and M.W. Shelly (eds.), *New Perspectives in Organizational Research*. New

York: John Wiley & Sons, pp. 289–304. A landmark publication in which the authors formulated a concept of the organization as decision maker. Also they set forth the fact that organizations are constantly attempting to adapt to their external and internal environments and that fully rational adaptation is constrained by some strong limits on the cognitive capacity, the computational speed, and the internal goal consistency of the organization.

Dale, E., and Urwick, L.F. 1960. *Staff in Organization.* New York: McGraw-Hill Book Company. This book attempts to provide a framework for understanding staff–line relationships and for using the staff concept in business and governmental organizations. The authors advocate adapting the military concept of staff to civilian uses. The book contains chapters on the military use of staff and the proper relationships between staff and line personnel. The second author is a retired British army officer and well-known authority and writer on organizational problems.

Dalton, G.W., Lawrence, P.R., and Lorsch, J.W. 1970. *Organizational Structure and Design.* Homewood, IL: Irwin-Dorsey. This book is concerned with the design aspects of organizations in relation to the kinds of technology used in the functions that are served by various organizational divisions. This approach has been termed "neostructuralist." The approaches of neostructuralists are important because they recognize that, for an organization to function effectively, both structure and functional behavior requirements must be taken into account.

Deutsch, M. 1949. "An Experimental Study of the Effects of Co-operation and Competition upon Group Process." *Human Relations*, 2, 199–231. This article is a technical report of a classical experiment concerned with the effects of cooperation versus competition upon group performance and member attitudes toward the group.

Deutsch, M. 1959. "Some Factors Affecting Membership Motivation and Achievement Motivation in a Group." *Human Relations*, 12, 81–95. This is a report of another study in which no relationship was found between group cohesiveness and effectiveness.

Deutsch, M., and Gerard, H. 1953. *Problems in Staff Relations: An Experience Survey.* Research Memorandum No. 23, Air Research and Development Command, Human Resources Research Institute, Maxwell Air Force Base, Alabama. This is the report of a survey conducted among Air Force officers concerning factors in effective staff functioning. The officers were interviewed concerning the functioning of various staffs on which they had served, what made each staff effective or ineffective, and problems encountered by these staffs. It translates to a general analysis of problem-solving groups.

Drabek, T.E. 1965. "Laboratory Simulation of a Police Communication System under Stress." Unpublished dissertation, The Ohio State University. This report describes a research project concerned with the effects upon a police communications system when it is under stress and faced with a large emergency in the community. This was the predecessor of project FORGE and project Cardinal Point reported in this book.

Drucker, P.F. 1999. *The Practice of Management.* Oxford: Butterworth-Heinemann. This book is a reprint of a classic in the study of management.

It has been one of the best and most stimulating books on management to appear for many years. It has been reissued by the European publisher listed here.

Drucker, P.F. 2001. *Management, the Individual, and Society*. Oxford: Butterworth-Heinemann. In this new book, the author carries on with his incisive analyses of management and of management as a social function.

Dubin, R. 1949. "Decision-Making by Management in Industrial Relations." *American Journal of Sociology*, 54, 292–297. This is one of the early reports in which emphasis was placed upon the way attitudes, values, and informal roles may develop within units within an organization and may conflict with structural controls.

Dubin, R. 1959. "Stability of Human Organizations." In M. Haire (ed.), *Modern Organization Theory*. New York: John Wiley & Sons. In this chapter, the author attempts to bring internal processes into his analytic system. Primary emphasis remains, however, upon structure. The chapter shows that even now there is recognition that disregard of human variability may have seriously disruptive effects upon an ideally designed organization.

Edwards, W. 1954. "The Theory of Decision Making." *Psychological Bulletin*, 51, 380–417. This paper contains a review of decision theory and makes the point that most theories of decision making have their origin in economic theories of consumer choice.

Emery, F.E., and Trist, F.L. 1965. "The Causal Texture of Organizational Environments." *Human Relations*, 18, 21–32. A classical report on the effects of organizational contexts upon Effectiveness and performance.

Festinger, L. 1953. "An Analysis of Compliant Behavior." In M. Sherif and M.O. Wilson (eds.), *Group Relations at the Crossroads*. New York: Harper & Brothers. The author analyzes conditions under which individuals comply with group standards of behavior. He distinguishes between public compliance and private acceptance of the standards, and public compliance without private acceptance. He also discusses the effects upon the individual's behavior of these two types of compliance. The discussion has implications for discipline and morale.

Festinger, L., Schachter, S., and Back, K. 1953. "The Operation of Group Standards." In D. Cartwright and A. Zander (eds.), *Group Dynamics: Research and Theory*. Evanston, IL: Rowe, Peterson and Co., pp. 204–222. This is the definitive article on group standards (norms) and their operations. Excellent examples offered about how group standards operate in life.

Flanagan, J.C. 1954. "The Critical Incident Technique." *Psychological Bulletin*, 51, 327–358. John Flanagan, the inventor of the critical-incident technique for assessment of performance and for identifying requirements of jobs, describes the technique and discusses its potential benefits and values.

Foegen, J.H. 1955. "Should You Tell Them Everything?" *Advanced Management*, 20, 28–32. This article presents arguments for providing personnel with full information concerning matters that affect them. It discusses the pros and cons of information programs and concludes, "Too much communication is impossible."

French, J.R.P., Jr. 1941. "The Disruption and Cohesion of Groups." *Journal of Abnormal and Social Psychology*, 36, 361–377. This is the report of an experiment concerning the effects of group frustration upon the cohesion of small groups. It shows that frustration can have seriously disrupting effects upon group performance.

French, J.R.P., and Raven, B. 1959. "The Bases of Social Power." In D. Cartwright (ed.), *Studies in Social Power*. Ann Arbor: Institute for Social Research, University of Michigan. This article analyzes the sources of power (influence) and discusses each source in relation to its potential Effectiveness.

French, R.L. 1949. "Morale and Leadership." In *A Survey Report on Human Factors in Undersea Warfare*. Washington, DC: Panel on Psychology and Physiology, Committee on Undersea Warfare, National Research Council. In this article, "an effort is made to outline what seem to be the major problems" concerned with group effectiveness and morale. Group effectiveness is defined, methods of measuring it are discussed, and consideration is given to a variety of factors related to it. Special attention is given to the question of leadership in relation to group effectiveness with a review of definitions and questions on the selection and training of leaders.

Galbraith, J.R. 1995. *Designing Organizations: An Executive Briefing on Strategy, Structure and Process*. San Francisco: Jossey-Bass. The author shows how organizations' designs support policies, behavior, and performance.

Gardner, B.B., and Moore, D.C. 1950. *Human Relations in Industry* (rev. ed.). Chicago: Richard D. Irwin. This well-known book is concerned with the informal social structure of work organizations, with social equilibrium and change, and with management principles and practices. Although written in the terminology of business, the book contains many observations useful to other leaders.

Gellerman, S.W. 1963. *Motivation and Productivity*. New York: American Management Association. The three stated purposes of this book are to draw together the most significant achievements in the study of motivation; to present a theory that puts most of this research into a simple, understandable perspective; and to show the practical implications of all this research and theory for management policy. The book succeeds in its objectives and is recommended for anyone who desires a highly readable, understandable, and generally applicable discussion of motivation in all sorts of organizations.

Gibb, C.A. 1954. "Leadership." In G. Lindzey (ed.), *Handbook of Social Psychology* (Vol. 2). Cambridge, MA: Addison-Wesley Publishing Co. This is a survey and analysis of the social psychological literature concerned with leadership. The major sections discuss leader behavior, group factors in leadership, psychodynamics of leader–follower relations, types of leadership, succession of leaders, and theories of leadership.

Gibb, J. 1964. "Communication and Productivity." *Personnel Administration*, 27(1), 8–13, 45. This easily readable article presents an incisive analysis of leader communication. The merits of persuasion versus problem-solving techniques in relation to organizational effectiveness are also discussed.

Gill, D.L. 1977. "Cohesiveness and Performance in Sport Groups." In R.S. Yeeton (ed.), *Exercise and Sports Sciences Review* (Vol. 5). Santa Barbara, CA: Journal Publishing Affiliates. This article is interesting because it describes cohesiveness and its development in sports teams.

Gilman, G. 1962. "An Inquiry into the Nature and Use of Authority." In M. Haire (ed.), *Organization Theory in Industrial Practice*. New York: John Wiley & Sons. This article is an outstanding attempt to develop a systematic picture of what authority is and the role that it actually plays in human affairs. Highly recommended for anyone who desires an understanding of the important implications underlying the concept of authority.

Goetzinger, C., and Valentine, M. 1964. "Problems in Executive Interpersonal Communication." *Personnel Administration*, 27(2), 24–29. This article discusses some of the problems facing executives as they make decisions, implement old ideas, and create new ones and as they engage in such communication activities as receiving, analyzing, evaluating, synthesizing, and transmitting information. Twelve problems are cited that are common to most organizations, the presumed recognition of which provides a start toward the improvement of interpersonal communication and leadership.

Greenbaum, C.W. 1979. "The Small Group under the Gun: Uses of Small Groups in Battle Conditions." *Journal of Applied Psychology*, 15, 392–405. This article is a report of an extensive review of studies of small military units in combat (World Wars I and II, Yom Kippur War, Korean War). Greenbaum concludes that properly led individuals in combat units will develop strong bonds of identification with one another and that these bonds are functional, serving to control individual fear and helping the individual to be effective in his or her work, and this leads to cohesiveness in small groups.

Griffith, J. 1988. "Measurement of Group Cohesion in U.S. Army Units." *Basic and Applied Social Psychology* 6, 51–60. This article is concerned with the techniques for measuring group cohesiveness in U.S. Army units.

Griffith, J. 1989. "The Army's New Unit Personnel Replacement Policy and Its Relationship to Unit Cohesion and Social Support." *Military Psychology*, 1, 17–34. This article is concerned with the effect of stability in an organization and its effect upon cohesion. The Army's personnel policies for replacement were changed in the late 1980s and personnel were allowed to stay in units much longer than formerly. This resulted in higher unit cohesion and the provision of emotional support from various members to each other.

Gross, E. 1954. "Primary Functions of the Small Group." *American Journal of Sociology*, 60, 24–29. In this article, Gross reports on a study of small work groups within the Air Force and found that satisfaction with the Air Force and personal commitment to group goals were directly related to group cohesiveness.

Habbe, S. 1952. "Does Communication Make a Difference?" *Management Record* 14 414–416, 442–444. The author reports the results of a study of the effects of communication upon group performance by industrial workers.

Haire, M. 1956. *Psychology in Management*. New York: McGraw-Hill Book Company. In this popular book, students and leaders are offered a "statement of a set of psychological principles and their implications for some problems of industrial management." Although written for a business audience, the basic material covered in the book is applicable to any context, is readable, and is readily understood. The book contains much useful information.

Haire, M. 1959. "Biological Models and Empirical Histories of the Growth of Organizations." In M. Haire (ed.), *Modern Organization Theory*. New

York: John Wiley & Sons, pp. 272–306. This is the editor's introduction to the book and traces the history of organizational theory and discusses some of the ramifications of change in organizational theory.

Haire, M. (ed.). 1962. *Organization Theory in Industrial Practice*. New York: John Wiley & Sons. This book is a collection of papers describing the application of organizational theories to actual practice. Although mostly concerned with business operations, several articles have useful relevance to other organizations.

Halsey, W.F., and Bryan, J., III. 1947. *Admiral Halsey's Story*. New York: McGraw-Hill Book Company. These are the battle memoirs of Admiral Halsey. The book contains helpful commentaries on many principles of organization.

Harbord, J.C. 1936. *The American Army in France*. Boston: Little, Brown and Company. Quoted in C.I. Barnard. 1938. *The Functions of the Executive*. Cambridge, MA: Harvard University Press. This book is an account of the American Expeditionary Force in World War I, by the onetime chief of staff to General Pershing.

Harris, P.R., and Moran, R.T. 2000. *Managing Cultural Differences*. Houston: Gulf Publishing Co. This book has easy-to-read case studies with guidelines to improve leadership skills for dealing with globalization, communications, and negotiations and with strategic alliances, cultural change, cultural synergy, and diversity in the workplace.

Hart, B.H.L. (ed.). 1953. *The Rommel Papers*. New York: Harcourt, Brace and Company. This is the German General Rommel's account of his campaigns, as taken from his personal papers by editor Hart. Contains numerous analyses of Hitler's contributions to organizational failures of the German Army, which occurred because of his interference.

Hayes-Roth, B., and Hayes-Roth, F.A. 1979. "A Cognitive Model of Planning." *Cognitive Science* 3, 275–323. Just what the title implies. A heavy emphasis upon cognitive aspects of decision making and ignores the circumstances under which the decision maker is acting.

Helson, H. 1964. "Current Trends and Issues in Adaptation-Level Theory." *American Psychologist*, 19(1), 26–38. This paper is a highly technical discussion of a significant psychological theory that accounts for the many complex factors affecting a particular instance of behavior.

Hemphill, J.K. 1949. *Situational Factors in Leadership*. Monograph 32. Columbus: The Ohio State University, Bureau of Educational Research. This is the technical report of a series of experiments designed to study group factors affecting leadership.

Henry, W.E. 1949. "The Business Executive: The Psychodynamics of a Social Role." *American Journal of Sociology*, 54, 286–291. This article is a discussion of the characteristics of high-level executives. The author contends that the successful executive represents a crystallization of many of the attitudes and values generally accepted by middle-class American society. The characteristics are listed and discussed in detail.

Herbst, P.G. 1957. "Measurement of Behavior Structure by Means of Input-Output Data." *Human Relations*, 10, 335–346. In this article, it was found that middle-size groups sometimes produce better than smaller ones or larger ones.

Herman, C.F. 1963. "Some Consequences of Crises Which Limit the Viability of Organizations." *Administrative Science Quarterly*, 8, 61–82. This is an excellent analysis of the effects of crisis upon organizations and their abilities to function effectively. It presents various pitfalls or events that can occur because of a crisis.

Herzberg, F., Mausner, B., and Synderman, B.B. 1959. *The Motivation to Work* (2nd ed.). New York: John Wiley & Sons. This book reports a study of motivation in which more than 200 industrial employees were interviewed to provide insights into the effects of attitudes upon performance. Both factors influencing attitudes and their effects are discussed along with implications of the results. A major finding was a confirmation of the hypothesis that some factors influence attitudes only in a positive direction, and others, only in a negative direction as contrasted to the idea that any given factor can have both a positive and negative impact upon morale.

Hite, J. 1999. *Learning in Chaos: Improving Human Performance in Today's Fast-Changing, Volatile Organizations*. Houston: Gulf Publishing Co. This book explains how change is a functional characteristic of any organization.

Homans, G.C. 1950. *The Human Group*. New York: Harcourt, Brace and Co. This book is one of the classic sociological studies of human groups. Presented from the standpoint of a sociologist, it was one of the major books at the time of its publication.

Hovland, C.I., Janis, I.L., and Kelley, H.H. 1953. *Communication and Persuasion: Psychological Studies of Opinion Change*. New Haven, CT: Yale University Press. Based on a program of coordinated research on the modification of attitudes and beliefs through communication, this report analyzes the effectiveness of arguments and appeals, personality factors underlying susceptibility to persuasion, and the influence of social roles on resistance to acceptance of new ideas. The importance of motivation and the higher thought processes, their relevance to social influence in everyday life, and the problems of effective mass communication are stressed.

Hunt, E. 1980. "A Cognitive Science and Psychometric Approach to Team Performance." In S.E. Goldin and E. Thorndyke (eds), *Improving Team Performance: Proceedings of the Rand Team Performance Workshop*. Santa Monica, CA: The Rand Corporation. This is an interesting paper, one of several appearing in the report of the 1980 Rand Corporation Conference on Team Performance. The paper desribes some interesting concepts concerned with cognition and team performance.

Indik, B.P., and Seashore, S.E. 1961. *Effects of Organization Size on Member Attitudes and Behavior*. Ann Arbor: Survey Research Center, Institute of Social Research, University of Michigan. In this study, the authors report that they found no relationship between size of work group and productivity in automotive dealerships but did find that productivity was higher in small groups within a package-delivery organization. It appears that for some types of work, organization into smaller groups leads to improved performance; for other kinds of work, size of the group may be irrelevant for productivity.

Jackson, J.M. 1959. "The Organization and Its Communications Problems." *Advanced Management*, 24(2), 17–20. This article is an excellent discussion of communication problems in organizations and some of the reasons for them. The author concludes that communication problems are often only symptomatic of other difficulties within the organization.

Jackson, J.M. 1959. "Reference Group Processes in a Formal Organization." *Sociometry*, 22, 307–327. This is the report of a study concerned with factors determining the extent to which an individual will like the group of which he or she is a member.

Jacobson, E., Charters, W.W., Jr., and Lieberman, S. 1951. "The Use of the Role Concept in the Study of Complex Organizations." *Journal of Social Issues*, 7(3), 18–27. This is a discussion of the concept of "role" and its use in understanding behavior in organizations.

Janowitz, M. 1960. *The Professional Soldier*. Glencoe, IL: The Free Press. This book explores the changes taking place in military organizations and the military profession in consequence of twentieth-century developments in military technology and international relations. Central among these changes in the armed forces is a shift from a traditional military to a constabulary role, that is, one calling for continuous readiness to act, using minimum force, with the objective of viable international relations rather than victory. The author contends that the future of the military profession depends in large part on the manner in which military organization and personnel policies adapt to the demands of this new role. Basic concepts have application to all types of organizations.

Kahn, R.L. 1960. "Productivity and Job Satisfaction." *Personnel Psychology*, 13, 275–287. This report shows that job satisfaction and productivity are not necessarily complementary.

Kahn, R.L., and Katz, D. 1953. "Leadership Practices in Relation to Productivity and Morale." In D. Cartwright and A. Zander (eds.), *Group Dynamics: Research and Theory*. Evanston, IL: Row, Peterson and Company. This chapter in one of the first books concerned with group dynamics is a survey of research conducted in the Survey Research Center at the University of Michigan. The authors discuss the findings of a series of studies concerned with the effects of various leadership practices in relation to productivity and morale. The conclusion is that the leadership practices have an important impact upon both productivity and employee attitudes.

The authors summarize research up to 1953 conducted in business and industry to identify the characteristics of supervisors who lead relatively productive crews. Relatively little has changed in 50 years.

Katz, D. 1964. "The Motivational Basis of Organizational Behavior." *Behavioral Science*, 9(2), 131–146. This is an interesting discussion of motivation in organizations. The author concludes that if an organization is to survive and function effectively, it must require not one but several different types of behavior from most of its members, and the motivations of these different types of behavior may also differ. The author tries to answer the basic problem: What is the nature of a person's involvement in an organization or his or her commitment to it?

Katz, D., and Kahn, R.L. 1952. "Some Recent Findings in Human Relations Research." In E. Swanson, T. Newcomb, and E. Hartley (eds.), *Readings in Social Psychology*. New York: Holt, Rinehart & Winston, pp. 650–665. This chapter in one of the early social psychology textbooks is an excellent presentation of much of the Lewinian approach to research upon human relations in industry. Not much has changed since the publication of this chapter.

Katz, D., and Kahn, R.L. 1953. "Human Organization and Worker Motivation." In *Industrial Productivity*. Ann Arbor, MI: Industrial Relations Research Association. This is a useful discussion of the ways that organizational factors influence the motivations of personnel. The authors stress the importance of social psychological factors but warn against overemphasis upon these variables at the expense of formal organizational requirements.

Katz, D., and Kahn, R.L. 1966. *The Social Psychology of Organizations*. New York: John Wiley & Sons. In this book, the authors attempt nothing more than a complete explanation of organizational behavior within Systems Theory concepts. The attempt was reasonably successful in putting into proper perspective such ideas as interchange with environments, operation by process instead of procedure, and the interrelationships among functional units.

Katz, D., Maccoby, N., Gurin, G., and Floor, L.G. 1951. *Productivity, Supervision and Morale among Railroad Workers*. Ann Arbor: Institute for Social Research, University of Michigan. The study makes comparisons of the attitudes of railroad workers in high- and low-producing groups. The major conclusion is that leadership is as important to productivity as are the attitudes of personnel.

Katz, D., Maccoby, N., and Morse, N.C. 1950. *Productivity, Supervision and Morale in an Office Situation*. Ann Arbor: Institute for Social Research, University of Michigan. This report presents findings from a study of clerical workers in the home office of a large insurance company. Differences in group motivation are seen to be related to differences in supervisory practice and philosophy.

Katzell, R.A., Barrett, R.S., and Parker, T.C. 1961. "Job Satisfaction, Job Performance, and Situational Characteristics." *Journal of Applied Psychology*, 45, 65–72. In this study of the effects of situational characteristics upon job satisfaction and performance, it was found that smaller work unit size leads to higher productivity.

Kelley, H.H. 1951. "Communication in Experimentally Created Hierarchies." *Human Relations*, 4, 39–56. A report of a study concerned with the quantity and type of communication transmitted up and down the chain of authority. Differences in the quantity and types of information communicated upward and downward were found to be related to the position of the individual and with whom he or she was communicating.

Kelley, H.H., and Thibaut, J.W. 1954. "Experimental Studies of Group Problem Solving and Process." In G. Lindzey (ed.), *Handbook of Social Psychology* (Vol. 2). Cambridge, MA: Addison-Wesley Publishing Co. This article summarizes the technical literature concerned with group problem solving. The analysis places special emphasis on the communication process and on interaction within small groups while producing solutions to various types of problems.

Kemp, G.O., Munger, M.T., and Spencer, L.M. 1977. *Analysis of Leadership and Management Competencies of Commissioned and Noncommissioned Naval Officers in the Pacific and Atlantic Fleets*. TTD EG-33. Boston: McBer and Co. In this report, some of the pioneering methods for identifying and assessing leader competencies are identified. Although it identifies competencies for Naval personnel, the important part of this report is concerned with the methodology for accomplishing the identification.

Kerr, W.A., Koppelmeier, G.J., and Sullivan, J.J. 1951. "Absenteeism, Turnover, and Morale in a Metals Fabrication Factory." *Occupational Psychology*, 25, 50–55. This is one of the more classical analyses of determinants of absenteeism, turnover, and morale in a heavy metals factory.

Kline, B.E., and Martin, N.H. 1958. "Freedom, Authority, and Decentralization." *Harvard Business Review*, 36(3), 69–75. This article is an excellent discussion of freedom to act within the limits of assigned responsibility. The main focus is on the nature of freedom in an organization, its effects, and ways of fostering it among subordinates.

Knickerbocker, I. Summer 1948. "Leadership: A Conception and Some Implications." *Journal of Social Issues*, 4, 23–40. This article presents the classical argument for viewing leadership in terms of what the leader does to meet the requirements of his or her organization and the situation rather than in terms of personal traits and characteristics. It also discusses several means by which a leader may direct the activities of people.

Landsberger, H.A. 1961. "The Horizontal Dimension in a Bureaucracy." *Administrative Science Quarterly*, 6(3), 299–332. This is a study concerned with the effects of varying amounts of communication and interaction between leaders occupying equal organizational levels.

Laver, M.E., and O'Connor, J.R. 2000. "Competence Modeling: Ready, Set, Research." *The Industrial-Organizational Psychologist*, 37, 4. The authors bring up-to-date the methodology for identifying and assessing competencies and for competence modeling.

Lawrence, P.R. 1958. *The Changing of Organizational Behavior Patterns*. Boston: Division of Research, Harvard Business School. This book deals with decentralization and the attendant problems of changing patterns of supervisory and administrative behavior among key business personnel.

Lawrence, P.R., and Lorsch, J.W. 1967. *Organization and Environment: Management Differentiation and Integration*. Boston: Harvard Graduate School of Business Administration. These two authors are among the writers labeled by Schein as "neostructuralists." They are concerned with design aspects of organizations in relation to the kinds of technology used and the functions served by various organizational elements.

Leavitt, H.J. 1951. "Some Effects of Certain Communication Patterns on Group Performance." *Journal of Abnormal and Social Psychology*, 46, 38–50. This article reports studies of the relationship between the behavior of small groups and the patterns of communication in which they operate. It was found that communication patterns within which groups work affect their behavior.

Leavitt, H.J. 1958. *Managerial Psychology*. Chicago: University of Chicago Press. An excellent examination of human problems within organizations. Deals with an examination of the individual and his or her behavior, effective influence in face-to-face situations, committees, and small groups, and the nature of business organizations, with some of the problems that seem to arise only in large organizations.

Leavitt, H.J. (ed.). 1963. *The Social Science of Organizations*. Englewood Cliffs, NJ: Prentice-Hall. Organizational problems are analyzed from four perspectives: the psychological, the applied anthropological, the economical, and the sociological. Areas covered include people in organizations, organizational decisions, structure of organizations, and relationships between tools and equipment versus structure, decision processes, and people.

Leighton, A.H. 1959. "A Working Concept of Morale for Flight Surgeons." *The Military Surgeon*, 92, 170–180. This is an insightful discussion of morale in which the author, a well-known psychiatrist and social scientist, stresses the importance of each individual's attitudes toward his or her organization and its leaders.

Levinson, D.J. 1959. "Role, Personality, and Social Structure in the Organizational Setting." *Journal of Abnormal and Social Psychology*, 58, 170–180. This is a technical analysis of the psychological factors in individual functioning within an organizational setting. The article contains a useful discussion of the concept of "role."

Lewin, K. 1942. "Time Perspective and Morale." In G. Watson (ed.), *Civilian Morale*. Boston: Houghton Mifflin Company. In this article, a famous social psychologist analyzes morale. The main theme is that the actions, emotions, and morale of an individual depend on his or her aspirations in relation to his or her time perspective.

Lewin, K. 1947. "Frontiers in Group Dynamics: Concept, Method, and Reality in Social Science; Social Equilibria and Social Change." *Human Relations*, 1(1), 5–42. A highly theoretical and difficult formulation of some "field theory" concepts by their originator, Kurt Lewin, "the father of group dynamics." Valuable for historical significance.

Lewin, K. 1953. "Studies in Group Decision." In D. Cartwright and A. Zander (eds.), *Group Dynamics: Research and Theory*. Evanston, IL: Row, Peterson and Company. This article is a summary of the famous "group-decision" experiments that demonstrate the effectiveness of group discussion and consensus upon behavior change.

Lewin, K., Dembo, T., Festinger, L., and Sears, P. 1944. "Level of Aspiration." In J. McV. Hunt (ed.), *Personality and the Behavior Disorders*. New York: The Ronald Press. This is a technical survey of research on level of aspiration. It also contains a discussion of level of aspiration in terms of Lewin's field theory.

Lewin, K., Lippitt, R., and White, R.K. 1939. "Patterns of Aggressive Behavior in Experimentally Created 'Social Climates.'" *Journal of Social Psychology*, 10, 512–532. This is the classical report of the experimental variation in leadership style and the effects of such variations upon member behavior in small groups. The senior author, Kurt Lewin, is known as the father of field theory and group dynamics in social psychology.

Likert, R. 1959. "A Motivational Approach to a Modified Theory of Organization and Management." In M. Haire (ed.), *Modern Organization Theory*. New

York: John Wiley & Sons. The author presents an understandable theory of organizational leadership and management. The theory is based on substantial research findings that show the character of the better practices and principles developed and used by managers and supervisors who the author contends are achieving the highest performance in American business.

Likert, R. 1961. *New Patterns of Management.* New York: McGraw-Hill Book Company. This is a readable book that presents a theory of organization based on research conducted mostly by the author. Although the theory is derived and discussed in terms of business and civilian governmental organizations, the book contains much that will be of use to anyone interested in leading an organization.

Likert, R. 1967. *The Human Organization: Its Management and Value.* New York: McGraw-Hill Book Company. The classic book by Rensis Likert in which he proposed a fourfold typology of organizations and concluded from extensive research that more successful organizations tend toward "System Four" management. System Four organizations are characterized by a supportive climate, group decision making, considerable group self-control, and high performance goals. The major variables appear to be the nature of the management climate (directive versus supportive) and the individual versus group orientation. Likert also advocated an overlapping group structure, which is his well-known "linking pin" concept.

Lindzey, G. (ed.). 1954. *Handbook of Social Psychology* (Vols. 1 and 2). Cambridge, MA: Addison-Wesley Publishing Co. This two-volume work contains survey articles pertaining to the major areas of social psychology. Volume 1 deals primarily with theoretical or systematic positions and methods employed in social psychology. Volume 2 focuses upon the substantive findings and applications of social psychology derived from these theoretical viewpoints.

Lindzey, G., and Aronson, E. (eds.). 1968. *The Handbook of Social Psychology* (2nd ed.). Reading, MA: Addison-Wesley Publishing Co. A review and survey of social psychology circa 1968. In five volumes, containing 45 chapters. Chapters that especially pertain to this book are:

Cyert, R.M., and MacCrimmon, K.R. "Organizations." Vol. 1, pp. 568–613.

Deutsch, M. "Field Theory in Social Psychology." Vol. 2, pp. 412–487.

Gibb, C.A. "Leadership." Vol. 4, pp. 205–282.

Sarbin, T.R. "Role Theory." Vol. 1, pp. 488–567.

Vroom, V.H. "Industrial Social Psychology." Vol. 5, pp. 196–267.

Lippitt, R. 1954. "Methods for Producing and Measuring Change in Group Functioning: Theoretical Problems." *General Semantics Bulletin*, 14, 15 (Winter–Spring), 28–33. This article is a discussion of problems in group functioning and of theory and methods used by professional consultants when attempting to develop or direct an organization.

Ludington, C. (ed.) 1959. *Communication in Organizations: Some New Research Findings.* Ann Arbor, MI: Foundation for Research on Human Behavior. This is the report of a seminar on communication in organizations. It presents reports of four distinct research efforts directed toward understanding communication problems, examining problems at the receiving end of communication systems, and studying communication systems in business organizations.

Lynn, W.M. Jr. 1963. "Decentralization." *Army* (January), 42–43. General Lynn discusses problems that occur when command channels in the Army become clogged. He attributes the problem to failure to properly delegate authority and suggests a number of principles pertinent to delegation.

Mann, F.C., and Neff, F.W. 1961. *Managing Major Changes in Organizations*. Ann Arbor, MI: Foundation for Research on Human Behavior. This is the report of a seminar concerned with accomplishing large-scale change in organizations. Four cases of organizational change are presented and analyzed in terms of (1) the state of the organization before change, (2) the recognition of a need for change, (3) planning for the change, (4) taking action steps to make the change, and (5) stabilizing the change.

March, J.G., and Simon, H.A. 1958. *Organizations*. New York: John Wiley & Sons. This book surveys the literature on organizational theory and proposes numerous propositions suitable for testing through research. The authors are mainly concerned with outlining fields of research. Accordingly, the casual reader will find this book difficult.

Marschak, J. 1959. "Efficient and Viable Organization Forms." In M. Haire (ed.), *Modern Organization Theory*. New York: John Wiley & Sons. This article sets out some of the more important issues in the question of organizational structure and design.

Maslow, A.H. 1954. *Motivation and Personality*. New York: Harper & Row. This book is Maslow's original presentation of his hierarchical theory of motivation, and it can be considered a landmark in the study and evolution of motivation theory.

Maslow, A.H. 1970. *Motivation and Personality* (2nd ed.). New York: Harper & Row. The second edition of Maslow's book, originally published in 1954. Maslow describes and expands upon his well-known model "Needs Hierarchy" theory of motivation. The theory is widely accepted, especially by practitioners, because the concepts are simple and understandable and make sense in the real world, especially in the world of organizations.

Mayo, E. 1933. *The Human Problem of Industrial Civilization*. New York: The Macmillan Company. The book that started it all. It discusses the famous studies at the Hawthorne Plant of Western Electric. There, researchers discovered the influence of the face-to-face informal group upon motivation and behavior in a work situation and triggered the human relations movement, which spread rapidly throughout the world.

McClelland, D.C. 1961. *The Achieving Society*. Princeton, NJ: D. Van Nostrand Company. This author attempts to isolate certain psychological factors and to demonstrate that these factors are usually important in the development or decline of societies. He defends the hypothesis that a particular psychological factor—the need for achievement—is responsible for economic growth and decline.

McClelland, D.C., Atkinson, J.W., Clark, R.A., and Lowell, E.L. 1953. *The Achievement Motive*. New York: Appleton-Century-Crofts. A technical description of the methods used in research that identified the achievement motive as one determinant of behavior.

McClelland, D.C., and Burnham, D.H. 1976. "Power Is the Great Motivator." *Harvard Business Review*, 54, 2. The senior author of this article is the well-known advocate of "Achievement Motivation." In this article, the authors concern themselves with power within organizations and the effects of power as a motivator and its effects upon human performance.

McClelland, W.A., and Lyons, J.D. 1968. *Guidelines for Manpower Training as Developed by the Human Resources Research Office*. Alexandria, VA: HumRRO Professional Paper, 43–68. These authors are well-known experts in training and training methodology. In this paper, they make the important distinction between training and education.

McCurdy, H.G., and Lambert, W.E. 1952. "The Efficiency of Small Human Groups in the Solution of Problems Requiring Genuine Co-Operation." *Journal of Personality*, 20, 478–494. This report concerns one of the early studies of problem solving in small groups. It sets forth some of the issues and some of the findings that were later confirmed by other researchers.

McDavid, J.W., and Harari, H. 1968. *Social Psychology: Individuals, Groups, Societies*. New York: Harper & Row. This is an excellent textbook for introduction to social psychology. The discussions of small groups and of teamwork are especially relevant and useful in application to real life.

McGregor, D. 1944. "Conditions of Effective Leadership in the Industrial Organization." *Journal of Consulting Psychology*, 8(2), 55–63. The main theme of this article is that a subordinate is dependent for the satisfaction of many of his or her vital needs upon the behavior and attitudes of his or her superior. The author identifies and discusses several conditions essential for subordinate Effectiveness.

McGregor, D. 1960. *The Human Side of Enterprise*. New York: McGraw-Hill Book Company. The highly readable book is a general discussion of some of the critical issues in leadership. The author examines the assumptions underlying conventional views of leadership and proposes an alternative approach to leadership of organizations. This book has become "the classic" in late-twentieth-century management literature.

McGregor, D. 1967. *The Professional Manager*. Caroline McGregor and Warren Bennis, eds. New York: McGraw-Hill. A collection of writings by Douglas McGregor, edited after his death by his wife and Warren Bennis. It describes McGregor's final thinking about leadership and management.

McLagan, P.A. 1997. "Competencies: The Next Generation." *Training and Development*, 51, 40–47. This is one of the most recent discussions of the competencies of individuals and the use of the competency concept in personnel management and training.

Medalia, N.Z., and Miller, C.D. 1955. "Human Relations Leadership and the Association of Morale and Efficiency in Work Groups: A Controlled Study with Small Military Units." *Social Forces*, 33, 348–352. This is a report of research conducted on small military units. It attempts to clarify the relationship between leadership, morale, and efficiency.

Meister, D. 1976. *Behavioral Foundations of System Development*. New York: John Wiley & Sons. This book addresses the issue of system technology and systems development. It is concerned mainly with simple systems of the input-output variety.

Mellinger, G. 1956. "Interpersonal Trust as a Factor in Communication." *Journal of Abnormal and Social Psychology*, 52, 304–309. This research report analyzes the effect of interpersonal trust upon quantity and quality of communication in a government research laboratory.

Merei, F. 1949. "Group Leadership and Institutionalization." *Human Relations*, 2, 23–39. This is a classical study of the way leadership evolves in groups and the tactics used by leaders to gain influence in groups.

Merton, R.K. 1940. "Bureaucratic Structure and Personality." *Social Forces*, 18, 560–568. This article is one of the earliest discussions of transition from strict bureaucracy and bureaucratic structure to recognition that attitudes, values, and informal goals develop within subordinate units despite structural controls and that these unintended consequences actually modify an organization's structure.

Merton, R.K. 1957. *Social Theory and Social Structure* (2nd ed.). Glencoe, IL: The Free Press. This book attempts to consolidate social theory and social research with emphasis on the procedures and qualitative analysis used in sociology. It includes analyses of reference group behavior and of the breakdown of social norms.

Miller, J.G. 1955. "Toward a General Theory for the Behavioral Sciences." *American Psychologist*, 10, 513–531. In this article, the author presents a general theory for the behavioral sciences. It closely resembles Open Systems Theory and has served as one of the bases of the development of organizational theory in the direction of Systems Theory.

Mills, T.M. 1967. *The Sociology of Small Groups*. Englewood Cliffs, NJ: Prentice-Hall. This book describes a sociologist's approach to small groups. While somewhat different from the ordinary social psychological approach, it contains some useful ideas about how to approach small groups and their performance.

Miner, J.B. 1963. *The Management of Ineffective Performance*. New York: McGraw-Hill Book Company. This book provides a synthesis of information available in 1963 on work performance and discusses methods of dealing with individuals who are not meeting established standards of effectiveness.

Mirabile, R.J. 1977. "Everything You Wanted to Know about Competency Modeling." *Training and Development*, 51, 73–77. This is another article about the competencies of individuals and competency modeling.

Mooney, J.D. 1947. *The Principles of Organization* (rev. ed.). New York: Harper & Row. This is a discussion of certain principles of formal organization considered by the author to be the fundamental bases for effective organizational functioning. The evolution of these principles within military, church, and business contexts is traced.

Morse, N.C., and Reimer, E. 1956. "The Experimental Change of a Major Organizational Variable." *Journal of Abnormal and Social Psychology*, 52, 120–129. This article reports an experiment conducted within an actual industrial organization to test the relationship between organizational decisions and both individual satisfaction and productivity.

Morse, N.C., Reimer, E., and Tannenbaum A.S. 1951. "Regulation and Control in Hierarchical Organizations." *Journal of Social Issues*, 7(3), 41–48. This article discusses the concept of control and considers degree of control and locus of control as significant factors in organizational functioning.

Newman, W.H. 1963. "Overcoming Obstacles to Effective Delegation." In J.A. Litterer (ed.), *Organizations: Structure and Behavior*. New York: John Wiley & Sons. This article examines some of the reasons that leaders are apprehensive about delegation and why subordinates hesitate to take responsibility.

Olmstead, J.A. February 1973. *Working Papers No. 2, Organizational Structure and Climate: Implications for Agencies, National Study of Social Welfare and Rehabilitation Workers, Work and Organizational Contexts.* [HumRRO Final Report, by Joseph A. Olmstead, August 1972], (SRS) 73-05403, Department of Health, Education, and Welfare, Social and Rehabilitation Service, February, 187 pp. This is one of a series of reports of field surveys conducted by the Human Resources Research Organization in a study of social and rehabilitation agencies, their work, and their work contexts.

Olmstead, J.A. 1980. *Leadership Training: The State of the Art.* Technical Report 80-2. Alexandria, VA: Human Resources Research Organization. This technical report presents an analysis of the current state of leadership training. The analysis includes training for military leadership, human relations, and people-related aspects of supervision and management in business and governmental organizations.

The report consists of 10 chapters, grouped into two parts. Part I is concerned with the present state of the field of leadership training and includes an assessment of leader training activities and a discussion of the state of leadership training.

Part II addresses considerations for improvement of leadership training through development of a leadership training technology.

Olmstead, J.A. 1992. *Battle Staff Integration.* IDA Paper P-2560. Alexandria, VA: Institute for Defense Analyses. This monograph contains an analysis of battle staff performance and identifies some critical aspects of performance. Puts the concept of Organizational Competence into an analysis of battle staffs. It provides the theoretical background of "battle-staff" integration and an analysis of processes of effectiveness and discusses implications for leadership and battle staff development.

Olmstead, J.A. 1997a. *Competency-Based Organizations: Theory and Practice.* Professional Paper 97-2. West Columbia, SC: The Vanguard Research Group. This paper describes the theoretical foundation and a conceptual model for the development and assessment of functionally competent organizations.

Olmstead, J.A. 1997b. *Leadership in Organizations.* Professional Paper 97-1. West Columbia, SC: The Vanguard Research Group. The purpose of this paper is to integrate significant research findings and to present a coherent framework for thinking about practical leadership in organizations. The effort was to present a straightforward but sound approach that could be useful to consultants and practicing leaders. The paper was a predecessor to the current book and contains many of the same concepts. However, it also contains a comparison between the leadership roles of first-line supervisors and high-level executives and an analysis of leadership training.

Olmstead, J.A. 1998. *Work Units, Teams, and Task Forces: Groups at Work*. Professional Paper 98-1. West Columbia, SC: The Vanguard Research Group. The purpose of this monograph is to present a coherent and integrated analysis of groups at work, their dynamics, and influences that impact upon their capabilities to perform effectively. The intent was to analyze the factors that are critical for effective group performance. An additional purpose was to propose a practical framework that is useful for understanding the dynamics of groups at work.

The discussion is organized around discussions of three broad types of groups: (1) Work Groups (work units, sections, departments); (2) Teams (work teams, crisis management teams, project teams); (3) Operating Groups (task forces, operational staffs, and high-level decision-making groups).

Olmstead, J.A. 2000. *Executive Leadership: Building World Class Organizations*. Houston: Gulf Publishing Company. This book provides an analysis of practical executive leadership and presents a workable model for use in developing functionally competent organizations. The final chapter of the book is devoted to a conceptualization of functionally competent organizations and a discussion of some of the implications for practice in executive leadership.

Olmstead, J.A., Baranick, M.J., and Elder, B.L. 1978. *Research on Training for Brigade Command Groups: Factors Contributing to Unit Combat Readiness*. Technical Report No. FR-ED(C)-78-1. Alexandria, VA: Human Resources Research Organization. This technical report describes a research and development program used with Army brigade command groups. The program was based on the concepts of functionally competent battle staffs, and the results demonstrated the validity of these concepts.

Olmstead, J.A., and Christensen, H.E. 1973. *Effects of Work Contexts: An Intensive Field Study. Research Report No. 2, National Study of Social Welfare and Rehabilitation Workers, Work and Organizational Contexts*. Washington, DC: Department of Health, Education, and Welfare, Social and Rehabilitation Service. This report presents and describes the results of an intensive field study of the organizational contexts within which social welfare and rehabilitation work is performed. It also identifies some of the effects of those contexts upon that work.

Olmstead, J.A., Christensen, H.E., and Lackey, L.L. 1973. *Components of Organizational Competence: Test of a Conceptual Framework*. Technical Report 73-19. Alexandria, VA: Human Resources Research Organization. An empirical study of organizational competence under simulated conditions. Identified and confirmed the validity of the "Adaptive-Coping Cycle" and its component processes as contributors to organizational effectiveness.

Olmstead, J.A., Christensen, H.E., Salter, J.A., and Lackey, L.L. 1975. *Effects of Work Contexts in Public Welfare Financial Assistance Agencies*. Technical Report 75-7. Alexandria, VA: Human Resources Research Organization. This is another report in the series concerned with Social welfare and rehabilitation organizations. This study concerned the performance, and effects of work contexts upon performance, of public welfare financial assistance workers. It was the second in the field studies conducted by the Human

Resources Research Organization for the Social and Rehabilitation Service, DHEW.

Olmstead, J.A., and Elder, B.L. 1980. *Organizational Process Performance and Unit Mission Readiness: Training for Battalion Command Groups.* Final Report. Alexandria, VA: Human Resources Research Organization. This was the final technical report on project Cardinal Point, and it describes the procedures and final data concerned with the process performance of Army battalion command groups engaged in field training.

Olmstead, J.A., Elder, B.L., and Forsyth, J.M. 1978. *Organizational Process and Combat Readiness: Feasibility of Training Organizational Effectiveness Staff Officers to Assess Command Group Performance.* Interim Report IR-ED-78–13. Alexandria, VA: Human Resources Research Organization. This was the first report on Project Cardinal Point and described the research procedures and initial outcomes of the use of Organizational Effectiveness Staff Officers (consultants) to provide training feedback to battalion staff groups.

Otis, J.L., and Treuhaft, W.C. 1949. "Good Communication Promotes Teamwork." *Personnel Journal*, 28, 83–90. The authors discuss some of the fundamentals of communication and its relation to teamwork.

Parsons, T. 1956. "Suggestions for a Sociological Approach to the Theory of Organizations, I and II." *Administrative Science Quarterly*, 1, 2, 3–85, 225–239. This article is a precursor to Parsons' 1960 book. It lays out an outline for a sociological approach to the theory of organizations. Parsons is one of the icons of sociology and the sociology of organizations.

Parsons, T. 1960. *Structure and Process in Modern Societies.* Glencoe, IL: The Free Press. Talcott Parsons sets out a systems approach to societies, governments, and organizations. A very understandable approach, but Parsons paints with a broad brush, and, accordingly, it is sometimes difficult to apply his concepts in specific ways.

Peabody, R.L. 1964. *Organizational Authority: Superior–Subordinate Relationships in Three Public Service Organizations.* New York: Atherton Press. This is the report on a study of authority in three public organizations. It contains theory and conclusions that are particularly relevant to authority. The author concludes that authority relations are basic to the achievement of organizational objectives but that conflicting attitudes appear to be a major source of tension within organizations.

Pepitone, A., and Kleiner, R. 1957. "The Effects of Threat and Frustration on Group Cohesiveness." *Journal of Abnormal and Social Psychology*, 54, 192–200. This is a landmark article demonstrating the effects of threat and frustration on experimental groups.

Peterson, G.W., and Rumsey, M.G. 1981. "A Methodology for Measuring Officer Job Competence." Paper presented at Division 19, American Psychological Association, Los Angeles. This paper is one of the first reports of job competencies and the methodology for identifying competencies and for developing them.

Porter, L.W., and Lawler, E.E. 1965. "Properties of Organizational Structure in Relation to Job Attitudes and Job Behavior." *Psychological Bulletin*, 64, 23–51. This article is a review of research concerned with the effects of organizational structure and variations of it upon job attitudes and job behavior of personnel.

Porter, L.W., and Lawler, E.E. 1968. *Managerial Attitudes and Performance*. Homewood, IL: Richard D. Irwin and Dorsey Press. This book, among other things, sets out the authors' concepts of expectancy theory and its impact upon organizational theory. The main result is that the authors have come up with a theory concerned with expectations that people have about their work, about their work situation, and about how moderator variables impact upon the influence of climate, organizational structure, and so on, and upon job attitudes and job performance.

Pugh, D.S. 1966. "Modern Organizational Theory: A Psychological and Sociological Study." *Psychological Bulletin*, 66, 235–251. An incisive critique of theoretical approaches to organizations by a noted British psychologist.

Pugh, D.S., Hickson, D.J., Hinings, C.R., MacDonald, K.M., Turner, C., and Lupton, T. 1963. "A Conceptual Scheme for Organizational Analysis." *Administrative Science Quarterly*, 8, 289–316. This article is a precursor of Pugh's 1966 article cited earlier.

Pugh, D.S., Hickson, D.J., Hinings, C.R., and Turner, C. 1968. "Dimensions of Organizational Structure." *Administrative Science Quarterly*, 13, 66–105. This article presents an analysis of some dimensions of organizational structure and their possible impacts upon organizational and human performance.

Rapaport, A. 1959. "A Logical Task as a Research Tool in Organization Theory." In M. Haire (ed.), *Modern Organization Theory*. New York: John Wiley & Sons. The author of this chapter is one of the later structural theorists who have attempted to bring internal processes into their considerations of organizational theory.

Raven, B.H., and Rietsema, J. 1957. "The Effects of Varied Clarity of Group Goal and Group Path upon the Individual and His Relation to His Group." *Human Relations*, 19, 29–44. A study that demonstrates the effects of clear and unclear goals upon relationships within a group.

Reitzel, W.A., 1958. *Background to Decision Making*. Newport, RI: U.S. Naval War College. An interesting and helpful discussion of military decision making. It indicates the approaches that psychology, the social sciences generally, and the mathematical sciences in particular are developing on the general subject of decision making. It examines the ways in which military decision-making processes are similar to, or diverge from, the other types of problem situations.

Richards, C.G., and Dobryns, H.F. 1957. "Topography and Culture: The Case of the Changing Cage." *Human Organization*, 16, 16–20. This article is an excellent illustration and analysis of how the physical arrangements within an office can have important influence upon the attitudes and performance of personnel and on the development of groups within organizations.

Riecken, H.W., and Homans, G.C. 1954. "Psychological Aspects of Social Structure." In G. Lindzey (ed.), *Handbook of Social Psychology* (Vol. 2). Cambridge, MA: Addison-Wesley Publishing Co. This is a survey and analysis of technical literature concerned with groups and social organizations. It discusses critical determinants of group performance and effectiveness.

Roethlisberger, F.J., and Dickson, W.J. 1939. *Management and the Worker.* Cambridge, MA: Harvard University Press. This is the definitive discussion of the results of the classical "Hawthorne Experiments." The authors stress that what is most significant in work environments are not conclusive answers to specific questions but development in the understanding of human situations, which help to improve personnel relations and aid in resolving the problems arising in them, when and where they occur.

Rogers, C.R., and Roethlisberger, F.J. 1952. "Barriers and Gateways to Communication." *Harvard Business Review,* 30(4), 28–34. This article presents a discussion of interpersonal communication by two well-known experts who are mainly concerned with removing barriers that impede understanding between people.

Sarbin, T.R. 1954. "Role Theory." In G. Lindzey (ed.), *Handbook of Social Psychology* (Vol. 1). Cambridge, MA: Addison-Wesley Publishing Co. This is a technical survey of the literature concerned with roles and theories of roles.

Schein, E.H. 1962. "Management Development, Human Relations Training and the Process of Influence." In I.R. Weschler and E.H. Schein (eds.), *Issues in Human Relations Training.* Washington, DC: National Training Laboratories, National Education Association, pp. 47–60. This article is concerned with the impact of groups upon the attitudes and behavior of individuals and with the potential for using group influences to assist in training executives.

Schein, E.H. 1965, 1970. *Organizational Psychology.* Englewood Cliffs, NJ: Prentice-Hall. A basic discussion of the fundamental issues in a rapidly developing new field—organizational psychology. An excellent discussion suitable for anyone interested in obtaining a better understanding of organizations.

Schoen, D.R. 1957. "Human Relations: Boon or Bogle?" *Harvard Business Review,* 35(6), 41–47. The article critiques and defends the "human relations" approach to leadership. The author presents some rational arguments for better understanding between superiors and subordinates.

Scott, E.L. 1956. *Leadership and Perceptions of Organization.* Columbus: Bureau of Business Research, College of Commerce and Administration, The Ohio State University. This report presents the results of a study of naval personnel concerned with the relationship between accuracy of role perception and both morale and effectiveness.

Seashore, S.E. 1954. *Group Cohesiveness in the Industrial Work Group.* Ann Arbor: Institute for Social Research, University of Michigan. This report describes a large-scale industrial study in which the author found that the morale of group members was related to group cohesiveness and that group influences were correlated to standards of work performance. He also found that groups of small size are more likely to have a high degree of cohesiveness than groups of larger size and that the degree of cohesiveness in a group is significantly determined by manager decisions concerning the size of work groups and the continuity of membership in the groups.

Selznick, P. 1957. *Leadership in Administration: A Sociological Interpretation.* Evanston, IL: Row, Peterson and Company. This book by a well-known organizational theorist is a sociological inquiry into the nature and quality of high-level leadership. The author contends that only through an understanding of organizations as responsive, adaptive organisms can an understanding of leadership be obtained.

Senn, L.E., and Childress, J.R. 1999. *The Secret of a Winning Culture: Building High Performance Teams.* Houston: Gulf Publishing Co. This book sets forth an allegedly proven series of principles and processes that ensure an organization's success when leaders change, mergers and acquisitions join cultures, change initiatives are introduced, and faster simply is not enough. Putting these ideas into action unlocks the power of high-performance teams, which, in turn, produces high-performance organizations.

Shepard, H.A. 1965. "Changing Interpersonal and Intergroup Relationships in Organizations." In J. March (ed.), *Handbook of Organizations.* Chicago: Rand-McNally & Co. In this chapter, the author stresses the importance of organizational leadership as the main integrating force in organizations, and he concludes that emphasis within organizations shifts from arbitration to problem solving and from delegated to shared responsibility as leaders see their organizations as organic rather than mechanistic and as adaptable rather than controlled by rigid structure.

Sherif, M. 1962. "Introductory Statement." In M. Sherif (ed.), *Intergroup Relations and Leadership: Approaches and Research in Industrial, Ethnic, Cultural, and Political Areas.* New York: John Wiley & Sons. In his introduction to an interesting book, this famous social psychologist sets forth some of the conditions leading to intergroup conflict and some fundamental bases for the resolution of such conflict.

Sherif, M. (ed.). 1962. *Intergroup Relations and Leadership: Approaches and Research in Industrial, Ethnic, Cultural, and Political Areas.* New York: John Wiley & Sons. This is a wide-ranging collection of articles concerned with conflict between groups, societies, and nations. The various papers, although somewhat academic in approach, contain many useful contributions to understanding of intergroup conflict.

Sherif, M., and Cantril, H. 1947. *The Psychology of Ego-Involvements: Social Attitudes and Identifications.* New York: John Wiley & Sons. This is a definitive work in the social psychology of ego-involvement. Although somewhat outdated, the book contains many useful illustrations of factors that affect the individual's involvement and identification with groups, organizations, and political systems.

Sherif, M., and Sherif, C.W. 1953. *Groups in Harmony and Tension.* New York: Harper & Brothers. This is the report of the classical "robbers cave" experiment in which groups were developed and studied under real-life conditions. It contains discussions of factors critical to the development of cohesive groups and to the development of cooperation between groups.

Sherif, M., and Sherif, C.W. 1956. *An Outline of Social Psychology* (rev. ed.). New York: Harper & Brothers. A basic textbook in social psychology. Discussions range from the influence of single social variables upon one individual to the development of complex social groups.

Sherif, M., and Wilson, M.O. (eds.). 1953. *Group Relations at the Crossroads.* New York: Harper & Brothers. This is a collection of technical papers concerned with various aspects of group relations.

Shils, E.A., and Janowitz, M. 1948. "Cohesion and Disintegration in the Wehrmacht in World War II." *Public Opinion Quarterly*, 12, 280–315. In attempting to determine why the German Army in World War II fought so stubbornly to the end, the authors have made an intensive study of the social structure of this army, of the symbols to which it responded, of the Nazi attempts to bolster its morale, and the Allied attempts to break it down. They found a key to many of the behavior and attitude patterns of the individual infantryman in the interpersonal relationships within the company—his primary group. The article discusses methods used by the Wehrmacht to foster high cohesion within its small units.

Simon, H.A. 1947. *Administrative Behavior: A Study of Decision-Making Processes in Administrative Organization.* New York: The Macmillan Company. This book is one of the landmarks in the evolution of decision theory. Simon retained the idea that decision behavior in organization is "intendedly rational" and that decisions are made by individuals within organizations and not by organizations as entities. He also recognized, however, the inadequacy of classical theory for understanding decisions in organizations. Accordingly, he distinguished between the role of facts and the role of values in decision making.

Simon, H.A. 1957a. *Models of Man.* New York: John Wiley & Sons. This book is a follow-up to Simon's 1947 book. In this one, Simon contends that the decision maker must "satisfice"—find a course of action that is "good enough"—rather than maximizing returns as would be possible with full knowledge of the consequences attached to every alternative. This concept of satisficing opened new vistas in theories of organizational decision making.

Simon, H.A. 1957b. *Administrative Behavior: A Study of Decision-Making Processes in Administrative Organization* (2nd ed.). New York: The Macmillan Company. This is another continuation of Simon's expansion of his theories of decision making, and his pointing out the contrasts between classical economic man and his administrative man emphasizes an important point. Rationality is central to behavior within an organization; however, if the members of an organization were capable of the kind of objective rationality attributed to economic man, theories of organization would have no purpose. Simon contended that the need for administrative theory is the fact that there are practical limits to human rationality. These limits are not static and depend upon the organizational environment in which the individual's decision takes place.

Simon, R. 1955. "Are We Losing Sight of Communications Principles?" *Personnel Journal*, 34 206–209. This is a discussion of principles of written communication, with particular emphasis upon communication with personnel in large numbers. Instances of good and bad communication are cited from government and business.

Stacey, R.D. 2001. *Complex Responsive Processes in Organizations: Learning and Knowledge Creation.* Philadelphia: Psychology Press. Over the past decade, practicing managers and organizational theorists have been drawing attention to the centrality of information and knowledge in economic and social processes, the so-called knowledge economy. This book argues that most of the literature on these matters and the ways in which most practitioners now talk about them reflect systems thinking and that its information processing view of knowledge creation is no longer tenable. The purpose of this book is to develop a different perspective of relating, that of Complex Responsive Processes, which draws on the complexity sciences as a source domain for analogies with human action. The result is a radical questioning of the belief that organizational knowledge is essentially codified and centralized. Instead, organizational knowledge is understood to be in the relationships between people in an organization and has to do with the qualities of those relationships.

Stacey, R.D., Griffin, D., and Shaw, P. 2000. *Complexity and Management: Fad or Radical Challenge to Systems Thinking*. Philadelphia: Psychology Press. This book covers issues such as predictability, creativity, and relationships as it considers how complexity and its central principles of emergence and self-complexity are being used to understand organizations.

Steiner, I.D. 1972. *Group Process and Productivity*. New York: Academic Press. This book is an excellent analysis of group processes and their effects upon performance and group productivity.

Stogdill, R.M. 1950. "Leadership, Membership, and Organization." *Psychological Bulletin*, 47, 1–14. In this article, the author outlines some of the critical factors in organizational functioning and in leadership. He contends that leadership must be viewed from the standpoint of influence upon organizational activities.

Stogdill, R.M. 1959. *Individual Behavior and Group Achievement*. New York: Oxford University Press. This book presents a theory for describing both the structure and the achievements of groups. Variables are developed using personality and group constructs. Research findings are cited to support the theory.

Stogdill, R.M. 1966. "Dimensions of Organization Theory." In J.A. Thompson (ed.), *Approaches to Organizational Design*. Pittsburgh: University of Pittsburgh Press, 1–56. This article by one of the central figures in the study of leadership and organizations is an attempt to bring some order out of the chaos of organizational theory. He approaches it from the standpoint of dimensions of organizations and attempts to make a case for a dimensional study of organization theory.

Stogdill, R.M. 1974. *Handbook of Leadership*. New York: The Free Press. A detailed survey of theory and research on leadership to 1974, conducted by Ralph Stogdill, one of the icons in the field of leadership. Contains all you would ever want to know about leadership at that time.

Strauss, G. 1963. "Some Notes on Power-Equalization." In H.J. Leavitt (ed.), *The Social Science of Organizations*. Englewood Cliffs, NJ: Prentice-Hall. This article is an incisive and unbiased critique of the so-called human relations movement, which increasingly exercised potent influence upon thinking about leadership and organizational practices. The author identifies the fundamental issues and discusses the pros and cons of each. This article will be helpful to anyone who wishes to understand more about the practical issues involved in the question of "democratic" versus "authoritarian" leadership.

Swanson, G.E., Newcomb, T.M., and Hartley, E.L. (eds.) 1952. *Readings in Social*

Psychology (rev. ed.). New York: Henry Holt and Company. This book of readings presents illustrative selections of the ways in which the influence of social conditions upon psychological processes have been studied. Topics include influence and interpersonal relationships, collective problem solving, recurring interaction patterns, effects of interaction patterns on individual participants, and some social psychological approaches to public issues.

Tannenbaum, A.S., and Georgopoulos, B.S. 1957. "The Distribution of Control in Formal Organizations." *Social Forces*, 36, 44–50. This article presents an analytical framework for study of the distribution of control in formal organizations. Four major concepts are explained: active control, passive control, orientation of control, and sources of control.

Tannenbaum, R. 1949. "The Manager Concept: A Rational Synthesis." *The Journal of Business*, 22(4), 225–241. This article differentiates "managerial" services from "nonmanagerial" services by isolating those functions performed exclusively by "managers." The author defends the thesis that "managers" are those who use formal authority to organize, direct, or control responsible subordinates so that all contributions will be coordinated in the attainment of an organization's purpose. As used in this article, the term "manager" might equally apply to leaders in any type of organization.

Tannenbaum, R. 1950. "Managerial Decision-Making." *The Journal of Business*, 23(1), 22–39. This is an analysis of decision making in organizations. The interindividual and intergroup relationships that make it possible for the decisions of one person to affect the behavior of another are explored. Some conclusions are presented concerning the work of managers (leaders), indicating how managers affect the behavior of their subordinates and how other people affect the behavior of managers.

Tannenbaum, R., and Masserik, 1957. "Leadership: A Frame of Reference." *Management Science*, 4(1), 1–19. The frame of reference described in this article takes into account three separate aspects of leadership: the leader and his or her psychological attributes; the follower with his or her problems, attitudes, and needs; and the group situation in which followers and leaders relate to one another. Leadership is treated as a process or function rather than as an exclusive attribute of a prescribed role.

Tannenbaum, R., and Schmidt, W.H. 1958. "How to Choose a Leadership Pattern." *Harvard Business Review*, 36(2), 95–101. This article discusses the apparent conflict between two ways of leading an organization: the democratic, participative approach and the authoritarian, one person method. The authors contend that no such conflict should exist. They believe that there is a large spectrum of possible leadership attitudes, and different approaches are appropriate for different situations. The successful leader is described as the person who recognizes the nature of the particular problem with which he or she is dealing and adapts his or her methods of leadership to it.

Taylor, D.W. 1965. "Decision Making and Problem Solving." In J.G. March (ed.), *Handbook of Organization*. Chicago: Rand McNally & Company. This article is an excellent presentation within March's handbook in which the author provides an analysis of decision making and problem solving within complex organizations.

Thelen, H.A. 1954. *Dynamics of Groups at Work*. Chicago: University of Chicago

Press. This book is a comprehensive analysis of the dynamics of problem solving and work groups. It contains many practical comments upon the functioning of small groups. The book is divided into a section of theory and a section illustrating the application of theory in various practical situations.

Thompson, J.D. (ed.). 1996. *Approaches to Organizational Design*. Pittsburgh: University of Pittsburgh Press. This book is a symposium concerned mainly with organizational design and organizational structure.

Tiede, R.V., and Leake, L.A. 1971. "A Method for Evaluating the Combat Effectiveness of a Tactical Information System in a Field Army." *Operations Research*, 19, 587–604. In addition to the primary objective of the article, it presents an excellent method for evaluating the effectiveness of military units in simulated or training situations.

Triandis, H.C. 1959. "Similarity in Thought Processes in Boss–Employee Communication." In C. Ludington (ed.), *Communication in Organizations: Some New Research Findings*. Ann Arbor, MI: Foundation for Research on Human Behavior. The study reported in this article was concerned with the relationship between communication and similarity in thinking between superiors and subordinates. Findings and a discussion of their implications are reported.

Urwick, L. 1957. *Leadership in the Twentieth Century*. London: Sir Isaac Pitman and Son. In this short book, a well-known management consultant, writer, and retired British Army officer discusses the need for leadership; the psychological basis of leadership; what the leader does; and the development of leaders.

Van Zelst, R.H. 1951. "Sociometrically Selected Work Teams Increase Production." *Personnel Psychology*, 5, 175–185. This article is a good example of how people whose attitudes are favorable toward each other work more productively and with better performance than those who do not like each other.

Vecchio, R.P. 1998. *Leadership*. Notre Dame, IN: University of Notre Dame Press. This book sets out one of the latest approaches to leadership. It is fairly comprehensive in its coverage of the subject.

Viteles, M.S. 1953. *Motivation and Morale in Industry*. New York: W.W. Norton & Company. This is a basic work on motivation and morale in industry. It contains wide-ranging discussions of factors affecting morale and performance.

von Bertalanffy, L. 1956. "General Systems Theory." *Yearbook of the Society for General Systems Research*, 18, 21–32. The first lucid application of General Systems Theory to social phenomena, including groups and organizations. A landmark publication in the evolution of organizational theory.

von Neumann, J., and Morgenstern, O. 1944. *Theory of Games and Economic Behavior*. Princeton, NJ: Princeton University Press. This is the famous article on game theory that started a change in decision theory to take into account probabilistic decisions.

Vroom, V.H. 1969. "Industrial Social Psychology." In G.I. Lindzey and E. Aronson (eds.), *The Handbook of Social Psychology* (2nd ed., Vol. 5). *Applied Social Psychology*. Reading, MA: Addison-Wesley Publishing Co. This is an excellent chapter on the issues involved in industrial social psychology in the late 1960s. The issues have not changed much since the chapter was printed.

Weber, M. 1947. *The Theory of Social and Economic Organization* (reprinted and translated). Glencoe, IL: The Free Press. This is a reprint and translation of Weber's original statement of the theory of social and economic organizations, which sets out his analysis of bureaucratic ideas. The concepts of organizational structure and design enter into these discussions.

White, R., and Lippitt, R. 1953. "Leader Behavior and Member Reaction in Three 'Social Climates.' " In D. Cartwright and A. Zander (eds.), *Group Dynamics: Research and Theory*. Evanston, IL: Row, Peterson and Company. This was the famous original study of the ways that democratic and authoritarian degrees of control affect group life. The study examined the effects upon individual and group behavior of three variations in social atmosphere labeled "democratic," "authoritarian," and "laissez-faire." Leadership behavior is described from the viewpoint of both the leader and the members of the group.

Whyte, W.F. 1959. *Man and Organization*. Homewood, IL: Richard D. Irwin. This book is one of Whyte's earliest and is very well known. It considers the effects of the place of man in organizations and the effects of the organization upon his performance.

Whyte, W.F. 1961. *Men at Work*. Homewood, IL: Dewey Press and Richard D. Irwin. This comprehensive book presents research cases, the analysis of cases, and a theoretical scheme to explain them. There is discussion of such questions as what factors account for conflict or cooperation in organizational relations, what conditions lead to high morale among organizational members, what conditions lead to high productivity, what the job means to the worker, what conditions account for the cohesion of work groups, and how people in organizations react to changes.

Williams, H.B. 1957. "Some Functions of Communications in Crisis Behavior." *Human Organization*, 16, 15–19. This is an excellent article and one of the few that discuss crisis behavior. Here, the impact of faulty communication in crises situations is emphasized, but what happens to organizations in crises is an important aspect of this article.

Williamson, O.E. (ed.). 1995. *From Chester Barnard to the Present and Beyond*. New York: Oxford University Press. This is a collection of papers celebrating the 50th anniversary of the publication one of Chester Barnard's remarkable and still influential publications.

Zaleznik, A., Christensen, C.R., and Roethlisberger, Fl. 1958. *The Motivation, Productivity, and Satisfaction of Workers: A Prediction Study*. Boston: Graduate School of Business Administration, Harvard University. This is one of the better-known studies to come out of the Harvard Business School concerned with motivation, productivity, and satisfaction of personnel.

Zaleznik, A., and Moment, D. 1964. *The Dynamics of Interpersonal Behavior*. New York: John Wiley & Sons. This book is concerned with interpersonal relations within organizations. It is somewhat in conflict with the group dynamics authors and with the descendants of Lewin. It is a semisociological report of human behavior.

Zander, A.F. 1950. "Resistance to Change—Its Analysis and Prevention." *Ad-*

vanced Management, 15–16, 9–11. This is an analysis of the factors leading to resistance to change. The article also gives suggestions for preventing and overcoming such resistance.

Zander, A.F. 1961. *Effects of Group Goals upon Personal Goals*. Technical Report No. 12 (Factors Determining Defensive Behavior in Groups). Washington, DC: Group Psychology Branch, ONR, National Training Laboratories. This survey report reviews various findings relevant to members' acceptance of a goal provided them by their group. Level of aspiration is analyzed in relation to personal and group objectives. The nature and origin of efforts to cope with demands that are higher than the individual can fulfill are also discussed.

Author Index

Subject Index

About the Author

JOSEPH A. OLMSTEAD is Vice President, Product Development, The Vanguard Research Group, West Columbia, S.C. Previously he was with the Human Resources Research Office of the George Washington University (now The Human Resources Research Organization), where he served as a senior staff scientist and program director. Dr. Olmstead is a Fellow of The American Psychological Association and was also Chief of Training and Management Development at Eli Lilly. He is the author of more than 50 papers, monographs, and technical reports.